/35.95

SWINDON
ENGINEMAN

by

GORDON SHURMER & MIKE FENTON

WILD SWAN PUBLICATIONS

ISBN 1 905184 22 0

Designed by Paul Karau
Printed by Amadeus Press, Cleckheaton

Gordon's best years on the railway were the seven he spent in No. 1 Link firing for Bill Hinder, as chronicled in Chapter 6. Here they are seen at Chippenham signal box with No. 5009 Shrewsbury Castle, working the 1.18 Paddington to Weston-super-Mare. Gordon made great progress during his time with Bill. He'd passed his passenger fireman exam with Inspector Charlie Pullen in February 1947, not long before joining Bill in the top passenger link, and the following year was elected as Improvement Class Instructor on 4th January 1948. On 24th August 1950 he passed his examination for driver which meant that he could now take the controls when required in an emergency. During these years, the most lucrative run on No. 1 Link was the overnight run to Leicester and back, part of a through service to York. On this trip a GWR crew had the chance to meet up and compare notes with their LNER contemporaries from Marylebone. The distances between Swindon—Leicester and Leicester—Marylebone were exactly the same and the Leicester runs were operated alternately with GWR and LNER crews as part of a mileage agreement between the two companies. Gordon and Bill would discuss features on their engines with the LNER men, just sitting on one of the footplates. LNER crews envied the GWR cabs because there was no bare metal in the firebox, it being covered all over with cleating, as compared with their bare upper firebox stuck out in the cab. But the GWR crew were worse off in the comfort stakes, their spartan wooden tip-up seats for the driver being outdone by their rivals' bucket seats! KENNETH LEECH

Published by WILD SWAN PUBLICATIONS LTD. 1-3 Hagbourne Road, Didcot, Oxon, OX11 8DP

INTRODUCTION

I first met Gordon Shurmer in 1995 while in Swindon visiting an ex-Malmesbury shed engine cleaner and top-link Swindon engineman Fred Hinder. In conversation with Fred, he mentioned that there was a fellow just around the corner in Churchward Avenue who 'had a tale to tell'.

And so it proved. Right from our very first meeting I fell under Gordon Shurmer's spell – there were indeed many tales to be related, and it became evident to me that, whilst there was much in published print relating to the famous Swindon Works and its place at the very core of the history of the Great Western Railway, there was little co-ordinated information in print about the working of Swindon's locomotive shed, and this was a golden opportunity, through Gordon's life and work, to properly chronicle a missing link in GWR history.

Naturally, other projects, other commitments, and the need for one's living to be made, have conspired to hold up progress towards a finished work, but my visits to Gordon have continued over a ten-year period, and many times I left his home not just with a feeling of satisfaction at the quality of the information gleaned but also full of an emotional response to Gordon as he always impressed the listener not just with his knowledge, but his love of life, his pride in what he achieved, the knowledge he passed on to others and his dedication to his career.

I, like Gordon, have an affection for Swindon, and wish I had spent more of my life there. My family came to Swindon in April 1949 when I was nine months old when my father took a post in the Borough Engineers' Office and we moved to a grey, austere council house at 2 Barton Road in Moredon. So I have some Swindon connections and, had we remained in the town instead of moving to Middlesbrough in 1953, I would have attended Moredon Junior School, where, by sheer coincidence, I took up my first teaching post when I returned in the Autumn of 1970. I loved the old Railway Museum in Faringdon Road, in the old 'barracks', the oddly-Gothic building once provided by the GWR for housing unmarried employees of the Company, and which, I observed, like Pannett Park Museum in Whitby, always looked and smelt like museums used to do!

It was at Moredon Junior that I met my first wife, Tricia, in 1971, who introduced me to her home town, Malmesbury, where I spent many years researching the history of the town's branch railway in order to produce my first book for Wild Swan in 1990. I passed my driving test in Swindon and remember vividly negotiating the test car gently past scores of bicycles as hundreds of workers spilled out of the Works onto Rodbourne Road. I've begun and ended many a journey from the old GWR station, upon whose refreshment rooms Brunel once commented so unfavourably, and I even wrote a song there one cold, windswept night in the early '70s while waiting for a dmu to Gloucester. I once sang in the folk song club which existed in the Greyhound by the corner of the GWR Park in Faringdon Road. I've been to the County Ground many times over the years (to support Middlesbrough, not Swindon!) and once had a conversation with Swindon's favourite son, Don Rogers, who was the

Town's most notable player in the '60s, in the sports shop he ran in Faringdon Road for many years, shortly after his team had given my team a 4-1 drubbing, I can remember him commenting "They weren't as good as last year".

So I have tangible connections with Swindon which I value highly. I have always wanted to write something which would reflect my interest in Swindon, something that would express those personal connections that I treasure and at the same time add something to the fabric of the town's railway heritage. Meeting Gordon gave me that chance, and it was a culmination of years of coming to Swindon to research railway history on other projects that I first met Gordon. When I researched Malmesbury, I found that there were many railway people who had worked on the old branch still resident in Swindon. In Stratton St. Margaret, Len Hillman filled me in on parcel porters' work at Malmesbury in the '40s. In Crombey Street, Arthur 'Buller' Reeve put me back inside Malmesbury engine shed at the time of the Great War, whilst in the Railway Village in Bathampton Street, Charlie Hurley explained to me the details of signalling alterations at Little Somerford after the Malmesbury branch was diverted there in 1933. I could not have gleaned the information these fine old railwaymen imparted to me any other way. On other topics, another inhabitant of the Village, Jeff Pegler, explained to me how actual operations on the banking engines at Brimscombe shed were not always as shown in the Working Timetable. I remember spending hours in the *Evening Advertiser* offices up in Old Town, poring over the bound volumes of the paper before they were put on microfilm, trying to find snippets on Malmesbury and examine some of the political intrigue concerning the history of the abortive Wilts & Glos Railway of 1864. I loved the old GWR Museum in the former 'barracks' in Faringdon Road. Railway history always came alive for me in Swindon.

The very existence of Swindon, a sleepy village on a Wiltshire hilltop with a population of less than 2,500, overlooking the western end of the Vale of White Horse, was changed forever by Isambard Kingdom Brunel's decision to install the GWR's main locomotive operations and eventual Works on the flatter land a mile to the north of Old Swindon, to precipitate a century and a half of honest industry and a working railway culture with which the town will always be associated. The rumblings of the future were heard first on the hilltop in 1840 when the new main line was extended through to Hay Lane near Wootton Bassett.

The Great Western Railway were paternalistic and enlightened employers, and very self-contained – it is said that they only ever bought screws, and everything else they made themselves – and not merely content with ensuring that the new imported workforce had somewhere to live locally, they also took on responsibility for subscribing to the moral, educational, medical and social welfare of the inhabitants of New Swindon, providing housing, a church, a school (some 25 years before the Education Act of 1870), a market, hospital, medical insurance, swimming and Turkish baths, a recreational park, and in the Mechanics' Institute there existed the first public library in the country some years before local councils made such provision. The back-to-back stone cottages of the Railway Village were a unique development, an example of early planned industrial housing which had a great impact on the country. It survived intact, a quiet enclave with an almost self-contained community of railway families, and there was little social distress here, little poverty, no slums, as New Swindon escaped most of the worst deprivations of the Industrial Revolution because of the caring attitude of the GWR Company towards its employees. The GWR encouraged loyalty and received it in good measure from its workforce, in that very patriarchal society of those times. As a factory worker or fireman and his family relaxed in the GWR Park on a Sunday afternoon and listened to the music of a brass band from local militia playing in the bandstand, free briefly from the rigours of railway work, they may have imagined that their pattern of life could go on for ever.

Swindon became the last Borough to be created by Queen Victoria, with the road named after her symbolically linking the Old and New Swindons. By 1901, the population of the incorporated Borough was 44,996, of which 12,500 were employed in the Works, and larger and larger locomotives emerged from those Works, under the guidance of George Jackson Churchward, who lived at Newburn House. All railwaymen lived in the town back then, including the top brass. The railway executives of that era belonged more completely to Swindon than their modern-day counterparts at Honda and Plessey.

In truth, the end of the railway era was more of a cultural loss than an economic one. The one-industry town has always been vulnerable to market fluctuations and social change, but positive winds of change were in the air as early as 1952, the year I first left Swindon, when it was designated as a London overspill town and gradually the area began to attract new industries. Even by the mid-60s Swindon was offering a variety of industrial employment, although the emphasis was still at that time on unskilled and semi-skilled work – car accessories and components, soft drinks, light engineering, packaging, plastics, and, of course, the long-time providers H.O. Wills tobacco and Garrards Engineering with their sound and reproduction equipment. So there was already a manufacturing base to assume the economic mantle. By the 1980s there was a large influx of middle-class professional people taking skilled jobs in high technology and service industries as the town expanded to the west, and today, in the 21st Century, there is a population of over 180,000, a virtual doubling since the '60s. This is not a population increase commensurate with recession and failure.

In St. Mark's churchyard, behind the church itself, where many of the folk of Victorian Swindon are buried, there are tangible reminders of the importance of the railway to Swindon in this secluded spot in the middle of town, memories of another age which has passed, and yet can never be forgotten. Across the railway tracks beyond the northern fence of the churchyard, one is aware of remaining buildings of the Works standing in silent testimony to the expert work that was once undertaken there, a quiet occasionally punctuated by the abrasive rumble and hiss of a blue-liveried First

Great Western diesel train on the main line between Paddington and Bristol, its pause to call at Swindon's station seeming to be a token salute in recognition of the town's railway heritage. On this line once ran *Lord of the Isles* and *Vulcan* and the cream of the GWR's fleet of engines, on tracks which were Brunel's original brainchild, the 7 foot Broad Gauge. Indeed, where the STEAM museum proclaims its attractions to passengers on the main line, is exactly the spot where Swindon's original locomotive running shed was situated in the 1840s, something of which I really had no idea until I began researching for this book. History is all around, from the weathered gravestones of the 19th Century (many recording children) to the remaining carriage works wall enclosing the east end of the churchyard; from the overlooking water tower to nearby Bristol Place, where the sombre imposing grandeur of Park House is a reminder of how generations of aspiring young railwaymen from all over the system went there to undergo their medicals as they sought entry to the ranks and subsequent promotions. Here in St Mark's, so close was the railway/church connection that a vicar here was once entitled to hail a train and have it stop for his convenience, and then travel free!

Here in the churchyard, one gravestone merits extra attention. Here lies Minard Rea, who died 18th June, 1857, aged 35 years. Rea was Manager of the Locomotive Works and was responsible for the building of the GWR Mechanics' Institute. Dating from 1843, this Swindon landmark provided a library, reference library, reading rooms, rooms for billiards and chess, and for many years educational classes and lectures were a feature of the Institution. After its Large Hall was destroyed by fire in 1930, this part was rebuilt as a theatre with a dance hall underneath. Sir Daniel Gooch was an early president, a role also taken on by F. W. Hawksworth, the GWR's Chief Mechanical Engineer, in the '30s. At time of writing, there are plans afoot for the Mechanics', but there is some disagreement between private ownership and local council as to its future use.

To say that Swindon has changed is a glib truism which can only be understood by looking at the social forces which enforced that change. The social structure which once made it possible for a whole town to go on holiday at the same time no longer exists. That change has been irrevocably taking place for fifty years, from the designation as a London overspill area in the '50s, to the demise of steam as the principal motive power, to the closure of the locomotive shed in 1964, to the final demise of the Works in March 1986, and as Swindon extended, primarily westwards, to provide homes for those who came to work in the new diversified economic structure of the town as new industries moved in.

Today Swindon is but a denuded shell in railway terms, with modern high-speed trains saturating track space, and with old buildings now posing as heritage centres, although this is not to deride this function in any way. I cannot say if the railway age in Swindon was a good thing or a bad thing compared to the Swindon of today, only that it happened. The changes that have come to pass are happening – they just don't seem as valid or attractive because we always tend to

Looking along a rainswept Commercial Road sometime in the 1950s, with the Market in evidence to the left. Gordon's Mum did most of her shopping for provisions here, just two minutes walk.
CTY. SWINDON LIBRARIES

view the past through rose-tinted lenses. But life in a railway works was a rough existence if we believe Alfred Williams' account in *Life in a Railway Factory*. He worked there as a steam hammer man for much of Queen Victoria's reign and paints in his words a very gruelling picture, for which he was castigated by many of his workmates – that old Company loyalty again. But GWR Swindon was not as idyllic as local myth would suggest. I am fascinated by the life and lore of GWR Swindon, but my fascination exists from a distance. I am deluding myself if I believe that living in a society where most men smoked, where the limit of their horizons was the pub and one day away in Barry Island every year, and where the grind of the workplace was regulated four times a day by the most unmusical of factory hooters, are the norms by which I want to live my life in the 21st century!

Amongst those children I taught in Moredon in the early 1970s, there were many rolled r's and a distinct West Country flavour in the accents. What price finding that attractive burr now? We live in an internet society, and the computer itself encourages solitary behaviour as well as a form of communication devoid of face-to-face contact. The imported citizenry appears to venerate technology and there is a fear that they have lost the roots that their forebears took for granted. But we must respect history as a moral and social backdrop, and let us not forget that New Swindon was founded with an

imported workforce – the skills of the railway age simply were not available in rural north Wiltshire in 1840. Swindon has evolved, as it did in the 19th century, but differently, with a host of information technology companies – it is a mobile society now and the workplace has become as electronic as it is geographical.

The Swindon of today presents me with a myriad of culture conflicts. Yes, it has certain disadvantages – no river, no large civic centre, no university, no major concert hall, although I did see that American songstress Dionne Warwick was appearing in the last show of a UK tour at 'The Oasis'. I recall going out with the Moredon teaching staff to see Anthony Booth starring at the newly-opened Wyvern Theatre in 1971, and clearly recollect how the introduction of a fine modern theatre venue was hailed as a great cultural advance for the town. But there's something in me reacts against the marauding Americanisation of the Orbital Shopping Park even if there is easy parking there. On the other hand, when I was a young green schoolteacher in Swindon during 1970–72, I could little have imagined visiting a Barnes & Nobles bookstore near Haydon Wick or essaying to do research in a Swindon-based National Monuments Record. And there's a reference library in the centre of Swindon in a building which appears to have long since outlived its usefulness, but Roger Trayhurn and his staff

This 1963 aerial photograph of Swindon, looking north, illustrates the centre of Swindon and encapsulates much of my life.

1. The house at 56 North Street where I was born, 31st January 1921.
2. The house at 50 Havelock Street where our family moved in 1926, my home until 1955 when Hazel and I married.
3. Sanford Street Boys' School, where I avoided the cane from the headmaster until just before I left!
4. The Sunday School I attended in Downing Street.
5. Milton Road swimming baths, one of many facilities built by the GWR for its workforce. A swim cost 3d and you could stop in there all day if you could stand the pink chlorine!
6. Perkins' Grocery, where I had my first part-time employment. The lady who ran it was a Mrs. Crook (née Perkins) who was married to Clem Crook, an engine driver at Swindon shed. The family had one of the first Ford cars in Swindon, for which they paid £120.
7. The site of the 1908 tram disaster at the foot of Victoria Hill, still talked about today a century later. The brakes failed as the driver applied them before the curve on its way down from Old Town and it went over onto its side. Several people were killed and there is a local story about one fellow who jumped off and ran off down Princes Street as he had a train to catch!
8. Victoria Hill, the main road link between the lower part of Swindon near the railway and Old Town on the hilltop. Swindon Town station, the Midland & South Western Junction's station, was off camera to the south, about 300 yards behind the photographer.
9. The Savoy Cinema. I can remember seeing it being built in 1937, over a period of two years, being particularly impressed by the large square section where the screen was to be mounted. The first movie shown there was Captain January starring Shirley Temple.
10. The older Regent Cinema. The first film ever shown there starred Ronald Coleman in Bulldog Drummond.
11. Whitehouse Bridge, where I first saw King George V, my favourite locomotive, while I was on my evening grocery round.
12. The Baptist Tabernacle, a very imposing place of worship with its Greek pillar facade. I only ever went in there once for a funeral.
13. Regent Street, the town's major commercial thoroughfare. A lot of my favourite shops were there — The Spot, Tompkins & Barrett, Chappell's . . .
14. Our local market, excellent for fish, fruit, meat and china!
15. Bristol Omnibus Company bus station.
16. The police station — 'the Nick'.
17. Bath Road Methodist Church.
18. Swindon Town Hall, an impressive building which towers over the less imposing library, still in wooden huts today and very poor for an urban area which now has city status.
19. The Ship public house, notorious because in 1903 a young barmaid was murdered by her former fiance, who was subsequently hanged in Devizes.
20. General Post Office.
21. Park House, where drivers and firemen went to take their technical and medical examinations.

Nos. 22-25 are locations where, as already mentioned with the swimming baths, the GWR provided many facilities for its local workforce.

22. The railway village, the housing estate built during 1843 for the new railway population.
23. The Mechanics Institute, the main recreational establishment built by the GWR here. It offered a theatre, library, reading room and billiard hall. Built in 1876.
24. The open expanse of Faringdon Road Park.
25. St. Mark's Church.
26. My route to work between Havelock Street and the shed, via Commercial Road, Milton Street, across Faringdon Road, into Shepherd Street to the main entrance to the Works, then through the tunnel which came out by the general stores (27). It was a 7-minute walk, although I could get it down to three at a brisk trot . . . thence through the brickyard to Swindon running shed (28).
29. The printhouse where I worked for the GWR first, which had a verandah where I loved to look out over the Bristol main line.
30. The General Offices, where I had my interviews with Mr. Smith in February 1937, prior to being taken on as an engine cleaner.
31. Swindon stock shed.
32. Swindon Locomotive Yard Signal Box.
33. Swindon West Signal Box.
34. Swindon East Signal Box.
35. Swindon Junction station.
36. Swindon Locomotive Yard sidings.
37. The Wesleyan Church which later became the GWR Museum, once sleeping quarters for railway employees.

Nos. 38-42 indicate key buildings in the Works.

38. Paint Shop.
39. Carriage & Wagon Works.
40. The Foundry (The Long Shop).
41. The Pattern Shop (woodworking).
42. Works turntable, 65ft diameter.

there were always so helpful and showed great interest in and support for this project.

But it is true that I have always, nearly always, valued Swindon's 'ordinaryness', and if it has moved with the times with its new highways, shopping malls and the new uses found for old railway buildings, you can still find some of that old atmosphere if you really want to, by talking with the native Swindonians such as Gordon Shurmer, by taking a walk along the footpath in Old Town that runs along the course of the old 'Tiddley Dyke' where it was once possible to catch a train between Swindon's *two* railway stations, or even at a remodelled County Ground where the football club continues its struggle in the lower reaches of the Football League, or by taking a walk by Coate Water and smiling at Gordon's tale of how he had to lock the gates each evening there during his first employment after leaving school, using a key which was attached to a large piece of an old oar to prevent him taking it home by mistake!

For some time after I began visiting Gordon, I was unsure as to what form a finished work would take. Then it gradually became clear that the aim of this work should be two-fold, to celebrate Gordon's life and times, and to chronicle as fully as possible through his life and work the running of Swindon's locomotive shed, including with it some history of the Broad Gauge and the working and allocations of the later shed of 1871 which became Gordon's workplace. He repre-

Swindon Works boilermakers outside 'A' Shop, grouped around a 'King' sometime in the early 1960s, with Gordon's Dad on the right in the front row and 'Barney' Owl, the chargeman, a Swindon Town football supporter, on the left. Those boilermakers were tough old boys. Gordon's Dad smoked forty cigarettes a day all his working life. Each night he'd take a puff of a cigarette before getting into bed, pinching it out as he put it on the bedside table. 'I always remember one morning when Dad was late, the hooter having gone at the Works, and from the next bedroom I heard my mother telling him in exasperated tones "I don't know — if this house was on fire you'd take a drag on that fag before you called the bloody fire brigade!"'
CTY. GORDON SHURMER

Author Mike Fenton learning to drive in the back garden at 2 Barton Road, Swindon, in 1950! I like to believe that I was woken up each morning by the busy progress of the Cirencester workmen's train on the Midland & South Western Junction line only a couple of hundred yards away. Twenty years after this photograph was taken, I returned to this same part of Swindon – Moredon – to begin a teaching career.

AUTHOR'S COLLECTION

sents the last of a tough breed of men, those who began their railway careers on the old Great Western Railway before the advent of the Second World War, and whose working life straddled the years of great change that ensued, and it is a tribute to his adaptability and versatility that not long after he finally attained his cherished ambition to become a driver of a steam locomotive, he also became one of the most respected tutors on the new diesel locomotives as steam approached its sunset on the nationalised railway network in the 1960s. His memories are a link with men who began their railway lives in the early years of the 20th Century, whose knowledge and belief in their work shaped his own attitudes and ambitions, as did a happy, supportive family life in a simpler, saner era, when a trip to the flicks to see Abbott & Costello, followed by sixpenny fish'n'chips and walking your girlfriend home to get her there by 10.30 p.m. was an innocent blend of simple treats and mature responsibilities. Talking with Gordon, I have thought many times how great it would have been if someone, armed with shorthand rather than a cassette recorder, had had the foresight to undertake research of this nature a century ago, and chronicled the memories of those first GWR men of the 1840s and 1850s who peer at us from beneath grizzled, hairy visages on photographs, those veterans of Swindon's first loco shed in Broad Gauge days.

So Swindon does retain a place in my cultural awareness, and I mourn the loss of an era that in truth did pass me by as a child. Many's the time I've stood on those same platform ends where Gordon spent hours as a boy observing the railway activity and knowing that he wanted to be part of it, in

my case simply wishing it was still possible to catch an evening direct train, indeed, any train, to the long-forgotten railway outposts at Malmesbury, Highworth, Faringdon and Marlborough, or longing to hear the crash of a signal lever in West Box which Gordon lucidly described so many times to me.

This book has been a collaborative effort, put together by taping Gordon's memories over a period of several years, then spending long hours transcribing the tapes and assembling the material into a readable account. For convenience, readability and atmosphere, I have kept the text in the first person, in Gordon's own words throughout the book, with the exception of this introduction and the appendix at the end which focuses on the history of the running shed provision at Swindon. Many hours have been spent poring over scores of photographs together in order to produce full, informative captions in the best Wild Swan tradition, with both Gordon and I reading and re-reading each chapter many times in order to ensure complete accuracy. Facts have been drawn from the records, as well as the memories of some of Gordon's old colleagues, and for me it is the human element that always shines through, to create some of the atmosphere of a bygone era. I wish I'd met Gordon much earlier, and indeed, I might have done so, recalling the days when as a young impoverished schoolteacher living in Beatrice Street, and for a short time, Emlyn Square, when I'd often catch the bus from Moredon to get into town at lunchtime to get to the bank, a local service which ran past the end of Churchward Avenue where Gordon and Hazel have lived since 1955.

Mike Fenton 2006

MEN LEAVING WORKS, SWINDON

The GWR workforce pouring out of the Bristol Street tunnel entrance to Swindon Works. The building on the right was the GWR hospital. I entered this establishment just once in my life, at the age of eight. I was chopping wood one lunchtime and I heard my Dad arriving from the Works through the back gate and I nearly chopped a finger off. Dad always forbade me to use his tools. A portion of my finger was hanging off and a nurse there in the hospital stitched it back together. I still have the mark it left.

CTY. MRS. CELIA FRASER

CHAPTER ONE

SWINDON BORN AND BRED

I first saw the light of day on 31st January, 1921, delivered at home at 56 North Street in the Old Town part of Swindon, a house that my maternal grandfather had purchased for £200. My mother and father were both born in 1898, Dad a Swindon boilermaker in the Works, like his father before him, whilst Mum, born Gladys Embling, came from Lambourn where her father ran a bakery. I was the first grandson in the whole family, christened Gordon Albert

George Shurmer. In those days you were normally named after your parents or relatives. The Great Western Railway was in my blood, and my earliest memory during our days at North Street is of a Trip Friday when I was four years old. This was the day that all the Swindon workforce of the GWR took special trains to Weston-super-Mare, Weymouth or Barry Island. Around four o'clock that morning we were the only ones who were out that early in North Street, as few

A busy Regent Street in Swindon, looking south at some point during my childhood, with the tower of McIlroy's department store visible in the distance on the right and Stead & Simpson's shoe shop advertising attractive offers in footwear for Trip week.

NATIONAL RAILWAY MUSEUM

Early morning special Swindon Corporation bus services were in evidence as Trippers converged on the station one Trip morning about 1930. Who knows, our family may even have been there among them!
WILTSHIRE LIBRARY & MUSEUM SERVICE TROWBRIDGE

Below: London-bound trippers. Bottom: A generation of hat wearers heading for Barry Island.
GREAT WESTERN RAILWAY MAGAZINE

A Paddington-bound Trip special passing Swindon East signal box on a misty July morning.

At work and at play in the 20s and 30s, an oft-heard question as July approached each year was "Where are you going Trip?" The GWR Swindon Works annual holiday, unpaid in those days, left the centre of Swindon like a ghost town for a week, as other employers locally followed suit with holidays. It started as far back as 1849 when the Company granted a special train to convey about 500 workers and their families to Oxford. By 1868, three special trains were running to London, Weston-Super-Mare and South Wales, and by the 30s the most popular destinations were London, Weston, Weymouth and Barry Island. There are even stories of Trippers going to smaller places such as St. Ives and Tenby where the local townsfolk would go down to the station to greet the visitors! I loved Trip, although we only ever went away for a day, not a week, on Trip Friday. It was simply economics; with paid holidays still a thing of the future, a week in a guest house for a family of four was very expensive. The Friday was followed by Trip Week, and by the Wednesday you could walk down Regent Street and hardly see a soul. My grandfather worked at the Home & Colonial grocers in Regent Street and on his suggestion I was able to save up money for Trip by taking back jam-jar empties. We used a lot of jam in our house and you'd receive a ha'penny back on the 1lb jars, a penny on the 2lb jars, and about a fortnight before Trip I'd put the empties in a wicker basket and take them to the shop and collect the money on them. A year's jam-jar empties could bring me up to 1s 6d pocket money for Trip!

The photo on the beach shows me with my cousin Harold at Weston-Super-Mare on a Trip Friday about 1930. We would have a donkey ride there, a great treat, but the thing I loved best about the day was going out of Swindon on the train and seeing all the new locomotives outside the Works. I loved the tunnels — Box if we were going to Weston, Severn Tunnel if we were going to Barry Island.

On the view of Trippers about to climb boarding steps, we are reminded that all departures took place around the station and the Works from ground level — Trip specials bearing away over 25,000 people could not all depart from the station platforms owing to their number and the need for regular diagrammed train services to work as normal. Buckets and spades were much in evidence. Shunters booked on very early, about 4.30 a.m., to assist passengers up into the carriages via little step ladders — a hefty grandma would have required a good push!

Preliminary arrangements for Trip were begun months beforehand and involved all railway folk locally, not just the Works. It was necessary for the GWR to find out from each employee the destination chosen so that a general idea could be formed as to the number who would take advantage of the special trains and the places to which those specials would have to be run. The train operating staff then had to make arrangements for the timing of the trains, to avoid clashing with regular passenger services, and to fit in the Trip trains to make such connections with cross-country and branch services as might be necessary. Places to which there were not sufficient holidaymakers to justify special trains being run had to be catered for by strengthening the ordinary passenger services. Assembling the specials at Swindon involved marshalling between 400-500 coaches. Special train services would also convey Trippers in from the outlying areas, such as Highworth, Marlborough and Faringdon, to link up with their special at an early hour. Our family would walk, of course, but there were special bus services, taxi-cabs and horses-and carts which brought folk in from areas further out on the edge of Swindon. On the morning of 8th July 1932, some 26 special trains left sidings all over Swindon.

Gordon (left) and Harold, at Weston-super-Mare on Trip Friday c.1930.

AUTHOR'S COLLECTION

A view of North Street, Swindon, in July 1941, looking west towards Pembroke Street. No. 56, the house where I was born, is the dark bay window on the right. The pillar box on the pavement beyond stood outside Cleal's general store. I had many happy times here and still visited my grandparents regularly here during the war, although I was working long hours on the footplate, especially on goods work.

CTY. MRS. MARY THOMPSON

Right: Neighbours in North Street in 1924, the Kents from No. 63. North Street was built during 1869 and was named as the northern limit of building at that time in Old Swindon, there being only fields between it and the newer railway community down at New Swindon.

CTY. MRS. BERYL WYNN

Commercial Road, Swindon

Commercial Road, looking east, around the time of my birth. You can discern the break in the houses (arrowed) which is the southern end of Havelock Street where we lived from 1926 in No. 50. Postcard views of Swindon side-streets are rare to see, only thoroughfares as this one receiving much attention. I do not recall Commercial Road being lined with trees — they must have been removed during my early childhood or even earlier. The Rolleston Arms features to the right whilst the market, with its roofed additions of 1903, is seen on the left. Mum did much of her shopping for food here. Even here, at the foot of Old Town, we were very much aware of the sounds of the railway. If the wind was in the right direction, you could hear trains leaving the station when you were standing in our back garden in Havelock Street.

in our part of town were railway folk, unlike down in the railway village area of Reading Street, Bathampton Street and Faringdon Road where the workers lived in terraces built by the GWR with the Works in 1843. I had my bucket and spade and, as we walked along our street on our way down to the factory sidings at the rear of St. Mark's Church to catch our train, I reached out and rattled my spade noisily along the railings! It was a lovely powerful feeling but I was swiftly scolded by my mother who exclaimed "You'll wake everybody in the street!"

Another early railway memory from that time was my first visit to Swindon Town station on the old Midland & South Western Junction Railway, a line I came to love with its fascinating history and unique atmosphere. My Uncle Les took me up there to pick up a puppy which was being sent on a train from Cheltenham. The little dog was named Radar and I can remember it grabbing at my uncle's shoes! I vividly recall the train coming in from Cheltenham under the Croft Road bridge, the hinges on the smokebox door showing up brilliant white in the fading light. When we got that little fella home he was so tired after all the travelling that he collapsed in his saucer of milk!

Trip Friday was a big day for the GWR workforce when I was a child. I recall the coaches on those trains were gaslit, and if you had to go through a tunnel, such as Box or the Severn Tunnel, the driver would sound the whistle and folk in the carriages would light the gas lights. They were clerestory roof stock, what we called 'pigeon-top' coaches. I can still see my Dad reaching up and lighting the mantles with a match. As you entered the tunnel they'd pull the windows up with the leather strap, and the closed windows would go blue in the tunnel with the fumes and the smoke.

The engine whistle would sound in the tunnel too as there would frequently be plate-laying staff in there working. There was no communication between the driver and the men on the line save for the whistle and plate-layers' lamps, which they'd raise to signal to the driver that they knew he was coming and would stand clear.

When I was five, my parents purchased a house at 50 Havelock Street (pronounced *Hav*-lock), Swindon, for £350, arranging a mortgage with the bank. The street dates from 1866 and was apparently named after a British General, Sir Henry Havelock, who fought in the Indian Mutiny of 1857. It was a simple move, which took us down near the market and much closer to what would eventually become my place of work, Swindon locomotive shed. My family did not possess a lot of belongings, and had virtually no furniture as we'd been living with Mum's parents. It was years and years before the front room was ever furnished because they just didn't have the money. In those days if you couldn't pay your rent, they used to make you sell your furniture; if you had a piano it had to be sold. When my grandfather was out of work, my parents and uncles and aunts all used to put in 1/6d a week to help them stay at North Street, although my grandparents eventually had to leave and live with my grandfather's sister in Manchester Road. But at least that kind of family support helped them avoid the last resort, the workhouse, that cruel institution where older couples would be split. I recall the move from North Street well, as the day we moved the Education Officer came to see my mother to enquire why I hadn't been sent to school. Mother explained that as the move to Havelock Street had been in the offing when I became of statutory school age, they'd thought it was pointless getting me settled in at an Old Town school when in a

Havelock Street from the air, my family home from 1926-1955. No. 50 is arrowed.

SIMMONS AEROFILMS

few weeks I'd be disrupted by the move. So I started school in the infants in College Street just after I became five years old.

What amazed me at Havelock Street was the size of the bedrooms, after the tiny rooms we'd been used to at North Street. The whole front of the upper floor was one large bedroom which was Mum and Dad's, with two smaller bedrooms behind it with the staircase in the middle. The door from the street opened into a tiny passage, then a front room and a middle room opened off that. You had to go through the middle room to reach the small kitchen, beyond which was a brick extension containing the wash-house. Here was the copper where Mum used to do the family washing. It was a huge bowl affair heated by a coal fire and she'd put the clothes in there and stir them with a long stick. She'd cook the Christmas puddings in there too! The wash-house was a spartan affair, with a sink and a tap and a single shelf containing saucepans, and the walls were just bare bricks which my Dad had painted over, cream above and green below, divided by a black line. I can see Dad now, with a piece of chalked string, which he'd use to give him the straight black line, pulling the string like a bow to give him two chalk lines on the wall so he could paint an accurate line. The dreaded mangle with its huge rollers was always kept outside against the back fence – it was never covered over and never came inside all the years we were there. There was no bathroom, just an outside privy in those days, although in later years the kitchen was enlarged and a bathroom added to the back of the house. Toilet rolls were a thing of the future, it was torn-up *Daily Mirrors* and *Evening Advertisers* in those days, threaded on a piece of string and hanging on a nail on the wall, and with all that print coming off, many a backside bore tomorrow's weather forecast and the latest Swindon Town match report!

There was a tiny back garden and out there Dad had a shed which he used as a small workshop. He'd be out there repairing shoes by candlelight with a piece of leather. I'd go with him to a shop called Chappell's in Regent Street where he'd purchase the leather at prices ranging from 1/3d to 1/9d. He'd take a piece out of the rack and smell it, bend it a few times, then when he was satisfied he'd take it home and cut soles and heels out of it in the shed. He'd cut the old soles off with his cobbler's knife and he had a big iron foot with three positions for different size shoes. He'd stick a lump of leather on there, tack it down and go round it with his knife and he had a burnishing tool which he'd use to polish and shine up the leather. That's how life was back then – my grandchildren's world is a throwaway existence, but in my childhood, if you didn't repair it, you didn't have it. It was simple economics.

Havelock Street was my home for almost thirty years until I married in December 1955. It was a typical town set of terraces, entirely residential in those days, no pub, although there were two general store-type shops, Mrs. Walker's opposite our house, and Mrs. Paisley's on our side of the road on the corner with Commercial Road. You could obtain provisions unofficially on Sundays at either establishment, if you ran out

of milk or another essential – you walked up the alley to be handed things from Mrs. Walker's side door, but her rival up the street preferred the privacy of her kitchen to sell goods on the Sabbath. There were originally tiny little front gardens enclosed with iron railings incorporating fleur-de-lys designs, that is, until the metal was removed for the War effort during the early 40s. Occasionally you saw a car on our street, but the pervading aroma was the horse mess from the regular visits of the rag-and-bone men, dustmen and milk deliveries. Our coal was delivered via the narrowbacks at the rear, our coal bunker being by the back window. We never had to cut our privet hedge at the back of our garden because the coalman's horse would regularly nibble at it. Mum always used to take a bowl of water out to the hard-working animal. The coalman was an expert in reversing that cart down the narrowbacks – with not a lot of room, you'd never see him hit the wall. I seem to recall that coal cost 1/9d a cwt in those days.

Our 'refrigerator' at Havelock Street was simply a wooden cupboard out back with a bit of gauze on the front. Of course, there was no actual freezing as such; it was simply where milk would be kept cool. A bottle of milk would be stood in a saucer of cold water and an old cloth would be draped over the bottle with its edges dangling in the water, and the water would be siphoned up around the bottle. That's all there would be in the cupboard. We never kept meat in there because you didn't buy it until you were ready to use it. In fact the butchers had no refrigeration either, so it was common in those days for the butcher to remain open quite late, maybe as late as 11 p.m., and people would wait outside the shop and buy their meat more cheaply that way. The butcher would cut his losses but still make as much as he could. So our Sunday joint would be bought late Saturday night and would have to do for Monday as well. Mum would put left-over meat through the grinder and make a shepherd's pie with it. Everything had to be used to its utmost. That was the accepted way of life. It was hard compared to life today, but we knew no different. My parents finally had an electric fridge at 50 Havelock around 1961, several years after I'd left home.

There was always something going on to interest us children in Swindon between the War. When you went out of our back gate you could see the fire station, to which we'd all run whenever the siren went. We'd run down the narrowbacks between the houses and stand out in front of the fire station to enjoy the action. Only three men were employed in three shifts, one man per shift, 6.0–2.0, 2.0–10.0, and nights, with the rest being volunteers. A Captain Baker was in charge and whenever the force was required you'd see the volunteers coming in on their bicycles, throwing their bikes into the station in their hurry and jumping on the fire engine as it left with all the hurried alacrity of the Keystone Cops! It was a fine sight! The main fire engine with the ladder was called 'Laddie' and had solid tyres, accompanied by a smaller one named 'Lassie', and we'd run along by the side of the fire engine for 30 yards or so, enjoying the burning smell coming off the tyres! Adjacent to the fire station was the Corporation yard, and I have a clear memory of Friday nights around 5.00, when the council workers would bring in the steam rollers from wherever they'd been working, and we'd watch the driver throw the fire out and move them into sheds where they kept them.

Simple childish pursuits varied with the season – marbles in the summer when the gutters were dry, conkers from Kingsdown Park or Coate Water in the autumn, whereas winter time you'd be more likely to be running with a steel hoop. If you had an old worn-out tyre you were king of the street, and you'd run for miles like that, batting it along with an old stick. You'd bowl those marbles along the gutter and try to hit your mate's marble and thereby claim possession of

it. Simple marbles were clay but if you were really keen you had a glass set, 'dazzlers', which you could buy in a pack of five at Tompkins & Barrett's for a halfpenny. Any dry time of the year was fag card season, propping them up against a wall and attempting to knock them down with other cards. I obtained a lot of my cards from my Uncle Les who smoked, but never from my Dad who rolled his own cigarettes. We'd see folk coming down the street smoking and simply go up to them and ask "Got any fag cards, mister?" They were never put in albums, I don't think we knew they existed, and they'd be dog-eared, black and indiscernible after a few uses in the street. Pea-shooters were available locally for the ubiquitous halfpenny, and we'd go down to the canal and take seeds of

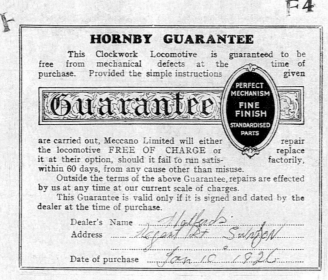

My fifth birthday present, with its original guarantee showing date of purchase, from Halfords in Regent Street, Swindon.   AUTHOR

Regent Street, Swindon, looking north about 1938. On the extreme right is the Savoy Theatre, which opened on the site of former numbers 38 to 42 in Regent Street on 1st March 1937. The building was designed by ABC's (Associated British Cinemas) own 'house' architect, W. R. Glen, and had a capacity of 1,906 people. It featured an RCA sound system and the first film shown there was 'Captain January' starring Shirley Temple. We had seven houses of entertainment in Swindon at one time, two theatres and five cinemas. On Trip days this street would be almost deserted as shops gave staff the day off. In the distance was a Swindon landmark, the tower of McIlroys department store, and well-known shops down the left side of the street included The Spot, and Lotts' Ironmongers, which had an aroma of its own with its paraffin, tools, barrows and various hardware. An interesting feature here is the dearth of motor traffic and the sole moving car coming towards the camera, its driver apparently not too bothered about adhering to the left side of the road!

CTY. SWINDON LIBRARIES

the hawthorn trees, put them in our mouths and have fun firing them at our mates!

The moment my future was sealed as a GWR engineman occurred on my fifth birthday, 31st January 1926. Mum was bathing me in a zinc bath on the living room table when Dad came in with a red box and put it down on the other end of the table. He removed the lid, pulled out a beautiful green clockwork engine and wound it up with a large key. I was mesmerised by the revolving wheels and when the spring had wound down and the wheels stopped, Dad returned the engine to the box and said, "When you've had your bath, it's yours. Happy birthday," he said. That was the quickest bath I've ever had in my entire life! When I'd been dried down and put on my pyjamas, I opened the box and played happily with my new toy on the floor until bedtime. It cost 12/6d and Dad was on a £2 a week wage in the Works. I still have that engine and its original guarantee.

On 23rd January 1927, my sister Betty Christine May was born, and I recall the midwife coming in and Dad boiling a lot of water. There was much coming and going up and down the stairs that night, and eventually Dad came down and announced "You've got a baby sister". And thus was our little family complete. Life was tough for women back in those times – beyond childbirth and child-rearing, it was a constant round of washing, ironing, cooking, shopping, sewing, altering clothes to squeeze a few months extra wear out of them, and many mothers would take in washing to supplement the man's wage to help make ends meet. Living close to the

centre of Swindon was convenient for Mum, who'd obtain most of what she needed in the nearby market and the shops along Regent Street, where she'd walk with a small wicker basket to carry her provisions. Life was a round of drudgery, but there was a spirit of comradeship in those streets of Swindon. Every street seemed to have its older matriarch who could be counted on for comfort, advice, and laying people out properly when they died. People were always glad to assist and rarely did any money change hands.

I started school in College Street and stayed there two years before transferring across the road to Sanford Street Boys School, where I remained until the age of 14. My clearest memory of the infant days at College Street is of the governess there, Miss Pickett, who kept sweets in her desk which she'd give, paradoxically, to children on their return from a dental appointment! Sanford Street Boys was a somewhat harsher regime – we were about 40 in a class, in rows, and there were monitors who had to fill the inkwells. There was one teacher who could leap onto the desktops from a standing position, walk across the desks and slash you across the back with his cane if you were talking! Another notorious member of staff was secretary of Swindon Town Football Club, and if they'd lost on the Saturday you had to watch out for yourself in his geometry class on Monday. He had a big gold ring and if you saw him take the chalk out of his hand and switch it to the other one as he came down the aisle between the desks, you knew you were going to get a tonker! There was a Sanford Street reunion some years ago and a cer-

'. . . just as the Town Hall clock struck nine, after which I'd run home, through the back gate of No. 56 North Street, down Western Street . . . ' Here's Western Street as I remember it, looking north with the tower of the Town Hall visible over the rooftops.
CTY. MRS. MARY THOMPSON

tain Mr Ruth was the only remaining member of staff who attended. One of the fellas remarked to him that in all the years he'd been taught by him in the school, he'd never found out the teacher's Christian name. Mr Ruth looked at him haughtily and replied "It's *Sir!*"

I discovered later, of course, that those school days were happy days, with discipline and security, and no worries about rent and bills. Discipline and efficiency go together. That's the difference today, isn't it? When I've been out in schools talking to children about the dangers of playing on railway lines, I've heard pupils call teachers by their Christian names! Another thing you could unfailingly expect back then was snow in the winter time. There's proof of global warming right there! We only ever seem to get a brief dusting of snow these days, but back then, as a child, I heard stories of the Swindon trams being dug out of a snowdrift, and the Winter of 1947 has lived long in the memory, with icicles hanging from eaves and guttering like glittering daggers.

Even after our move to Havelock Street I continued to spend many happy hours at my grandparents' in North Street, where I'd had many piggy-backs upstairs when I was tiny. They had a cellar there where I'd delight in watching coal deliveries being tipped down the chute from the street. I'd spend hours down there indulging in one of the great passions of my youth, making models from scrap materials. I'd use cake foil, cardboard boxes, chicken wire, and produce mostly railway buildings – bridges, platforms, tunnels, stations – fashioned from papier-mâché, decorated with Humbrol paints and bonded with glue from a tube. There was always a great satisfaction making models from scrap material and the interest has remained with me throughout my life. In 1954, with a fireman named Reginald Dan ('Texas' Dan) we founded the Swindon Model Railway Club.

An evening's modelling in the cellar would always end in the same way. Gran would invariably bring me a cup of cocoa just as the Town Hall clock struck nine, after which I'd run home, through the back gate of No. 56, down Western Street, along Crombey Street, down Newhall Street and into Havelock … by the time I reached my teens my mother's brother, a bachelor uncle, had built a smashing workshop in a shed at the back of the house in North Street, and my modelling activities continued there. I loved it in Old Town and for years after I would often go round the back and peer over the rear fence at the house where I came into the world. Christmases there were wonderful – especially with what they used to put on in those hard times with little money! Every house seemed to have a piano in those days, whether anyone could play it or not, but there'd always be someone in the extended family circle who could lead a Christmas sing-along with it! Then there'd be the silly games, *Find a Ring, Musical Chairs* or *Poor Pussy,* where you sat blindfolded on someone's lap with a cushion and they'd utter 'miaow' and you had to guess whose lap you were sitting on! There'd be about twenty-two or so aunts, uncles and cousins gathered on Christmas Day, and when my grandparents became too old to host the festivities, my mother took it all on at Havelock

Street, where Mum used to have two sittings for Christmas tea because the house was so full! Dad used to have some old planks in the yard, very thick ones about nine inches wide, and he'd put sheets on them for two sittings, mounted on two chairs, one at each end, so we could seat everybody. One strange indelible memory I have of Christmas at North Street is of a friend of my father's bringing me some chocolate animals, which were placed on the mantelpiece in the front room ready for next day. Mum always gave me a piggy-back upstairs to bed, and I can still see myself looking longingly through the banisters towards those out-of-reach chocolates!

My Dad was a fine man, a devoted family man and proud of his work. After serving in France, he emerged from World War I with a slightly odd way of walking, after a kick from a mule disfigured one of his feet. He told me many stories about his war experiences and he had more time for the Germans than the French! He reckoned the French would rob you of your bootlaces! He recalled a German PoW who etched out Dad's regimental badge and number with a nail

In view of my lifelong interest in model-making, this carpentry session is an appropriate inclusion. I was aged six at the time of this photograph taken in the Woodfield Studio in Old Town.
AUTHOR'S COLLECTION

G.W.R. PARK, SWINDON

Below: *Children's Fete tickets from 1932, including a roundabout ticket still exhibiting greasy cake stains!*

Among many of the boons provided for the local community by the GWR Mechanics Institution, one that remains fresh in my memory is the children's fete, held every year in August in the GWR Park in Faringdon, an amenity also provided by the Company. For this event, the GWR also organised trestle tables at a cost of £35 to accommodate up to 11,000 children. There were many stalls — the two-headed calf, the bearded lady, a boxing booth, shooting range, and a popular stall was the chocolate king where they'd put pieces of chocolate in a white bag and keep adding to it — " . . . and one on top for the baby . . . a shilling, who'll give me a shilling?" It was

terrible chocolate and people used to say it fell off a lorry but I reckoned it was run over by one! All the children were given a free lump of fruit cake from the Henry Street bakery, which would be packed in a little paper bag with a ticket for a free ride on a roundabout, which, by the time you exchanged it for the ride, would be fairly greasy from being enclosed with the cake. This was a very big thing for us youngsters as there wasn't much free in Swindon in those days. They'd stamp your hand to prevent you trying to get a free second ride. I have a vivid memory of me eating that cake as I was going up and down on a carousel. My Uncle Arthur used to be on the gate opposite The Grapes public house from 2.0 to 8.0 p.m., for which he was paid five shillings. At 8 o'clock everyone was allowed in free to see the fireworks, and Uncle, being one for the booze, would head straight for the pub, and with beer at 6d a pint, would consume ten pints and then walk home to Hinton Street in Gorse Hill. He used to boast that he could drink 14 pints and still walk straight as a die — and he could. A good job too, as we always thought that if he was to lean sideways, the beer would leak out of his ears! He was twice married and had seven children by each wife! They were lovely gardens in the Park; there was a park keeper who lived there and gardeners to maintain it, and Works employees and their families could relax from the rigours of the factory at weekends and listen to brass bands playing in the bandstand. Bertram Mills' Circus would set up there, too, when in town.

AUTHOR'S COLLECTION

A studio portrait of me aged six, from Palmer's, Cromwell Street, Swindon. I am sure I dressed more casually than this at the fete!

Round-about
1932.

G.W.R. Institution,
SWINDON.
ANNUAL FETE
1932.
3d.
0380

G.W.R. Mechanics Institution
SWINDON.
20
JUVENILE FETE
SATURDAY, AUGUST 6th. 1932.
CHILD'S TICKET for Cake, Tea,
Switchbacks or Roundabouts, 3d.
E. H. PHILLIPS, Sec.

on a cigarette case and how impressed he and his comrades were with this. Conditions were awful – he once related to me how they'd sit in the dugouts using lighted candles to burn lice out of the seams of their jackets. He lost many of his mates going over the top, and when he returned from the War it was a source of bitterness to come back to 'a land fit for heroes' and find Garrard's, the Swindon engineering firm that made gramophones, offering employment at 6d a hour.

I have no recollection of how Dad met my Mum, but after their marriage, they settled in with my Mum's parents in North Street and Dad was able to gain employment as a boilermaker by virtue of his father having been one in the Works before him. Those boilermakers were a tough breed. Dad was very thin, but strong and wiry, and I have vivid memories of him coming home from work on a hot summer's day and saying to Mum "Look at my shirt" and it would be dripping with slime and sweat, his back glistening with perspiration. There were no automatic rivet guns in the Works in those days – they used 7-pound hammers to smash those rivets down, and Dad had corns on his hands like acorns. All those rivets you see on locomotive fireboxes were hammered down by hand, and Dad spent a lot of time in the fireboxes on this work. There were two boxes, of course, the inner being made of copper, the outer of steel. He liked his pint and was a member of the Milton Road Working Men's Club, where he was on the committee and spent a lot of time organising the old men's charabanc outings to Symonds Yat and Weston-super-Mare and a number of other venues. These were basically men-only boozing expeditions, of course, with dinner in a café, tea in a pub and plenty of crates of beer along for the ride!

My pocket money as a child was one penny every Friday dinner time. Mum was always there with a cooked lunch. My usual plan was to split the penny into two ha'pennies and head for Tompkins & Barrett on the way to school on Friday afternoon and buy a halfpenny bag of broken biscuits. As well as the biscuit fragments, there'd be sweets, tiger nuts, a locust bean, a little game where you could try and get a ball in a hole, and a triangular sherbert dab with a piece of toffee on the end of a stick. The stick had enough wood in it to start a bonfire! All for a ha'penny! And the shop made a profit! A 'Big Lot', they called it. Tompkins & Barrett's shop was like a letter 'L', with entrances in Regent Street and Market Street, with Briggs' Shoe Shop in between. The other halfpenny would usually be spent in a little sweet shop in Brunel Street, Dunn's, where you could purchase a glass of Tizer and drink it there in the shop.

By the time I was about eight, there was a new demand upon my week's pocket money, as my fascination with the railway assumed obsessive proportions! For a penny you could buy a platform ticket for Swindon Junction station, and, especially on Saturdays in the summer, that's where my precious penny went. I didn't usually receive any extra, as times were tight financially, although on a balance week Dad might give me an extra penny with which I could go to the

THE HALF-CROWN, THE CAT AND THE CANDLE

During my childhood in the twenties, the gas meter man would come round and empty the meter of shillings. He'd pack up the coins into a little blue bag, then he'd work out discount on a scrap of paper. There'd always be a bit of discount to come back, and on this one particular day, he said to Mum, "Oh, you've got a fair bit to come back this time. Do you mind if I give it to you as a couple of half-crowns instead of shillings?"

So Mum took the half-crowns and put them on the mantelpiece and away he went. It was approaching dinner-time and Dad was due home from Swindon Works at half past twelve. Well, it was pay day, being a Friday, and he came in all cheerful, as every other week they used to get what they called a 'balance week', when they'd receive extra.

Dad announced "We've had a good week this week!" and of course Mum replied "They've read the meter and we've got five shillings back." She tipped out the half-crowns onto the table and one of them rolled off and fell on the floor. Well, in those days we weren't too well off and in that house we could never quite get the linoleum to reach neatly against the skirting board. Mum was always buying remnants to fill the gaps, so of course at certain points the floorboards were exposed. That errant half-crown continued its roll, hit the skirting board, then edged its way along the board until it stopped right over a gap in the floor boards, where it turned and dropped down out of sight.

Well, this was disastrous! Half-a-crown was a lot of money. You could go to the pictures for sixpence so that was five nights at the cinema. You could go to the theatre for a tanner, and to Dad 2/6d was five pints of beer. So Mum looked at Dad and he said, "Well, we'll have to get the floorboards up and find that half-crown. We can't leave that kind of money down there. We can't do anything about it now. We'll deal with it when I come home from work tomorrow", which was a Saturday. In those days they worked in the factory from 8.0 a.m. to twelve noon, so it was Dad's plan on Saturday afternoon to get those floorboards up and retrieve the half-crown. I'm not saying Mum was anxious to find that money but she met Dad half-way up the alley that afternoon with a screwdriver in her hand! But Dad was determined to have his dinner first, which he did, then turned his attention to the lost coin.

All the furniture had to come out of the living room into the kitchen, the table, four chairs and a settee. The floorboards reached from one side of the room to the other, so the lino was rolled back and Dad got that screwdriver and prised one up. Then he peered into the darkness and reached down with his hand, but he couldn't feel the coin. So a second floorboard had to come up; he looked down into the gloom but there was still no sign of it. He said to Mum "We'll have to get a light." We had no torch so Mum found a candle in the kitchen, lit it and passed it to Dad, who reached down and placed it on the dirt surface some nine inches or so below the floorboards. At first he could see little, but as his eyes became used to the gloomy space, he eventually shouted, "I can see it! You won't believe this, it's gone halfway across the room!" Mum handed him a walking stick and he used this to reach across to the half-crown and gingerly drew it towards the opening in the floorboards, whereupon he reached in, picked up the coin and handed it to Mum with a relieved "There y'are! What a caper!"

Now, everything had to go back together. Down went the floorboards, back went the lino and in came the furniture. And Mum said "Bet you could do with a cup of tea?" Dad agreed, so Mum made a pot of tea, and she no sooner had it ready and was pouring it out when a sudden thought struck her. "Where's the candle?"

It dawned on them, in their relief at finding the half-crown, they'd left a lighted candle in that shallow space beneath the floorboards … so, out went the furniture, back up came the lino, and up came a floorboard, only one this time as it was quite easy to reach the candle. Then Mum warned, "Don't put that floorboard back yet. The flame was near enough reaching the underside of the floor. Leave it for a bit to make sure there's no smoke coming out."

So they left it open a while, Dad drank his tea, and when they'd decided it was quite safe, down went the floorboard, back went the lino, and in came the furniture again. Dad was heard to comment "What a day for a half-crown!" They were talking when all of a sudden we heard "Miaow, miaow!"

Mum said "What's the matter with the cat?", and Dad replied "Never mind *what's* the matter, where IS the bugger?"

… out went the furniture, back up came the lino, and the floorboards, and out jumped little Willie! To this day my sister and I often laugh as we recall the escapade with the half-crown, the cat and the candle!

The west end of the down platform at Swindon as I remember it about 1930, when this very spot was one of my key vantage points as I watched the railway activity as a boy. West signal box, seen here, dated to a major resignalling of 1912-13 and took the place of two older boxes, and its lever frame first contained 135 levers with 24 spare. By 1918 this had become 138 levers with 21 spare. The resignalling was long overdue — with Swindon being an early centre of GWR operations, things had become fairly antiquated by the dawn of the 20th century. A 1913 report stated that 'the whole place has been resignalled' and further referred to 'an additional junction of the Gloucester branch with the Up main line and general re-arrangement and improvement in the running lines'. The hut next to the signal box was the Loco Inspector's room, where the official would be based from 10.30 a.m. to 7.30 p.m. In my firing days, Charlie Blackford was the Inspector here, although in the Christmas Day escapade (see Chapter 6) it was my old friend Inspector Pullen who emerged from this building to ask Freddie Browning and me to hang around to deal with a horse-box. The down side carriage shops can be seen to the left. The fine array of signals and the regular movements on these gantries was a great source of interest as I sat here as a boy.

C. L. MOWAT, CTY. W. R. BURTON

Arcadia on what they called the *Tuppenny Rush* and enjoy a western with Ken Maynard, Hopalong Cassidy or Tom Mix. So the lure of the GWR was indelibly etched into my life as I'd spend those precious Saturdays on the platform at the station, enthralled by the passenger expresses as they roared through on the main lines between Paddington and South Wales. I'd leave about eight in the morning with a paper bag of cheese sandwiches in my pocket for lunch, and although I'd sometimes have a mate with me, few of my friends were as keen as I was, so I'd usually be alone. I'd have a notebook and pencil with me, but in truth, I wasn't really a great engine name or number collector – I was simply enthralled by the atmosphere and wanted to be a part of it.

I'd usually be found at the end of one of the main platforms where you'd have a good view of the expresses going through, sometimes on the up side, sometimes the down, and I'd invariably be there all day until about tea time. One of the things that most concerned and fascinated me as a child was when a slow goods train went through the station, then a few minutes later a fast passenger express would come hurtling through at a speed in excess of seventy mph on the same track! How on earth could this be? What was going to happen to the goods in front when the express caught it up at such a speed? Then another slow goods would come

through soon after the passenger and I used to wonder how the freight could be so close behind the express? Of course, it wasn't until a lot later that I learned about loops where slow trains could be sidetracked by the signalman, out of the path of the fast train, and then I realised that the goods following behind the express had already been sidetracked.

Swindon station was alive with sound. I was particularly entranced by the sounds emanating from the signal boxes, East Box on top of Whitehouse bridge, West Box at the end of the West platform. You'd hear the tinkle of the bells and I got to know the different codes – if you heard a tinkle and four consecutive bells, that was a passenger express, three-pause-one was a stopping train, with different codes for the freights. You'd hear the clump of the signalman's boots and the creak of the floorboards as he walked along the cabin floor, the crash of the levers as he pulled them over, and you'd see the signal wires dance and hop and the semaphore signal come off to the oblique position to herald the approach of a train. There'd be a pause, then in the distance you'd hear the rumble of the approaching train, increasing in its intensity as it came into full view, then a whole world of people roared by, until it vanished again and the signal resumed its horizontal 'on' position and you'd hear the sequence in reverse, then calm would ensue. All of that's gone now, of course, no

Swindon station, looking east about 1930.   C. L. MOWAT, CTY. W. R. BURTON

Pennyhooks Farm, Shrivenham, where I spent many happy hours as a boy. I'd collect the eggs from the chickens for my Uncle Frank to earn a little pocket money. On one occasion, he sent me and some friends from Swindon out into the woods to collect firewood. We weren't satisfied, apparently, with the logs we found, so, using one of Uncle's axes, we cut a tree down! He later cycled into Swindon to complain to Mum!

CTY. LYDIA OTTER

Shrivenham station in June 1934. It was my great delight to accompany my Uncle Frank here each night when we were staying at Pennyhooks as children. We'd ride in a horse and trap with three large milk churns, which we left on the Up platform where they would be picked up by the 8.10 stopping train from Swindon. I used to love watching the station porters bowling those huge heavy churns along the platform to the train. Shrivenham was the site of a fatal accident on 15th January 1936 when Old Oak Common driver Ernest Starr was killed when his Up Penzance passenger train collided with a brake van and coal trucks on the up line here in advance of the up distant signal. The van and trucks had become detached from an Aberdare to Old Oak coal train at 5.20 in the morning as a result of the breaking of a drawbar hook on one of the coal wagons.

C. L. MOWAT, CTY. W. R. BURTON

smoke, no steam, no signal boxes, just control centres tucked away somewhere, no signalmen leaning from the box to check that there was a tail lamp on the end of the train, to prove that the train had cleared their section complete.

I got to know the staff, especially the ticket collectors, and I got to know the train services – the 'Red Dragon', and 'Bristolian', the 'Cheltenham Flyer', which ran all stations from Cheltenham through the Chalford Valley to Swindon, then non-stop to Paddington.

From the age of about ten, a visit I loved was to stay with my Uncle Frank at Pennyhooks Farm out at Shrivenham. He was my grandfather's brother but we just called him Uncle Frank. I used to go with him in a horse and trap to take his milk churns to Shrivenham station, where they were picked up by the 8.10 night stopper from Swindon which called at all stations to Reading on its way to Paddington's No. 14 platform with the milk traffic. I loved the times out there on that farm and can still see in my mind my Uncle Frank milking those cows. We first went there when I was very young, when my Dad was unemployed and we could earn our keep by Dad helping with the haymaking. They were happy times on that farm and the perfect way for a town boy like myself to become acquainted with the countryside. Later on, when I was in my teens, I used to cycle out there with several mates and we'd take a tent and camp. Uncle Frank had about 40 cows there and I can always remember being horrified as a child when I saw Uncle remove an insect which was embedded in a cow's skin! I remember the farm was the first place I ever saw a dead cow. I can still picture the large animal lying on its side with flies buzzing around it.

I hazily recall that electricity was introduced into Havelock Street about 1934, with electric lights replacing the old gaslit ones. I can still see the old lamplighter in my mind's eye, coming along on his bike, and he was that clever and practised that he'd remain mounted while he reached up with his long pole and use the hook on its end to click off

THE DOCTOR SAT AT HIS DESK WITH THE CANE BEFORE HIM

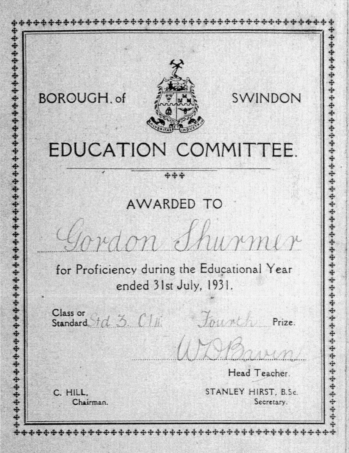

My remaining souvenir of schooldays. In July 1931, I was presented with a book, The Dampier Boys, *a schoolboy's tale, for 'Proficiency during the Educational Year'. I recall asking Mum what the word 'proficiency' meant and she told me "You must have been good at something. Maybe you were a model pupil?" Of course, I then asked her what 'model' meant, and when we looked it up, it said 'a small replica of the real thing'. The picture showing the headmaster's office with the cane on the table was the only illustration in the entire book, and is a reminder of the only time I had the cane from the headmaster at Sanford Street, Mr. Bavin. I was very proud of the fact that I'd never been caned by him, then during my very last month before leaving, several of us boys were accused of stone-throwing at this woman's daughter. We weren't guilty, but stone-throwing was one thing for which Mr. Bavin would not stand. He would not listen to our protests and several of us received three strokes each on the palm. A deputation of mothers with sleeves rolled up went up to the school to protest, but the damage was done and my clean record was broken!*

What is striking to me about this photograph looking down Swindon Road is the complete absence of litter in those pre-packaging days. Just off the picture to the right were the railings where I noisily rattled my spade early one morning on a Trip Friday in 1925.

CTY. MRS. MARY THOMPSON

the light each night. Yes, in those days they turned off street lights individually, before they became automatic with a time clock. Electricity also saw the advent of the Radio Relay, which introduced a new sound and atmosphere into our house. For 1/6d a week we could hire a wireless from a shop at the bottom of Victoria Hill, and the whole family could listen in, a big improvement on the old crystal sets where you heard it through headphones. We got our money's worth from the Relay, keeping it on virtually all day right through

to 'God Save the King' and sign-off! We enjoyed hearing the news broadcasts, *Workers Playtime* was a favourite, and I used to love listening to comedians such as Frankie Howerd and Al Reed.

However, my 5th birthday present had sown its seeds with a profound inevitability – I wanted to drive those great expresses. I liked all locomotives, but best of all I idolised *King George V*, the first of just 30 engines in the 'King' class built in 1927 in Swindon Works, for the remarkable price of £7,546.

The old Empire Theatre, which was situated at the foot of Victoria Road, just where the famous tram accident happened in 1911. Originally built as Queen's Theatre in 1897, it was renamed early in the 1900s. When I was on the right turn of duty at the shed, I used to go regularly every week. It was a cinema too, of course, and the first colour film shown there, I think, was The King of Jazz starring Al Jolson. Mum and Dad had reserved seats there every Saturday night. On occasions when they couldn't go, they would have me call in at the theatre to let them know. I saw many well-known stars there – Martha Rae, Alan Jones who sang 'The Donkey Serenade', Max Miller (the Cheeky Chappie), Rob Wilton, Georgie Wood, and, of course, Laurel & Hardy, who stayed at the Bear Hotel in Hungerford. I remember Alan Jones being drunk in his dressing room and the manager had to come out and apologise. Stars of the theatre in those days could perform the same routines for years, going round the provinces, but today everyone can see an act once on television and it's finished. You could sit in the stalls, in one of two balconies, or for an extra sixpence you could go up in the gallery, 'in the Gods'. It was a wonderful theatre acoustically – people could easily project their voice from the stage, no microphones in the old days. Local drama groups used to perform there too. Our running shed Foreman, Herbie Scarratt, used to work at the Empire as a stagehand, as did several other drivers and firemen. By the time the Empire closed in January 1955, the dearest seats were four shillings. I remember Mollie Tanner rehearsing her dancers for an 'Aladdin' pantomime but it never got started. The theatre was demolished in 1959. CTY. SWINDON LIBRARIES

Right: *I remember the trams very well from my early childhood. They were gone by 1930. This one was heading down Victoria Road towards the Empire Theatre on the corner at the bottom of the hill.*
SWINDON MUSEUM

Regent Circus in May 1930. I had to look twice to make sure the little boy wasn't me! It shows the Regent Cinema advertising 'talkies', and behind the very ornate drinking trough for horses is the 'omnibus waiting room' of the Bristol Tramways & Carriage Company, with their sign over the window. The old church to the right became the Town Museum. The No. 67 Corporation bus was probably bound for Coate Water as this service left from this spot. The wall visible at right is the edge of the Town Hall.

CTY. SWINDON LIBRARIES

Our family at the back of 56 North Street — my father Harry Albert Shurmer, my mother Gladys, and my sister Betty. This was taken in 1931 by my grandmother on a visit to my grandparents, probably a Sunday judging by my suit and tie and Dad's waistcoat. We were living in Havelock Street by this time. We looked much like this when we went out for a family walk on Sunday evenings after Sunday tea, as I recall the stiff collar I'd have to wear and the little walking stick I carried! We usually used to go to Coate Reservoir across the fields as they were then, nine fields one way and seven coming back the other way. Alternatively, we'd go up to Springfield Road and walk down Mill Lane as far as Rushey Platt, and come out by the signal box and Barnes' wood-yard, one of my later vantage points for viewing express railway activity on the main line, then back home via Wootton Bassett Road and Faringdon Road. Sometimes we would go up to Dad's allotment on Okus Road to see what he'd been growing up there. Grandfather had one there too. AUTHOR'S COLLECTION

A close-up of the shop fronts of Mac Fisheries and The Spot in Regent Street, with shoppers' bicycles parked along the kerb. The fishmonger is advertising cod at a shilling a pound, as well as lobster tails, Scotch kippers and salmon at unseen prices! The Spot was a legendary Swindon shop, a wonderful place, a treasure trove at No. 60 Regent Street. The place was a child's dream — they sold toys, train sets, Dunlop tennis rackets, cricket bats, dartboards, and I remember a board bearing scouts' knives in several different sizes. As the sign above the shop proclaims, the shop was a distributor for Raleigh, Humber, Rudge and Hercules bicycles — I remember a Hercules bike was £4 10s 0d, £1 dearer than a Raleigh. On one occasion, they were advertising Hornby Dublo train sets with engine, wagons and everything for £4 10s 0d. "What's the matter w'it?", I recall enquiring. "Nothing at all", came the reply, "we've got to get rid of them, there's too many in the warehouse!"

SWINDON LIBRARIES

Twelve years old in the back garden at Havelock Street. You can clearly see the red bricks which formed the back path to the rear gate down the side of the yard. Dad built the trellis fence. The window behind me was the middle room in our house, with the wash-house extension being off the photo to the right. I am wearing my school clothes. Our headmaster used to like us to wear school caps, with red letters 'SSS' for Sanford Street School on a black material. They cost 1s 9d each, although a better-quality one could be purchased for 2s 6d for Sunday wear!

She was 135 tons in working order and was built by men in the Works on £2 a week. She was the kingpin of the GWR fleet, always my favourite. She boasted 30,400 pounds tractive effort and 2000 horse power, and later in 1927 went to the USA at the invitation of the Baltimore & Ohio Railroad to celebrate their centenary as the first USA railroad to carry passengers. On a run between Washington and Philadelphia, she achieved a speed of 75 mph, and was presented with a brass bell from the B&O which was placed on her front gangway between the buffers.

Dad would sometimes come home from work with the tantalising information that they'd had her in the Works for repair, but it wasn't until 1935 that I saw *King George V* for the first time. I was on the verge of leaving school and I had a job at Perkins Fruit Shop in Market Street, delivering groceries to customers in a little trolley. The owner there had one of the first Fords in Swindon, costing £120 – he took me out in it once. I worked Thursday and Friday nights from 5.30 to 7.0 and a Saturday morning turn from 9.0 till 1.0 pm. I received 2/6d a week for this. I'd have about six orders in wicker baskets on the trolley and sometimes would have to go back and fetch another load. On one particular night I had to deliver to a house in Station Road, and as I was passing close to Whitehouse bridge, an express came over the bridge above, and to my delight I recognised her as *King George V* from the B&O bell on the front. I clearly remember saying to myself "Yes mate, one day I'm going to be in charge of you!"

During my year between leaving school and going into the GWR drawing office, 1935–6, I attended night school in Sanford Street and a favourite jaunt when school finished around 9.0 p.m. was to cycle down to Rushey Platt to see the South Waler go through around 9.20. I'd have a vantage point in the wood yard there and you could see the sparks shooting up into the sky well before she came into view. She ran from Paddington non-stop to Newport and was a real hard hitter, always headed by a 'Castle' 4–6–0, a class of locomotive I came to respect and love working as my career on the railway progressed. It was also at Rushey Platt that the GWR used to link up with the Midland & South Western Junction Railway, but the fittings and points for the connection between the two lay unused for nearly twenty years from the early years of the 20th Century before the GWR finally consented to finalising the link, so that MSWJ trains could use Swindon Junction station, by which time the GWR had taken over its persistent neighbour in the Grouping of 1923.

My first sight of *King George V*, my first remunerated part-time employment, the arrival of the wireless in our home, and those evening trips to Rushey Platt, were all beacons signalling the end of childhood as I knew it. With the GWR in my genes, the railway was the prime interest in my young life. I was surrounded by the lure of the Great Western in what was still very much a railway town, and began to think about confronting an apparent annoying hereditary hurdle in my desire to be an engine driver.

One of the great train-watching locations of my youth, with the Great Western main line passing under my beloved Midland & South Western Junction line at Rushey Platt. This is the spot referred to on page 22 where I'd come after night school, the exact viewpoint being down on the Wootton Bassett Road by Barnes wood yard which was just down the embankment from Rushey Platt signal box, seen beyond the bridge on the right. 'A' Shop in the distance was where my father was employed as a boilermaker. On the MSWJ line a Cheltenham-bound train, the 2.38 Andover Junction to Cheltenham on 14th April 1949, is seen behind a Mogul class 63XX, with the Rushey Platt starter signal in the off position to accommodate its progress northwards. On the extreme left, visible above the embankment, is the travelling crane for the sawmills. The white sighting panel painted on the bridge allowed clear vision of the signals to the Up loops at Rodbourne Lane and the yellow distant for Rodbourne Lane Signal Box was accompanied by a sighting board in black.
S. C. PHILLIPS

The flagship of the GWR, my favourite, No. 6000 King George V, on No. 1 road outside Swindon shed, with her commemorative B&O bell resplendent on the front gangway in the middle of the buffer beam. I first saw her in 1930, first fired on her just after the war when relieving Old Oak Common men on a down passenger working on No. 3 link at Swindon, first took charge of her as a driver sometime during 1957 (see page 177), and still see the old girl today every two weeks when I talk to the visitors on her footplate at the Steam Museum on Saturday afternoons. When I look in that firebox now, 11ft 6in long, I wonder how on earth I managed to throw the coal to the far end of that box when travelling at 80 mph.
PHOTOMATIC

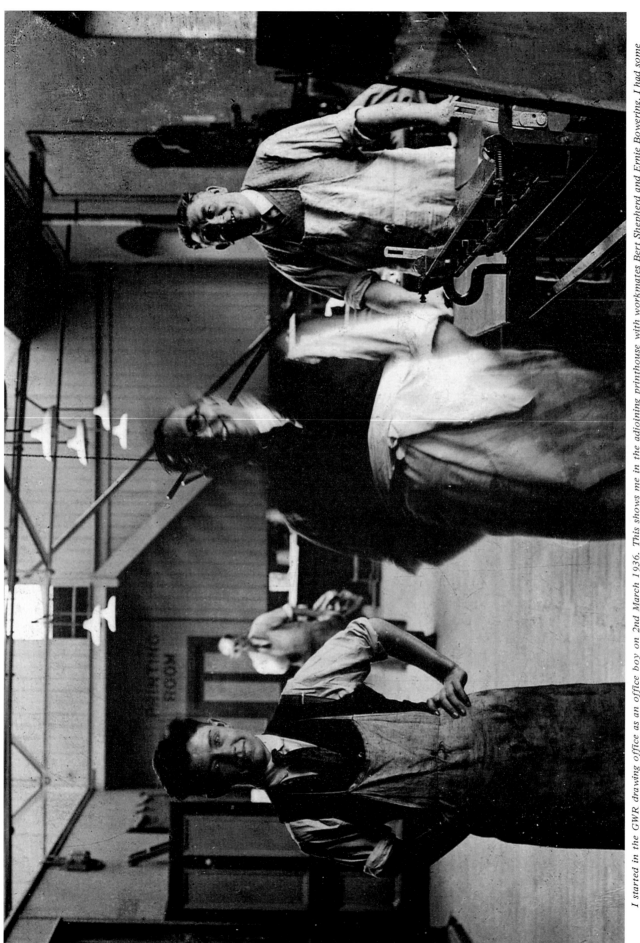

I started in the GWR drawing office as an office boy on 2nd March 1936. This shows me in the adjoining printhouse with workmates Bert Shepherd and Ernie Bowering. I had some great times working in that printhouse – it was here that they did the blueprints off the draughtsmen's tracings on the printing machine. Bert was a great friend and used to give me 6d every Friday so I could go to the pictures. He had been on the footplate but transferred to the printhouse because of trouble with his ears. On one occasion he took me to London – our engine was No. 4015 Knight of the Grand Cross, and Bert's influence got me onto a footplate for the first time, further fuelling my dreams of becoming a driver. It was a memorable day on which we visited the four main London stations, St. Pancras of the LMS, Paddington of the GWR, the LNER's King's Cross and Victoria on the Southern. Ernie's main job was to mount vellum tracings on calico to go to the Record Office, and his nails were black from contact with the developer in the darkroom. The machine on the right was for trimming the edges of transfers. The windows on the right looked towards the station, and I'd regularly look out of them and say to myself 'One day I'll be on one of those locos, in charge!'

AUTHOR'S COLLECTION

CHAPTER TWO

FIRST RUNGS ON THE LADDER

MY father and grandfather had both been GWR boilermakers, and when boys in railway families left school in Swindon they went what they called *inside*, which strangers might think referred to prison, but of course it meant inside the Works. At that time there were only three major employers in Swindon – the engineering firm of Garrards, the tobacco company H. O. Wills, and the Great Western Railway. I left school in 1935 when I was 14 and had a job out at Coate Reservoir as a gate attendant where my pay was 10/6d a week.

The usual practice was for sons of GWR employees to go as office boys in one of the workshops in the Works. After registering, they appointed you to wherever you were needed, while waiting for an apprenticeship which lasted five years, and usually took you up to the age of 21. Then you were dismissed from the GWR and expected to go out and better yourself elsewhere. You could re-apply to return if you wanted to do so when vacancies came up, which most people did. The GWR apprenticeship was a thorough grounding for young lads in developing a good work ethic and gaining experience in the workplace. At the end of it, you had a trade at your fingertips, and if you went elsewhere you had the benefit of an association with the Great Western.

So on 2nd March 1936 I went as an office boy in the GWR drawing office on three shillings a day. Adjoining the drawing office was the print house where they used to do all the photographs that were taken of new locomotives, new machinery and even the photographs that used to go in the passenger carriages at that time. It was a 9-5 job and I would assist Bert Shepherd who did the blueprints off the drawings of the draughtsmen. They'd come into the print house to request a copy to be made off their drawing. It was like a tracing on celluloid and it would go through the machine with the blueprint underneath. That was the copy that was sent to the Works, so the men there would have a plan from which to work when they were producing new parts for locomotives, carriages and wagons. I'd roll them up and give them back to the draughtsmen. Bert was great to me – he even used to give me 6d pocket money every week so I could go to the pictures, and he once took me to London for a day

Scenes at Coate Water, Swindon, about the time I was in my first remunerated employment, as a 10s 6d a week gate attendant while waiting to be called by the GWR. I loved Coate Water and remember being thrilled at getting a job there on leaving school. My first duty after booking on was to take a bucket and wash the varnished wooden sparred seats, dry them down, then inspect the toilets. The graffiti in the female lavatories in those days was worse than the fellas! I had to work around Coate in the evening to lock the gate. It snowed heavily that winter and it was like a fairyland out there with the lake and the trees. There was a Bill Stevens who worked in the boathouse building boats. He'd take the side of a skiff out, and just have the ribs left, then he'd slot pieces in there, riveting with brass and copper washers – quite immaculate. If there was a new fishing punt wanted, the lorry used to come out to Coate with a load of mahogany and he'd be in the top boat shed for about a month building that new craft. If anyone went in there he would stop work, preferring to hang on to the secrets of his trade. I used to take a flask of tea every day and share it with him, and he'd share his lump of cake with me. That was my introduction to a working week. I'd pay 2d a week insurance and take home 10s 6d to Mum for my keep and she'd give me half-a-crown back and that provided me with five nights at the cinema.
CTY. SWINDON LIBRARIES

Paddington GWR station, much as I remember it from my trip there with Bert Shepherd in 1936, with the Post Office and bookstalls close to Platform 1. The pannier tank had just brought in coaching stock from Old Oak Common for a main-line train.

PUBLIC RECORD OFFICE

out. Our train engine was a big passenger 4–6–0 locomotive, *Night of the Grand Cross*, and when we arrived in Paddington station Bert got me up on a footplate for the first time. The driver was very accommodating and I can still hear him saying "Yeah, come on up, kid. You know anything about Mathematics? Well, this is the reversing lever, and I can increase the speed of the train by bringing the lever back from full gear towards mid-gear. And up there, there's all the different cut-offs so I can reduce the travel of the valves to increase speed." It was a great occasion, a great thrill for a teenager, and of course it further cemented my ambition to be an engine driver. But how could I have known at that moment that in later years I'd be going into Paddington hundreds of times in charge of a passenger train?

The Works photographer, George Smith, was also based in the print house and if there was a new machine established in the Works or if a new locomotive had been completed, he'd go and photograph it and I'd go with him to carry his equipment. I'd also assist by holding up his flash equipment for him to provide more light inside. This was a tray full of powder, which I would hold up and, when he shouted to me, I'd pull the trigger and the powder would be ignited, and as

it flashed he'd take the photograph. On one occasion I had the tray held up and he took longer than usual to prepare himself to shoot the photograph, so that my arm began to sag and when he finally called to me it had sunk so low that the flash singed my eyebrows!

I enjoyed my time in the drawing office and print house, but my days there were numbered, and the day soon arrived when my Dad received the papers from the Company to go into an apprenticeship. "I put you down to go as a fitter," Dad explained, "but there's no vacancies at the moment. So they've offered you boilermaker, tinsmith, coppersmith or painter. So which one are you going to choose?"

Seeing all those photographs of locomotives in the print house had fuelled an ambition which had been burning in me for years, as had my trip to London with Bert Shepherd. Further, the office in which I worked overlooked the main line to Bath and Bristol and the Gloucester branch, and I had spent every spare minute leaning over the parapet watching the trains go by. So there was only one reply possible:"I don't want any of those, Dad. I want to be an engine driver!"

Dad gave me little encouragement. "You haven't got a snowflake's chance in a baker's oven!" he told me. "Unless

Aged sixteen at the Empire Studio.

Park House, Swindon, where generations of railwaymen from all over the GWR system came for their medicals. Its architecture was very impressive, with its neatly-cut bargeboards in the gables and the mullioned windows. It looks exactly like this today. Behind the left-hand bay window on the first floor was the room where I had my medicals for passenger fireman and driver. The eyesight test included the legendary exercise where prospective crew men had to sort out different shades of coloured wool. Medicals were very strict here – they had to be because only the fittest and healthiest could become engine drivers. So this was also the place where the hopes of many aspiring young enginemen were dashed as a result of failing a medical – you might pass on practical but fail on eyesight. The tram tracks were still present on Faringdon Road here, indicating that this was the late 1920s.
WILTSHIRE LIBRARY & MUSEUM SERVICE, TROWBRIDGE

your Dad is someone in the operating department, such as signalman, driver or passenger guard, you just can't get onto the footplate". "Well," I said, exuding a confidence I didn't necessarily feel, "I'm going to see the Chief Draughtsman, Mr. Smith, and see if he'll help me."

So, cap in hand, I knocked very nervously on Mr. Smith's door, and entered the office where the Chief Draughtsman worked which incidentally overlooked the running sheds for the Gloucester branch.

"Well, young man, what can I do for you?"

"Well sir," I began, my fingers nervously fidgeting with my cap, "I've just had my papers for my apprenticeship. I have to go out into the workshops. They've offered me tinsmith, boilermaker, coppersmith or painter."

"What's wrong with that?" replied Mr. Smith. "It's no good for you to stop here in this office."

I held my ground and told him, "I want to be an engine driver, sir."

Immediately Mr. Smith leapt out of his seat, grabbed me by the arm and led me over to the office window. He pointed to the engine sheds below his window.

"See all that dirt and dust down there? You'll be down there Sundays when you should be in church! You'll be there Christmas Day when you ought to be at parties. You'll be there at night when you feel like being home in bed asleep. You don't want any of that, my boy – go back home and think about those four jobs they've offered you and come back next Wednesday and tell me what you want to be."

So, the following Wednesday I returned and knocked on Mr. Smith's door. There was a stern "Come in," and I remember him looking over the top of his glasses as he enquired of me,"Well, young man, what do you want to be?"

"I want to be an engine driver, sir."

"THEN SO YOU BLOODY SHALL!" he announced, and thumped his desk with his fist! I owe my career on the footplate to Mr. Smith.

Funnily enough, my pal Freddie Simpson, who started on the shed at roughly the same time as me, had a slightly different and easier passage onto the locomotives. His father had been a machinist in the Works and Fred first joined him there on leaving school. He, too, started as an office boy but actually began his apprenticeship in the Works as a brass moulder, a job that produced the brass for boiler parts and coach doors. He lasted a year but felt too 'shut in' in the Works and managed to get accepted at the shed by way of a letter from his mother to the Shed Foreman, Mr. A. M. Duck! Freddie and I still meet up today.

Before I could report to the shed to start my cleaning duties, I had to attend a medical at Park House, overlooking the GWR's Faringdon Road Park where Dr. Bennett told me "You have a hollow tooth at the back. It's only a shell. Get it removed and come and see me again and I'll pass you!"The GWR were very strict in such circumstances.

And so it was that on 1st February 1937, just after my 16th birthday, I started down the Swindon running shed as an engine cleaner on four shillings a day. My first day on the

A pre-war view, looking north, showing the very heart of the Swindon Works complex, dominated by the huge L2 (tenders) shop in the centre, with the boiler testing house to the left and, behind at centre right, the chimneys of the Central Boiler station. Adjacent to the factory sidings and the main GWR line is the massive iron foundry, and at lower left the Works 65ft turntable.

This aerial view of the mid-1920s provides a good view of the Broad Gauge engine shed at Swindon in relation to the Works and the junction with the Gloucester line. At this time the old Broad Gauge shed was in use as part of the Works, mostly for 'finishing-off' type work such as repairs to sandboxes, engine buffers, cleaning and painting. It was known as 'A' shed and was eventually demolished in 1930 under a Government loan scheme for the relief of unemployment, to make way for modernisation of the engine repair shops.

1. The original Broad Gauge engine shed.
2. The 'B' Shop with the printhouse and its balcony where I leaned over many times as a teenager to watch the railway activity outside.
3. The Main Office building where Mr. Smith, the Chief Draughtsman, worked, the man to whom I owe my career on the footplate. The top floor of this building was added in the early years of the 20th century, at which time the stone bas-reliefs of the Broad Gauge loco, which once were on the ends of the old shed, were incorporated in the architecture of the office block, where they remain today as a tangible reminder of the Broad Gauge shed at this point.
4. The down side carriage shops of the Works.
5. The down side carriage siding from which the 'Royal' Carriage shop pilot made its timetabled run every day to take new carriages across to the north side for finishing work in the carriage shops there. This is also the point at which I joined a Cardiff paper train one night in the early 1950s on No. 1 Link, standing on the main line to wave down my driver Bill Hinder so I could get up on the footplate and not miss my turn.

6. The foundry.
7. 'B' Shop.
8. 'A' Shop.
9. Loco Yard sidings with crane sidings where I did my first ever firing turn.
10. Brunel's offices.
11. L-2 Shop.
12. Spring Shop.
13. Paint testing house.
14. Hooter house, which issued its summons to the town each day at 7.25 a.m., 7.30 and 7.40.
15. Chimneys of Central Boiler station at Swindon Works, each chimney built from six boiler barrels from Dean Goods engines.

NATIONAL RAILWAY MUSEUM

shed began rather inauspiciously. Being used to office hours, I was an hour late reporting to Mr. Duck, and he took me to task very sternly.

"Young man, you are late for duty. This is not a good start to an illustrious career. You are not in the drawing office now and the sooner you realise that the better. We start at all hours of the day and night here and *your* time is 8 o'clock."

Thus chastised, I settled in quickly. The first locomotive I ever cleaned was No. 2014, a pannier tank shunting engine, and I also recall working on 2070 and 1797, also panniers, very early on. The first large passenger engine upon which I worked was No. 2947 *Madresfield Court*. The cleaners were a mischievous bunch, about sixty in all at the shed in those days, and there were several initiation techniques used to wel-

Swindon locomotive shed in July 1935, the year in which I left school. This is the way I remember it when I arrived there as a cleaner in February 1937. The ordered air of quiet industry suggested by this photograph is very much a false impression which belies the noisy, smoky and grimy intensity of the work inside. The forest of smoke vents is a reminder that men were employed full time on shed roof and smoke stack repair — the sulphur from the fire below was very corrosive. The locomotive visible on the extreme left was 'Bulldog' class 4–4–0 No. 3376 River Plym. L&GRP

19th August 1934, a hidden mystery to me at this time, the interior of Swindon shed, my future workplace, with a variety of tank engines around the turntable. From left to right, ignoring the partially visible loco on the left, the engines are identified as '3571' class 0–4–2 No. 3580, an '850' class saddle tank 0–6–0 No. 2007, a '48XX' class 0–4–2T No. 4833 and an ex-Midland & South Western Junction 0–6–0 Beyer-Peacock No. 1008 (ex-MSWJR No. 24). This view provides a good look at the smoke ventilation hoods above the locomotives with the part-glazed roof above.

These instructions to drivers were suspended from a roof truss in the shed. I always thought it was rather unnecessary as it was accepted knowledge at the shed that you couldn't get a large engine round the small turntable.
GORDON GRAVETT

come new recruits to the shed. They might grab you at the beginning of a shift, or right at the end as you were leaving, when Mr. Duck wasn't around, and rub axle grease in your hair, douse you with water from a hosepipe, lock you in a boxvan, and what they did to new boys with condensed milk, egg shells and brick dust down your trousers doesn't bear thinking about! Strangely, the worst thing that I can recall happening to me was being sent to the stores to obtain red oil for the buffer plate, a trick which didn't catch me out!

So very strict were they in the running shed in those days that although the building was full of locomotives with fires in their fireboxes and the whole atmosphere was full of smoke and dust, and there were steam-raisers and lighters-up walking about with long shovels on their shoulders full of red-hot coals, there were notices everywhere stating *Smoking is Prohibited*! It always amazed me, because, although I didn't smoke, it seemed distinctly odd that with all this fire around, you weren't allowed to light a cigarette. I remember one occasion when Mr. Duck was walking across the big turntable, a driver lit up his pipe as he was oiling his engine with a feeder. The foreman's reaction was instantaneous: "Put out that pipe, driver! I will not have smoking in this shed.

When you're out on the road, standing in a station, you can do what you like, but here in *my* shed, no smoking, understand?"

Mr. Duck always handed in his pipe and tobacco at the door in Reading Street when he reported for work each day, before he walked down the tunnel to the running shed. He commanded a lot of respect, and as soon as he was seen to emerge from his office, word went round with all speed that "Duck is about" and everyone would be seen wiping away at nearby locomotives whether they were actually supposed to be working on them or not! That's how discipline was in those days. We knew if we looked after ourselves and toed the line we had a job for life. So permanent was a footplate job back then that we never paid unemployment insurance like everyone else did.

It wasn't long before I crossed Mr. Duck again. I was meant to be cleaning No. 3100, a large Prairie tank, which was destined to take Bertram Mills Circus on a night run from Swindon to Bath, and I distinctly remember the cleaner chargeman telling me "Make a good job of that engine." Well, on that day, a little dockside locomotive had come into the shed from South Wales. I was working with two other

On 17th May 1941 a couple of headlamps left on the ground, waiting to be added to a buffer beam, contrast with the cavernous interior of the locomotive shed with the countless roof trusses and imposing smoke hoods. Standing at the big turntable are two 0—6—0 tank engines of the '850' class, No. 2007 being a saddle tank dating from 1892, and its neighbour to its left, No. 868 from 1874, formerly a saddle tank and converted to pannier tank in 1922. I have heard of this class being described as the 'Terriers' of the GWR. Built at Wolverhampton, they were light but tenaciously strong, often being used on empty stock workings. No. 868 had been withdrawn by the time I arrived at the shed but 2007 remained in service until 1949. In the right background is a Dean Goods 0—6—0 and a 22XX class 0—6—0 freight engine. The shed was a daunting place for a new young cleaner and I remember being very surprised at the amount of dirt and grime in there.

H. C. CASSERLEY

new cleaners, Herbie Scarratt and Jack Beasant, and I'd never seen a locomotive like this one before. I was fascinated by the lockers in the cab. It was around the little turntable, and in our eagerness we forgot both our duties on 3100 and the fact that cleaners were not allowed on the footplate in Swindon shed. My mates clambered up first to have a closer look, but as I mounted the steps to follow them and looked across the cab, to my consternation I saw Mr. Duck standing on the other side, looking quizically at me. Jack and Aubrey had moved forward towards the controls, furtively out of the foreman's vision, so he wasn't aware of them, only me. He beckoned me across the cab and down the other side.

"What do you think you're doing, young man?"

"I was j-just interested in the loco, sir," I stuttered. "I've not seen one like it before."

"Why aren't you cleaning 3100?"

"I've finished it, sir."

"Finished it? There's always something you can do cleaning a locomotive. You will go home for the rest of the day!"

So I was banished and sent home, cruel as it seemed to me. Of course, I didn't go straight home, I just hung around in town until the end of my turn. I just didn't dare tell my Dad I'd been sent home from the shed, because even at the age of 17 and being a working man I'd have had a bloody good hiding and no sympathy! That's how it was. Strange as it may seem, cleaners were not allowed on the footplate, although I believe at some of the branch sheds with a single locomotive allocation and one overnight cleaner, things were rather more relaxed about such rules. But at major sheds they were very strict. There was an accident once when a cleaner had got on the footplate of a loco that was round the little turntable, and actually caused it to move forwards. The cleaner jumped off and the engine went into the turntable pit and turned over on its side. Although it was only a tank engine, it was a hell of a job getting it out again and, of course, it meant that the turntable was out of use until it could be removed. It was instant dismissal for the unfortunate cleaner, and of course it proves the point about safety and regulations. To be seen on the footplate, where the controls were, meant immediate suspension, as I'd found out very quickly in my youthful interest and enthusiasm!

A '13XX' class 0–6–0 pannier tank seen on one of the straights outside the shed. We cleaned these '13XXs' before breakfast in the 1930s, usually on the Saturday 6.0 – 12.0 turn, then enjoyed a tin of Heinz baked beans cooked on the shovel in the firebox. There were only six of this class built and most of them, 1366, 1367, 1368, 1369, 1370 and 1371, could be seen at Swindon shed. With their small wheelbase they were built especially for negotiating the tight curves in the factory sidings, so you rarely saw them anywhere else except the wagon shops duty. I worked 1370 many times as fireman.
LENS OF SUTTON

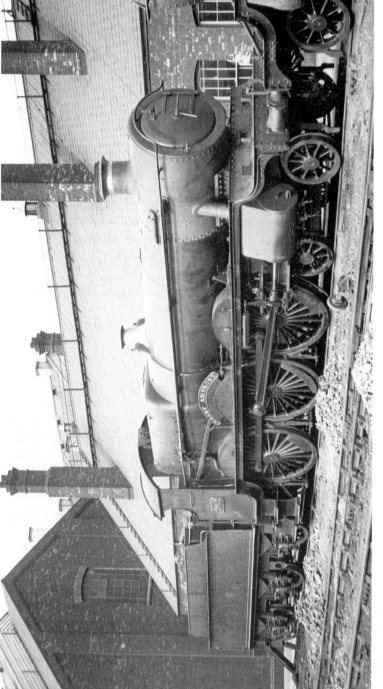

An undated view of No. 2912 Saint Ambrose standing at the stop-blocks outside the shedmaster's office waiting for its next turn of duty. This was a great locomotive to work for speed. With its two-cylinder engine, it was not as strong as a 4-cylinder 'Castle' class, but the 'Saints' really could move. The heaps of fire ash by the tracks indicate the fire-droppers had been at work here, dumping the rough firebox clinker on the lineside.
LENS OF SUTTON

A recently-outshopped large Prairie 2–6–2T No. 6154 outside Swindon shed on 29th September 1935.
L&GRP

In the old section of the shed, 'Saint' class No. 2902 Lady of the Lake *is seen on one of the straights on 10th May 1936.*   H. F. WHEELLER

Most of the '517' class tanks had been withdrawn by the time I arrived at the shed as a cleaner, so I never cleaned or fired one, but there were several still around, like this one, No. 1477, seen here in May 1934, which remained in service until 1937. A Wolverhampton-built 0—4—2T, they were usually allocated to pilot and local branch work, but from 1934 they were being replaced by the Collett 0—4—2 tank engines of the '58XX' class in the Bristol Division.
H. F. WHEELLER

A group of my engine-cleaning contemporaries at the rear of the running shed in 1938. I am not on the photograph because I believe this was taken during the time I was in the office doing the booking-on and off for the crews. Top: *Humphries, Simpson, Dunn.* Row of five: *Read, Martin, Townsend, Watts, Conlon.* Centre three: *Jeffreys, Scarratt, Tarrant.* Front: *Dowdeswell, Rumbelow, Cox.* Dougie Read is the only person who ever persuaded me to back a horse! He came to the shed one day and told me he had a cert and induced me to part with a shilling. When I caught up with him two days later and asked him about the race, he told me, "You'll never believe this! That horse dropped dead as they were taking him out of the stable!" I've never backed a horse since! George Watts also, like me, later became a tutor on the diesels. Herbie Scarratt later became shed foreman and features prominently in this book. Eddie Cox was the only fellow I ever saw with three sets of teeth! Freddie Simpson is still a good pal today. We once took a trip to London together to see a revue at the Prince of Wales Theatre, and happily recall the chorus girls shining lights on us from the stage! Freddie would often call for me in Havelock Street when we were both on the same shift. Freddie recalls that on callboy duty, if you were on the 10.0 p.m. shift at night, you would clean locos first, then go out calling crews from about 4.45 a.m., the men who were on the 6.0 a.m. turn. But if you booked on the 9.30 shift, you'd be calling all night. You would do a whole week on the 9.30, then a whole week on the 10.0 p.m. There was an adult callboy who used to make out the call sheets for the lads, and he would do the centre of town area himself. The rest of the town was divided into four main areas and we'd each do one area for a week — these were Rodbourne, Gorse Hill, Old Town and Pinehurst. We were issued with GWR bicycles painted brown and very stiff and hard to pedal. The bikes were fitted with oil lamps and were maintained by a chap called Jarman in Guppy Street. Those cleaners used to get up to some tricks — there was one lad who had to call drivers in Deacon Street by the cemetery and some of the boys got up ahead of him and dressed up in white sheets and scared the lad to death!   CTY. FREDDIE SIMPSON

Taken on top of the MSWJR railway bridge at Hodson Woods, this shows me during my early months of cleaning at Swindon shed with my new Raleigh tourer, purchased from The Spot in Regent Street, Swindon. Mum had bought it for me for £7 7s 0d and I was paying her back at a shilling a week out of my wages. I had it for years and polished it as lovingly as any of the locomotives in my charge. Chiseldon was to the left of the camera, Swindon to the right. The woods here were owned by a Colonel Burley and a friendly sign nearby read 'Trespassers will be prosecuted. Dogs will be shot'. We sometimes used to pick primroses here and were often chased away by a gamekeeper.

AUTHOR'S COLLECTION

We worked in gangs of four as cleaners, and we'd use our pay check to decide which two of us would clean the boiler and the wheels and which would do the tender. The pay check was an oblong brass strip with your pay number on, and you'd call "number" or "blank"! My number was 351. You picked up the check when you booked on, taking it out of a rack, and returned it when you left. All shed employees, excepting firemen and drivers, had to carry one. Whichever pair won, could choose which section they'd clean, and of course you'd prefer to do the boiler and brass around the chimney, the parts that people saw. You also tossed to decide who would go down underneath, where it became really filthy. Some of those dour old drivers used to come on duty and get down in the inspection pit and if you hadn't wiped the eccentric rods they used to play hell! There were about thirty cleaners on that 8 a.m.–5 p.m. shift. We had no break times allowed – we used to take our sandwiches in our pockets and pinch breaks when we could, climbing up into the motion underneath and sitting on one of the axles to eat our sandwiches as we couldn't go back in the mess room. The only washing facilities I recall were for the men at the coal stage. I had to strip down for a bath every night because you got so dirty. No showers in those days, of course – Mum would boil up the water in the copper and pour it into the zinc bath in the washhouse. There was no bathroom at 50 Havelock Street until the '60s.

The Chargeman cleaner would come round to check on the quality of the cleaning, to see that the brass and copper had been shined properly and that the underneath had received its proper share of attention. If an engine had been cleaned a day or two earlier, we used to like that because it would still be oily, so we'd just give it a 'rough-off', wiping it over with waste because there was still sufficient oil on the boiler and tender to render it shiny. Nothing was ever wasted – the waste that we used to clean the locomotive was collected up every day and was used by the lighters-up to start their fires on the engine. You were with different men all the time on the shed, as personnel would change constantly with promotions and transfers. We'd often receive special instructions to give a loco extra-meticulous attention if it was to be put on an especially prestigious run. One such situation was with the engine that was put on the overnight run to Leicester and back. This was because this run took a GWR train onto LNER metals, and in 'foreign territory' you wanted to show your rivals the quality of the GWR. The irony of that trip was that, of course, it was a night turn, so you wonder how many folk would have noticed the sparkling state of the locomotive at the dead of night!

We worked night shifts as well as the day, but you were not allowed to work a night turn until you were 18. When we worked nights we'd alternate between cleaning and calling. If you were on calling-up duties, you wouldn't be cleaning engines. As a call boy, your duty was to 'call-up' engine drivers and firemen between the hours of midnight and four in the morning. There'd be four call boys at work each night, with a wide area of the town to cover, and between 40–50 men to

be roused. Drivers had to live within the town boundary to be able to claim a call boy. They were also entitled to refuse to have one, but the responsibility was the driver's if he failed to report for work on time. I recall one taciturn old driver complaining "I don't want a dratted call boy! I've had 'em before and they wake up every bugger in the street except ME!"

I knocked up drivers many times. As a call boy you were responsible to the Shed Foreman and you were given a list of calls with the required times, which would be one hour before their booking-on time. I'd cycle as there'd be a lot of calls to make, spread over a wide area of town, and I remember there was one old boy who was habitually late on duty as he'd obviously dropped off again after being called and would always claim upon his eventual arrival that he hadn't been called. One of our number was so fed up with this bloke that on one occasion he called the driver, then took the gate off its hinges and brought it back to the shed and put in the foreman's office! Sure enough, the miscreant was late again and came on duty with his usual "I wasn't bloody called!" To which Mr. Duck replied "Well whose bloody gate is that over there?" There was a man in the office, 'the adult caller', we called him, and he used to go out with notes to advise a driver if he had been taken off his rostered turn of duty and put on another. He didn't do the calling at night.

It was a tough initiation in the running shed. They were a pretty rough crowd of fellows in that shed in 1938. If there was ever any trouble in the town, if cigarette machines had been broken into or whatever, the police always made their first port of call at the shed, to check where everybody was. There was a night watchman who used to walk around the factory, and he'd have to clock in to prove that he'd examined all the different workshops, but he'd never walk around the running shed at night on his own – that's the reputation the shed had. They were a good lot, a solid crowd, but there was that little certain amount of roughness there, especially when you were a new lad and you really got put through the mill during initiation. I daren't tell you some of the things that happened!

When I moved onto the 2.0pm–10.0pm and the night shift (10.0pm–6.0am) rostering, there were around 45 cleaners on those turns. On the 2.0–10.0 turn, one cleaner was designated to pick up all those roughers, the dirty waste left on the ground by the cleaners during the day's work, and this was dumped in a three-wheel truck for the lighters-up, which contained nothing but oily spent waste. On cold winter nights the shed was a comforting place to be with all that heat and warmth everywhere, and I particularly recall the braziers under the water columns to prevent them freezing up in the winter. Conditions were hard, though, and the work was tough. With the Health and Safety concerns of modern times, they'd never tolerate these days what we went through! When we cleaned the boiler of a locomotive, we'd jump up and put one leg on the handrail and just stand there cleaning. That just wouldn't be allowed now – they'd want scaffolding around the boiler! Another particular memory

I am seen here during my days as a cleaner, August 1938, my hand on the regulator of a 'Bulldog' class 4—4—0 outside Swindon shed. I should not even have been here on the footplate! I had borrowed the blue overalls and cap from a driver. I was just so keen to become a driver and this might have been my way of showing that enthusiasm — I just couldn't wait. I was made fireman the year after this was taken. Cleaning was a filthy old job. The three chargeman cleaners on each shift who were responsible for the three gangs at work would check the cleaning by wiping the backs of the spokes of the driving wheels with a piece of waste, and if there was still oil on there, you lost your bonus. We used to go along the side of the gangways, jump up and kneel on the handrail, then you'd pull yourself up and put your feet on the handrail to clean the brass of the safety valve cover and the copper around the chimney top, the only way you could get up there to do it. Kneeling on the boiler, the knees of your overalls became very dirty. We used to have a gritty abrasive paste but fellows were so keen that they used to buy a 4d tin of 'Brasso' themselves to clean the number and nameplates, the copper band around the chimney and the brass window frames. We never did claim for it. So interested and full of pride were we as cleaners, that if we were cleaning a loco on a day shift, 8.0 — 5.30, and the engine was going out on an evening turn, we'd rush home after work, get cleaned up, then go out as far as South Marston or up as far as Hay Lane just to see her go by. I remember one loco, No. 2978 Charles J. Hambro that was on the night Leicester, 9.40 ex-Swindon, and it was a regular thing to clean her, then go up to Gorse Hill and see her pulling out. She was a very old engine but she'd be spotless, and, of course, the great thing was that you could see everything moving — the rods, the pistons, etc. Steam locos were alive, even when they were in the shed and there was nobody on them, as long as there was a fire in the firebox and there were whiffs of steam coming out from different points.   AUTHOR'S COLLECTION

was that on nights when the wind was in the right direction, I was very aware of the railway as soon as I stepped out of our house in Havelock Street – you could hear engines leaving the station, especially if the loco was heavy starting, and as I got to know more drivers when I progressed to firing, I could often recognise individual drivers' styles – they each had their own distinctive technique.

One day Mr Duck sent for me and informed me that the booking-on clerk was to go into hospital for an operation. "I'll need you in the office for about three months," he told me. "You'll be booking the drivers and firemen on and off." I thought to myself "Bugger that!" because I wanted to be with the engines. So I worked 11.0–7.0 each day and every time a crewman booked on duty, I had to record the time he arrived, as opposed to when he *should* have been there. This was in case of a compensation situation – if he got hurt in any way, where was he? When they booked off, they'd throw their daily journal in to me and I'd copy the particulars off and book the time the ticket came in by the clock on the office wall. Of course, I got to know every Swindon man by

LABOURING ON SWINDON SHED

Many times when bringing an engine onto shed at the end of a turn, I thought of the men who worked tirelessly to ensure the locos were ready for their next turn of duty. Mostly these were dead-end jobs, eight shillings a day, with no pathway to promotion. Most shed jobs were undertaken by men who had fallen by the wayside, had failed examinations and had been offered a job on the shed to keep them in gainful employment. Most of the shed jobs could be undertaken by engine cleaners should a tube cleaner or smokeboxer fail to turn up – indeed, with the cleaners on four shillings a day, they would always be keen to double their normal wage. Labouring jobs included ash loaders and lighters-up, in contrast with the skilled tasks performed by the fitters and boilermakers. but it is worth remembering that the skilled jobs in the depot could only function properly with the contribution of the unskilled workers. Duties were clearly defined and separate, unlike at a smaller shed, such as Cirencester or Malmesbury, where a night cleaner would take on many labouring duties.

FIREDROPPERS
Before an engine was recoaled it was dealt with by the firedroppers, of whom there were six at Swindon, two per shift. When a loco came off its turn of duty, the driver would bring it in on what was known as the coal stage line, where these men would shovel out the clinker and ash that had accumulated in the firebox. If you had a loco that had been in service for quite a time and a tender empty of coal, then you had a firebox full of ashes and clinker. This was no ordinary ash – it was very rough and looked rather like lava lumps from a volcano, and had to be chiselled off the firebox bars. As the locomotive was working, beating and puffing, it acted like a blast on the fire, forcing the heating ingredients out of the coal. This caused all the minerals to fuse and it was just like a huge lump of concrete. On a 'King' class loco, it would take anything up to an hour to shovel all the ash and clinker out. When this was done, the firedropper had to get down in the pit and rake out the ashpan, because a considerable amount of ash would have fallen through the grate fire into here. If the firedropper could, he would try and save some of the fire, just a little, so that the lighter-up would have some fire left when they took over. If the fire was so dirty that it was impossible to save, then the firebox was completely emptied. A firedropper's pay was a basic 8 shillings on a shift. They were given 6d for

a tank engine, 9d on a medium or mixed freight such as a 43XX class, and a shilling on the larger engines such as 'Castles' and 'Kings'. This duty was the one exception to the principle of cleaners filling in at the shed when required – cleaners never did the firedropping, as it was such dangerous, arduous work. Incidentally, clinker was often bought by farmers for filling deep holes on their farm tracks.

COAL MEN
There were three coal men on each shift at Swindon. With what steam was left in the boiler, the driver on the coal stage line would bring the locomotive down under the coal tip, where the coal men would fill the bunker or tender. Their duties were to shovel coal out of wagons into drams (or trolleys) which were then wheeled to the tip and turned up on their end so the coal would shoot down into the tender. Each trolley held ten cwt of coal. Two men would perform the emptying out of the wagons into the trolley, whilst the third did the tipping. On a busy day, with new engines off the factory with empty tenders, it had been known for three men to shovel and tip ninety tons of coal in an eight-hour shift. With these trial engines, the axle bearings hadn't bedded themselves in on the pads, so the coalmen never put more than about five tons of coal on – anything above the height of the tender was considered unsafe as it might cause the axleboxes to run hot on trial. However, with large locos that were designed for 4000 gallons of water and six tons of coal, they frequently put much more than six on – by loading to well above tender height they could have up to ten tons on and think nothing of it. Locomotive coal arrived in the yard every day in a train from Rogerstone.

SMOKEBOXERS
Following coaling, it was the turn of the smokeboxer, whose duty it was to climb onto the front of the loco where, he would open the smokebox door by means of two handles. Depending on the journey and the work the loco had done, there would be varying amounts of ash in the smokebox. Sometimes it would be almost full of fine ash which was thrown out by the smokeboxer onto the ground. Builders would buy this ash and would mix it with water and cement to form breeze blocks used in their trade for the inner walls of houses. The ash was also used for many a garden or allotment.

ASH LOADERS
Working as a team of two, these men worked an arduous 6.0–2.0 shift every day, clearing the firebox ashes and loading them into trucks to be taken away. With about a hundred locomotives through that coal stage every day, all those dropped fires resulted in a great deal of red hot ash around, so they would douse it with water from a nearby hydrant before shovelling it up.

SHED TURNER
When the smokeboxer had finished, the loco was now ready for the shedman or driver to take from the coal stage and place it in a position ready for the shed turner. This man may have already been 'up the rank', and may have finished on main-line work through failed eyesight. He might chalk 'BT' on the side of the cab which indicated that the engine was to go to the big turntable. It was vital that it was the right way round for its next turn of duty, facing Up for London or Down for the West of England. When they put the engine over on the Bank (the name for the road onto the big turntable) the shedman took over and moved it down onto the table, and either turned it the right way round for its next turn of duty and brought it back on the straight road, or left it stationed round the big table on one of the 28 lines which radiated from the turntable itself. If the loco received by the turner was already the right way round for its next trip, he would simply chalk the number on the cabside of the appropriate road where the coal stage man was to take it. The shed turners worked as a team of four per shift, one driver and fireman on the engine, the other pair at the coal stage dropping the engines down. Not all locos were under cover of the shed, of course. It depended on where the shedman put it ready for its turn, but if the shed was full, it would certainly be left out in the open. It could be hell at 2.0am on a winter's morning preparing a loco out in the open.

LIGHTERS UP
These men, again working as a team of two per shift, would light fires by throwing bundles into the firebox ignited by oily waste discarded by the cleaners. Big lumps of coal would be piled on top, anything up to 5 cwt of coal, depending on how much fire had been left by the firedroppers. The lighter-up in fact worked as a team with the steam raiser, who, when the coal was burnt through, would push the fire over more of the grate, then add more coal. He ensured that when

the crew booked on for that particular loco there was sufficient fire in the firebox with red hot coals for the fireman to build on and sufficient steam in the boiler to get things going. At a branch shed, of course, the night cleaner would do these tasks, but a major shed such as Swindon had this team of two specifically for this function.

BOILERWASHERS

It might be that a locomotive would not be relit because it was due for a boiler washout. This happened about every ten days. A lot of silt and mud would accumulate in the boiler of a locomotive, so the mudhole doors at the top and bottom of the firebox would be removed, and boiler washout plugs would be removed to allow a hosepipe to be inserted. The boiler would be washed right out in a process which took about half-an-hour. Because the loco would invariably be warm, it was essential to wash it out with warm water – to put cold water into a boiler that was warm, being copper, there was a great danger of damage from contraction. Cold water washout was used if a loco had been stopped for two or three days and the engine was stone cold. It was a filthy job. One man would be with the pipe putting it into the different holes, while his mate worked the hydrant, turning the water on and off.

TUBERS

While the boiler washout was being done, another duo would be at work running long rods through the tubes. They would work from the smokebox and run the rods right down through the length of each tube pushing the clinker and ash through into the firebox. It was vital that these tubes were clean. The tubers also had to get into the firebox when it was cool enough, to knock all the clinker and ash off the stays, the rivets in the crown of the firebox, and clean off the brickarch.

SANDMAN

This employee, Sammy Brain, on one shift 8.0–5.30, had a little workshop with a furnace where he would dry sand and put it into trucks and take it around to bins stationed at frequent intervals around the shed – it was his duty to ensure these were kept full of dry sand, and it was one of the fireman's duties during the preparation of his locomotive to check the level of the sandboxes. Sand was important because when the rails were slippery, it could be released onto the rail to give greater adhesion for the wheels. If sand was required, the fireman would go to a bin with a scoop to fetch the necessary supply. Before a driver used sand he would shut the regulator and make sure there was no steam pushing the pistons backwards and forwards. If sand was applied quickly under spinning wheels, the sudden grip could cause the crank pins to snap and throw your rods. You would never drop sand on wheels under power. Each loco had four sandboxes, two at the front, two at the back, operated from a lever in the cab.

SHEDMAN CLEANER

This was one turn, one man a day, working an 8.0–5.30 shift. This duty involved swilling out the inspection pit with hosepipes, swilling the tops of the pits and keeping the shed clean.

TOOLMAN

Every new loco that came into the shed from shops at Swindon had to be equipped with all the tools it was going to need to carry out its duties – the fire irons, pokers, shovels, oil bottles, feeders, spanners, buckets, flat feeder, barrel feeder, all sorts for oiling different parts of the engine. The toolman had to see that all the tools were there, it was not the fireman's responsibility. It was quite a thing when a loco came out of the Works and required tooling. If the fireman came on duty and couldn't find a coalpick, he would go to the toolman who would then have to report to the Stores. At Swindon we used to equip locos which were going to other depots, so we carried a huge surplus stock of tools.

STOREMAN

Every time a driver came on duty, whatever the journey, he'd have to collect his allocation of oil from the storeman. The driver would make out his chit – 8 pints engine oil, 4 pints cylinder oil, 2 pints of paraffin for the headlamps, then he'd sign for it and the storeman would issue what he wanted. If a driver wanted extra oil, if the axleboxes were down, for instance, he'd have to go to the shed foreman and get permission for the extra. The storeman was also responsible for issuing uniforms, equipment, and everything for the locomotive.

THE LAMPMAN

This was a single daily shift which involved cleaning and maintaining locomotive headlamps. It was important that these lamps be kept clean. Everytime an engine came to shed and was stabled on the coal bank, the fireman would be responsible for taking his headlamps down into the stores where the lampman had his little corner. Later on, I recall he had his separate hut. Here he'd clean the lamps, fill them with paraffin and store them neatly ready for collection.

BUNDLEMAN

At Swindon this job was usually undertaken by a man who had been injured in the course of his work for the GWR, and was no longer fit enough for the rigorous outside jobs. He had a cabin just inside the shed and for most of the week he'd sit here making up the wooden bundles for the firebox, using twenty sticks nailed into a rough cube about a foot square. On Fridays, he served as the cash clerk and dished out your money. You shouted out your check number, and he'd give you your check which you'd take to the cash office. When you handed it over they gave you your money in a little tin. You took the money out and handed the tin back. If you'd had a big job there might be a white fiver in there and you were really rolling in it! If you were a cleaner and you'd had a relief firing turn with some extra labouring thrown in, you felt like a millionaire at the end of the week.

THE BRICKIE

His job was to repair the brick arches in the firebox. These only lasted so long because they were subjected to such terrific heat. Their purpose was to protect the tube plate at the firebox end, and assist in the correct draughting of the loco, to help to provide perfect combustion in the firebox. But they did burn, crack, collapse and fall down, so they had to be replaced periodically. He had a day shift of 8.0–5.30. There was always work for a brickie.

FITTERS

At frequent intervals during a shift, the running fitters would report to the booking-on lobby to consult the drivers' repair book. Every driver booking on duty would look at the repair book to check that the loco he was going to take out was fit for duty and that repairs booked by the previous driver had been carried out. There might, for example, be a piston gland requiring packing or joints blowing on a pipe. The driver would book it, the fitter would tear out the page and leave the carbon copy underneath so that the next driver could see what had been booked on that particular engine. There were also fitters at Swindon who dealt with locos that had been stopped for repairs – perhaps for valves and pistons which needed new rings. This would be a job on its own and the men involved would have nothing to do with repairs to running locos. There was a clear distinction between fitters assigned to repairs to locos in service and those working on engines stopped for major work. There were eight men per shift and always plenty of work for them.

BOILERSMITHS

These men dealt with leaking tubes or stays, and three were employed per shift. You could have tubes leaking at the smokebox or the firebox ends. The boilersmiths had expanders that they would put inside the neck of the tube to take up the slack and stop the leaks.

CARPENTERS

One carpenter worked a daily shift of 8.00–5.30. Anything involving wood was sent his way. He repaired hammers with heads on new wooden shafts, doors on the shed, furniture, and of course the wooden floor planks on the footplate of the locomotives.

ATC MAN

This was an electrician whose duty was to examine the Automatic Train Control apparatus which was fitted underneath each locomotive. It gave the driver an audible sound which repeated the indication of the signals – a bell rang in the cab if signals were at clear and a siren sounded, followed by an automatic brake application, if they were at danger. When the shoe under each engine passed over an ATC ramp in the middle of the track, that shoe lifted 2½ inches and if the signals were at clear then the ramp was electrified and as the shoe rose over it the electrical circuit was broken, but immediately restored and the bell rang. If the signals were at danger, the ramp was dead, not electrified, so the circuit was broken and not restored. In this instance the siren sounded and the brakes were automatically applied unless the driver overrode the system by operating a little lever on the side of his control box to cancel the siren. Today it's called AWS, Automatic Warning System. It was a wonderful invention. I have never known them fail.

name that way, and it wasn't very long before they'd come up to the window and say "Book us on duty, kid!" and I'd never have to ask for their names because I knew them, and it was on the paperwork. But what I didn't know were the 'foreign' men, those up from the West or from London, who would book off duty, and go to their lodgings if they were working 'double-home' jobs, then return next day, sign on again and work back. So they'd come in and shout "Book us off, kid, Brown and Williams!" We had a very prim and religious lady in the office who was due to marry one of our shift foremen and we also had a fellow who worked out the wages and had an awkward stutter. On one occasion, in came a set of London men who'd just worked a freight down to Swindon. It was a driver Ball and fireman Hall and they came in, slid the window back and shouted "Book us off duty, kid, Balls an' All!" Well, the poor lady was white with embarrassment and the wage clerk was stuttering away "F-f-f-fancy th-th-that!" It took us all afternoon to convince the delicate lady that what the driver had shouted was in fact quite proper!

On 3rd July 1939, I was promoted to Acting Fireman at the shed, which meant that I would now be able to get in valuable experience on the footplate with a driver, and it was to make a difference financially. Mr Duck called me in to his office and announced "You are going to be promoted to temporary fireman, which means that if you are required, you will go out firing, but if you are not needed you will return to your cleaning duties, but you will still be on the 9/6d a day rate instead of the 4/- cleaning rate."

This was an exciting time, and I remember the first locomotive I ever fired was a pannier tank, No. 1797, on the 2.0pm shift on shunting duties in the loco yard sidings which ran by the side of the Gloucester line. My driver was 'Topper' Moss, his nickname a reference to his habit of always arriving on duty looking smart and resplendent in a bow tie! Of course, within ten minutes on the footplate he'd be so dirty you could hardly see the bow tie!

The GWR records show that I went back to cleaning for a couple of months before being fully made up to fireman on 6th November 1939, but I have no recollection of this. It's a mystery to me as I am certain that once on firing I never went back to cleaning, and, now in the early months of World War II, the Company needed to move men through the ranks quickly to ensure that they had the crews available to cope with the expected increased traffic requirements of war work.

GWR '1854' class 0–6–0PT No. 1797, the first locomotive on which I fired, on the Loco Yard Sidings.
COLLECTION KIDDERMINSTER RAILWAY MUSEUM

Swindon shed on 13th August 1939, with (from left to right) 'Star' class 4–6–0 No. 4057 Princess Elizabeth, '517' 0–4–2T No. 1442, 'Aberdare' class 2–6–0 No. 2669 and '5500' class 2–6–2T No. 5614.

V. R. WEBSTER, CTY. KIDDERMINSTER RAILWAY MUSEUM

CHAPTER THREE

WARTIME PROMOTIONS

Collett class 0–4–2T No. 5802, a locomotive commonly allocated to the Malmesbury branch, on one of the roads leading from the big turntable in Swindon shed. The ring above was for water supply in boiler washout – it supplied hot water from a stationary boiler for the locomotives. The painted vertical post was for sighting in wartime – a black and white post aided vision when walking around the shed.
COLLECTION ROGER CARPENTER

I was a young fireman in the late thirties and dimly aware that storm clouds were beginning to loom in Europe. War broke out on 3rd September 1939, and it wasn't long after that I was made a temporary fireman, although it was a long time after war was declared that any action took place. I can remember being in the back garden at Havelock Street when I heard Chamberlain on the wireless talking to the country about the situation in Poland, and can still remember his exact words – "consequently we are now at war with Germany." With declared hostilities, promotions through the links became very much quicker than formerly, and cleaners like me were made firemen, and firemen were made drivers. Our duties were not classed as a reserved occupation, but they needed more crews to handle the extra trains needed to disperse imported cargoes which would normally have been warehoused at the docks where they were landed but when the German army over-ran France we were open to German air-raids and in the ports one direct hit on a warehouse would take out several ships' cargoes.

I had been to Park House for my medical examination to become a permanent fireman on 2nd July 1939, and when a vacancy came up I was duly appointed on 5th November the same year. So rapid were promotions during the war that I

have little recollection of some of the Swindon links, being in certain ones for a very short time indeed. However, I do recall that after some weeks on the Factory pilots, my first trip out on the main line on a firing turn was undertaken when I was on a spare turn on the Factory link on 27th January 1940, running a short pick-up goods train out on the South Wales Direct, as far as Hullavington and back, shunting all stations en route – Wootton Bassett, Brinkworth, Little Somerford and Hullavington. The locomotives on that turn that exciting week were two Collett 0–4–2 engines, Nos. 5802 and 5804, which were regularly seen on Malmesbury branch passenger services. Being inexperienced, I clearly remember that in my enthusiasm, I often shovelled far more coal than was required! In the week of 30th March that same year, a spare turn yielded my first passenger firing runs, with a morning trip on the Highworth branch with two Bristol Division B-set coaches hauled by No. 5413, an 0–6–0 pannier tank, and an afternoon run to Badminton with '14XX' class 0–4–2T No. 1442.

I was summoned down to Bath for an army medical and the old colonel who passed me asked me what branch of the army I'd prefer, and I told him I'd like to be in some section of the Railway Operating Corps. He informed me that this would depend on where I was required and that I'd have to go where they sent me; the only thing that was absolutely certain was that I'd be called up within ten days. He was wrong, however, because during that ten-day period in which I was waiting, the Government made footplate staff a reserved occupation, so I never made it into the services. Cleaners in earlier generations had had a long wait for promotion – you might not make it to driver until gone 50, and you retired at 60, but the war changed all that. I was only two years as cleaner but one disadvantage of the quick movement through the links was that I wasn't getting the experience that I should have had in each one. I was in the lower links from factory pilots up to the bottom passenger work from periods varying from six to eighteen months, then after the war I went straight into the Top Link, by which time things had slowed down again. We reached a situation often described as 'filling dead men's shoes', which resulted in my spending seven years in one link with one man, Bill Hinder, but this was the best period of my railway career. Promotion had been so fast during the war that it had exhausted itself.

The work for the drivers and firemen at locomotive sheds was organised in a series of turns known as Links, a means of assembling the great variety of work involved into a set number of rostered levels of factory, freight and passenger train work, ranging from short trips around the yard and factory sidings up to top passenger express duties. The principle was the grouping together of jobs of about the same difficulty on a cycle which repeated, often on a 12-week pattern, although this was not always possible, and, as ever, these procedures varied over the years. The passenger links, numbers 1–4 were all worked on this rota, so with a week at a time on each job you took three months to go round the link. You worked your designated turns of duty in one link at a time until you were moved on to the next link by promotion, and you did this individually.

There were eleven principal links at Swindon shed, although it is my recollection that they were numbered from one to ten with the lowest link, the factory pilots, unnumbered. You worked your way through each one as a fireman, then, once you attained the rank of engineman, you went through the whole process again, working your way from factory pilots to top passenger services. Within this framework, there were some exceptions to the general trend of promotion, as will be detailed. Of course, it should be stressed that these procedures varied over the years and jobs could be moved from one link to another, and it has been necessary to lean on the memories of some of my old colleagues to assemble these recollections of the work in the links, for, with the rapid promotions caused by World War II, young firemen tended to be rushed through the lower links and therefore not have great experience of the work involved. Hence my memory of these links is fairly jumbled as my career moved at a rapid pace until things slowed down after the War. Some of the links, such as the shed and coal stage link and the Old Town Link, were quite small and only used as promotion for firemen, not drivers, so there were only a limited number of places in them for this purpose. Therefore, if there were a large number of firemen in line for

promotion, they might miss out a link entirely on the promotion ladder. In fact, when I was first promoted to driver, I missed out the factory pilots entirely, going straight to the Transfer Link.

There was an inter-departmental committee, effectively a shop stewards' committee, usually three or four men, who would make out the links for the crews. The diagram would be sent to the shed committee from Paddington, but management used to leave it to the local men to form the links because they knew that if they, the management, did the job they'd only have to come to us to secure an agreement on it, so they would expect us to make up the rostering at local level and get the men to agree to it. So the links were made up, they were posted in the time office where the crews could look at them, and if there was any problem it could be dealt with at a branch meeting where the objection could be raised. Simply, the local committee had a better chance of working out a system that was practical than Paddington because they were the men doing the job. All the men on the local committee were elected by the workforce, and it was the job of those elected to put the diagrams into the links for the entire depot, and arranging them in this way was a whole week's office work.

When you booked on duty at the running shed, whichever link you were in, you were allowed ten minutes to study the K2 notice, to check your assigned turn of duty, check the route and any alterations, speed restrictions or single-line working, before going to prepare your locomotive. Your K2 book went with you but any late changes would be posted on the board and you had to study this and either keep it in your mind or make notes. A good friend of mine, Norman Wiltshire, who did 40 years on the footplate and was a member of the committee that worked on the links, used to say that the Swindon crewmen included some of the most responsible people with whom you could ever wish to work. Of course, those men who learned their trade in the days of steam received a long apprenticeship, maybe as long as 20 years on the footplate as firemen to gain experience and learn from drivers who in their turn had gone through similarly long years as the junior men. Sadly, today this has all been lost. Of the 250 drivers based at Swindon in 1940 you could count on one hand the number of drivers that firemen would avoid, given the chance. They were in the main excellent chaps, no question. There was just one man with whom no one could work, and I recall an amusing encounter with this driver's wife one weekend in Regent Street in Swindon. The lady asked me "Mr. Shurmer, 'ow does you get on with moi 'usband?"

"Well, to tell you the truth," I replied diplomatically, "some days I do, and some days I don't!"

"When oi married that man," she went on, "Oi thought I'd make 'im more loike me. But d'you know, the bugger's making me more loike 'im!"

Each link had its own relief system, known as spare turns, in which you were under the jurisdiction of the shed foreman responsible for locomotives. You booked on at the shed and stayed there, unlike on the Control Link where you reported to the Control Relief cabin. The foreman could ask you to do any footplate duty as long as you had knowledge of the road. Of course, you might not be given a job, and just spend the shift preparing locomotives. The best thing about being spare to a conscientious worker was the variety in the work, as every day it was something different, and sometimes nothing at all! Most links had two spare turns, except the factory pilots which had one only.

For instance, booking on at 2 p.m. Monday, you could be given a job up to London if you had the necessary road knowledge, then at 2 p.m. Tuesday you might be allocated nothing at all until 6 p.m. when the foreman might send you to Bristol 'on the cushions' to pick up a light engine, so you'd travel passenger to Temple Meads, then collect the engine from Bath Road shed. The older men used to say "Knowledge of road is finance", and the reason for that was that you could be on duty for five hours, waiting in the mess room with little happening, then the foreman would report that a driver had not turned up, so you'd start an eight-hour turn of duty, which paid you for 13 hours. If you had the necessary knowledge of road, you landed that job and reaped the benefits of that extra pay. We had a little pink form known as 'the dodger', which explained the shift.

Every link required relief at some stage, so this is why the spare turns were always present. They were for the purpose of covering absences occasioned by sickness, holiday or other eventuality. If a holiday absence was anticipated, the roster clerk would allocate the spare turn the day before.

At any locomotive depot, there was always a pilot, a locomotive prepared in case of the failure of a locomotive in service. It would be coaled, oiled, steamed up and held in the shed like a fire engine waiting for an emergency. If an express came down from Paddington and developed a problem, it would be stopped and the dagonet, the code word for 'new engine required' would be wired through to Swindon, whereupon the foreman would go to the messroom and instruct a relief crew to take the pilot off shed and "Change over with the down London, she's failing."

Safety was a paramount consideration with all GWR men, and there were in excess of 400 safety rules to be learnt by every crewman. When the number of crews at the shed was increased to 250 to help meet the demands of wartime, there were 109 steam locomotives based there, including shunting engines, diagram freight locomotives and top passenger classes. In addition, there'd be the extra engines just out of the Works after repair, awaiting allocation to another depot, and three crane engines, two of which I recall were called *Hercules* and *Cyclops*, which were used in the factory.

THE FACTORY LINK

The main work in this first link was on the factory pilot engines, clearly a link peculiar to Swindon, and this involved operating small shunting engines which worked the factory sidings and moved around whatever the Works required from one site to another. Every pilot engine in this link had two shunters attached to it, a head shunter and an under shunter, and these men travelled around the yard to reach their various tasks on a four-wheel open wagon called a 'shunting truck', known locally as 'The Chariot'. The factory pilots were a daytime shift, their hours being determined by the requirements of the Works and their hours. Clocking on was at 7.15 a.m., with 45 minutes allowed to prepare a tank engine, then the hours were 8 a.m. to 3 p.m. However, there were variations to this, as some of the pilot engines were used to do jobs early in the morning on the Van link – every opportunity was utilised in the diagramming to keep an engine busy if possible.

The shunting engines in this link were usually pannier tanks of the '37XX' and '57XX' 0-6-0 classes, and the wagon shops, for instance, had a set of six very small panniers of the '13XX' class. Numbers 1366–71 were built especially for the tight curves of the factory sidings, their short wheelbase making them very suitable for this work. If panniers were in short supply, it was quite common for '517' class 0-4-2 tank engines or one of the '58XX' Collett tanks allocated to the Malmesbury branch to appear on factory pilot duties. No. 1161 was a very old '517' which used to work the branches on local passenger services. It would work over to Highworth as empty stock early in the morning, bring the workmen from that town into the factory, then spend the rest of its day as the carriage shop pilot at the back of the main-line station. This was a typical situation in this link, whereby a factory pilot would be used on a little job early in the day before the Works were open, before going onto the factory sidings.

The factory link in my day comprised about 18 crews, an interesting combination of bright-eyed young firemen on the way up and sometimes older drivers on the way 'down', demoted because of failing health, eyesight or a misdemeanour higher up in the links. Failing eyesight was a common reason: the doctors who conducted the medicals at Park House were understandably very strict about this. These older men were usually assigned to the lighter duties of the carriage shop and transfer yard pilots. Those who were demoted as a result of, for instance, negligence in their work and causing an accident, were known locally as the 'Criminal Link', although I always thought the term was rather harsh because they were not criminals in that sense. The penalty for this form of down-grading was that there was no overtime available, for such men, nor any night work or Sundays, so they just earned the basic minimum.

The factory pilots were busy little engines pottering around the sidings, maybe a little frustrating for a former main-line driver, but good experience for the new young firemen fresh from cleaning duties – this was their first real start on a locomotive. Drivers on this link sometimes arrived from other depots – I recall one chap who arrived from Oxford where he'd somehow got his loco in back gear (whilst going forward!) and ruined the engine's motion while

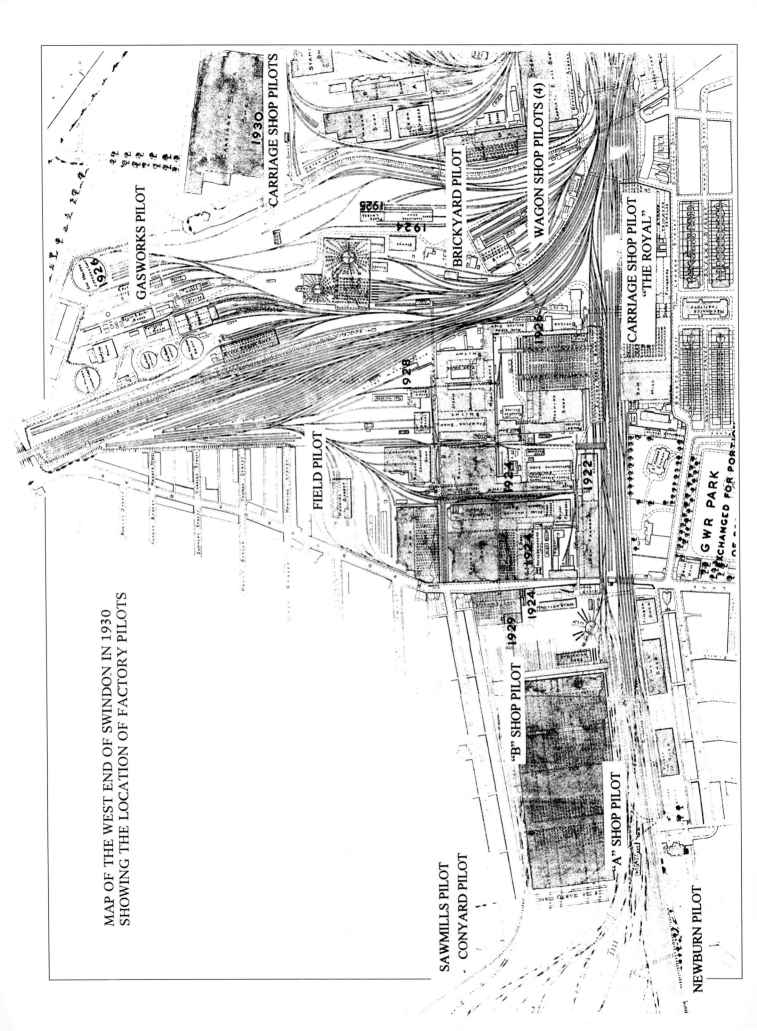

MAP OF THE WEST END OF SWINDON IN 1930
SHOWING THE LOCATION OF FACTORY PILOTS

SAWMILLS PILOT
CONYARD PILOT

NEWBURN PILOT

"A" SHOP PILOT

"B" SHOP PILOT

FIELD PILOT

GASWORKS PILOT

CARRIAGE SHOP PILOTS

BRICKYARD PILOT

WAGON SHOP PILOTS (4)

CARRIAGE SHOP PILOT
"THE ROYAL"

GWR PARK

working a train from Oxford to Didcot. For that expensive error he was sent to Swindon for light duties. But in all the years I worked on the railway, I never knew any driver who was sacked – a job would always be found on a demotion. But 'sent to Swindon' was a recognised punishment, and I recall we had men from Penzance and South Wales in the factory link at Swindon for such reasons.

You worked on a pilot engine duty for a week, Monday to Saturday morning, the Works being closed Saturday afternoons and Sunday. For instance, you'd be on the sawmills for a week, then switch to, say, the Newburn pilot, and so on. As fireman, you knew who your driver was, but you had to be prepared on early shift to be on a different locomotive. On the later shifts, it didn't matter. You'd relieve the engine crew and just take over the engine that was in use. During a quiet half-hour on a pilot you'd just put on a couple of shovelfulls of coal to keep the fire going. You didn't need maximum boiler pressure for yard work. You'd be keeping the footplate clean with your handbrush and watering the coal in the bunker to keep the dust down. Information during the day as to what jobs had to be done would come from the shunter who would receive his information in the mornings from the foreman in the wagon shops, as to what vehicles had to come out, on what road they were stood, and where they were to be moved. Shunters tended to

walk to jobs with the factory pilots where distances were not great, but the shunters trucks would be used to convey them over the longer runs, and also over on the transfer pilots at the goods sidings at the east end of the station. If you were working with a shunter in conditions of bad visibility, a whistle code had to be used, and it was crucial to avoid having more steam than was required because if steam was issuing through the safety valves you could not hear the whistles.

You would normally keep the same locomotive for a week's work on the factory unless it was required to go to the Works itself for repair. When the factory hooter went off at 12.30 p.m., the pilots would stop too and the crews would try to grab some lunch on the footplate, as their work was governed by the hours of the Works. The factory pilots performed their busy work well away from the public eye, the sidings, loops, necks and yards of the Works to which they went, being well away from public roads, and even parties of visitors to the Works rarely saw their activity. Young firemen of my generation moved through the ranks very quickly with hardly any experience on the factory pilots because of the speed of promotions caused by the needs of the War effort. I recall that there were about 20 turns in the factory link during the time I was associated with it.

In this 1949 view, pannier tank No. 2756 is seen on the factory sidings with a shunting truck, known locally as 'The Chariot' and used for conveying shunters around the yard safely to their various duties. This would have been on an 'A' or 'B' Shop duty, it is difficult to tell. These engines were commonly selected from withdrawn locos coming into the factory and among other jobs were used for pulling engines up from 'A' Shop to have their tenders attached and be coaled, as explained on page 52. The Pattern Shop features in the left background with, to the right, the Iron Foundry. Both buildings still exist in modern commercial ownership. The bridge girders at left carried the tracks over Rodbourne Road, below which would be thick with cycle traffic at peak times in response to the factory hooter.

A. C. STERNDALE

Rushey Platt Junction, looking east in 1953, with the Midland & South Western line diverging at right to run up to Swindon Town, and the roof of 'A' Shop in the Works visible in the left distance. The sidings visible in front of the factory were the areas worked by the Conyard pilot.

H. F. WHEELLER

Looking west towards Bristol with an Up passenger express for London headed by a 'Castle' class 4—6—0. In the distance between Rushey Platt signal box and the train, can be seen a permanent way gang working on the turnout to the Old Town line. The lower arm on the left post of the signal gantry was a fixed distant whilst the upper arm was the home signal for the MSWJ line. The arm on the other post controlled the road for the main line west to Bristol. The sidings at right were the mileage sidings of the up goods loop, flanked by a section of the Conyard sidings referred to on page 55. An interesting feature here was the three signalposts seen up on the embankment of the MSWJ line — these were not operational but were simply used by inspectors for administering eyesight tests to drivers.

COLLECTION JIM LOWE

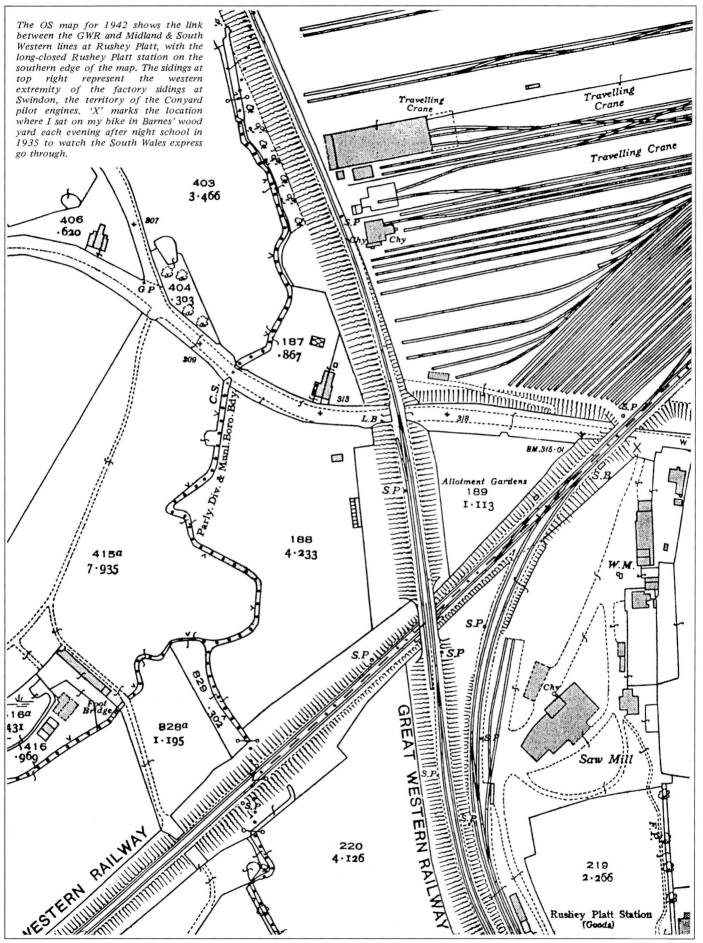

The OS map for 1942 shows the link between the GWR and Midland & South Western lines at Rushey Platt, with the long-closed Rushey Platt station on the southern edge of the map. The sidings at top right represent the western extremity of the factory sidings at Swindon, the territory of the Conyard pilot engines. 'X' marks the location where I sat on my bike in Barnes' wood yard each evening after night school in 1935 to watch the South Wales express go through.

From this extract of the same OS map, it is possible to see precisely where four of the factory pilot engines worked. The sawmill and Conyard pilots served Swindon's western yards which were both provided with travelling cranes, the Newburn pilot worked the lengthy carriage shed running parallel to the main line and stretching from Wootton Bassett Road to Dean Street, whilst the 'A' Shop pilot worked the sidings at top right.

SAWMILL PILOT

CONYARD PILOT

Travelling Crane

Travelling Crane

Travelling Crane

Travelling Crane

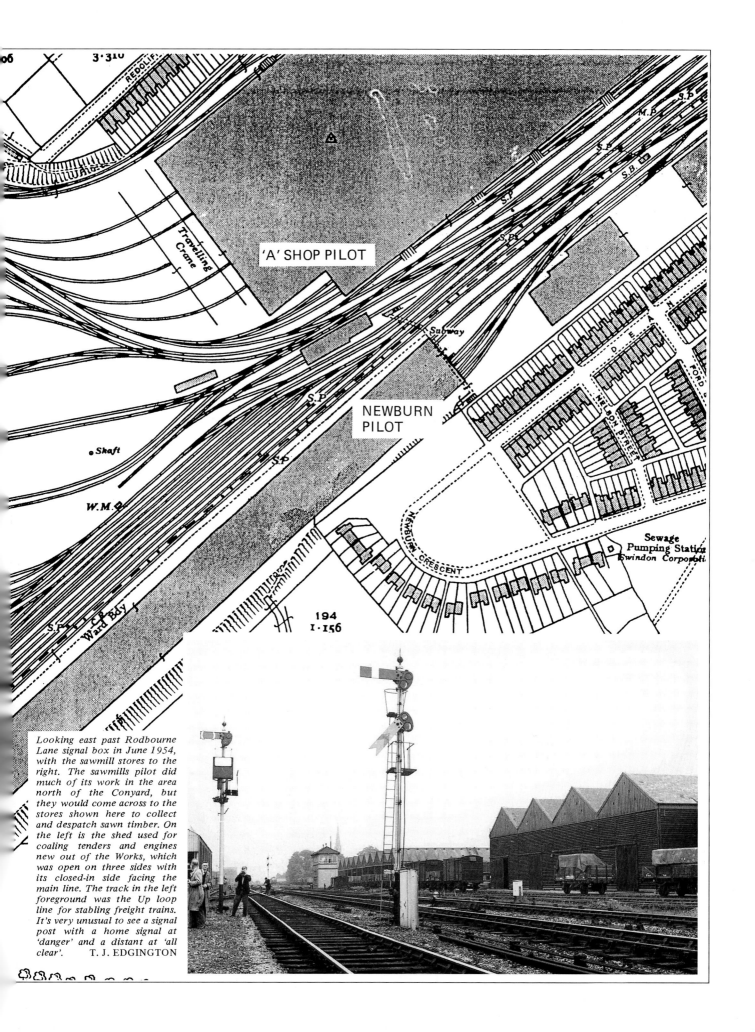

'A' SHOP PILOT

NEWBURN PILOT

Travelling Crane

Subway

Skaft

W.M.

Ward Bdy

Sewage Pumping Station Swindon Corporation

NEWBURN CRESCENT

194
1·156

06   3·310

Looking east past Rodbourne Lane signal box in June 1954, with the sawmill stores to the right. The sawmills pilot did much of its work in the area north of the Conyard, but they would come across to the stores shown here to collect and despatch sawn timber. On the left is the shed used for coaling tenders and engines new out of the Works, which was open on three sides with its closed-in side facing the main line. The track in the left foreground was the Up loop line for stabling freight trains. It's very unusual to see a signal post with a home signal at 'danger' and a distant at 'all clear'.   T. J. EDGINGTON

Sidings at the top end of the yard to the west of 'A' Shop.

Rough sawing was done at this sawmill on the north side of the main line just east of the Conyard, then wagonloads of sawn timber were moved to another sawmill on the south side of the main line near the carriage shops. Open trucks of raw logs were brought in here and left by the sawmills pilot engine. The cabin above was the control room for the overhead crane which ran along the horizontal gantry and removed raw logs from the trucks and moved them into the sawmill, the building in the foreground at right, for cutting. There was a little narrow-gauge tramway here where four-wheel trucks were used to move the sawn timber. They were pushed out by hand, then gangs unloaded the wood, which was stored in the open with offcuts between them to allow air to circulate around it.

This pannier tank No. 1542, seen in the sidings west of 'A' Shop in 1949, may have been on Conyard or Sawmills pilot duty.
A. C. STERNDALE

No. 3 road in the loco shed was where the factory pilots were stabled overnight, all the way back into the shed, and they could leave from either end, either via the turntable or by just going forwards. It was a great procession each morning as they all left the shed, and they were often referred to as the 'Channel Fleet'! There'd be a queue at the water column, although some of the drivers wouldn't wait – the wagon shops had water columns, for instance, so some pilots could take water elsewhere, especially if there were big train engines competing for the shed column. The shedman was responsible for seeing that the factory pilots were in the right order for getting out in the morning. He'd go in the office and check the duty sheets to see which jobs the engines were booked on, then as the pilots came in in the late afternoon, if they knew that an engine was needed at 4.10 a.m. for the Cirencester workmen's train, he would make sure that engine was at the front of the line.

CONYARD PILOT

The so-called 'Dump' originated from the Broad Gauge abolition of 1892, and was known locally as 'C' shop or the Conyard, short for Concentration Yard, or indeed, for condemned stock. The 'C' shop pilot shunted wagons of recovered scrap from the cutting-up shed,

and also towed condemned engines in there. Wagons were filled with copper scrap from burnt-off cables, lead, steel, iron and brass from cut-up engines, tubes from signal posts, old rails and girders in short lengths. Each night around 5.30, these wagons were shunted up to the Transfer Yard where trains were prepared to go to whoever had ordered specific scrap, be it wood from the sawmills or metal from the Conyard.

SAWMILLS PILOT

This pilot had an early booking-on, at 5 a.m., preparing the pannier tank for a 6 a.m. start. Their job was to deliver wagons of whole tree trunks to the sawmills, where they would be cut up into planks, then the pilot would pull them back out and they were stacked in the yard close by, with wooden slats in between so that the timber could weather and get seasoned. The pilot would also deliver trainloads of wood to anywhere in the Works that needed it. For coaches it would be best mahogany. With the early start, the early crew were relieved about 12.30 at the sawmills, and the driver and fireman would walk back to shed to book off about 1 p.m. The new crew would take over until 5 p.m. When they'd finished with the factory pilot work at 5 o'clock, they had only completed half their shift so they would be under foreman's orders until 9 p.m. I never actually worked the sawmills pilot for some reason, maybe because I was not on the factory pilots long enough to work round the link.

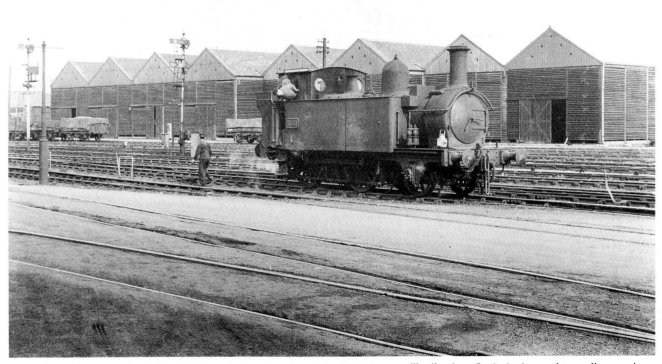

Alongside the sawmill stores No. 3561 may possibly have been seen here on a sawmills pilot duty. In the background tarpaulins covering wagons were used to keep loaded timber dry, while a shunter can be seen walking towards the nearby point handle to alter the road for the locomotive.
A. C. STERNDALE

This view was taken from a factory pilot on one of the factory sidings opposite Newburn shed. It shows a 'Hall' passing by with an eastbound express in early 1950. The MSWJ overbridge at Rushey Platt is dimly visible in the distance, with the Conyard sidings away on the right.

DAVE 'BRINKWORTH' JONES

Another view from the same factory pilot, showing the early morning goods train from the Transfer passing the weighbridge and sawmill stores on its way up to Swindon Town, headed by an unidentified pannier tank. Through the early morning mist it is not possible to tell if there was a banker on the rear, but on the occasions that the traffic warranted it, help would be provided at the rear for the climb from Rushey Platt up to Town, as referred to on page 89.

DAVE 'BRINKWORTH' JONES

'A' AND 'B' SHOP PILOTS

The job of this pilot was to move engines out of the factory, collecting them from the traverser and taking it with the shunters truck up the line to link up with its tender from 'B' shop. At the back of 'A' shop were several long sidings, to and from which were conveyed boiler tubes, machines for the 'AM' machine shop, rivets, copper sheets and many other pieces. These sidings were eventually connected to the traverser which ran between the 'A' shop and the 'Barn' where boiler repairs were undertaken. The 'B' shop pilot duty here was to marshall tenders from the Works. There was a long shed by the 65ft turntable in the factory close to the main up line and the engines would be coaled there and attached to the tenders which were delivered by the 'B' shop pilot. The 'A' shop yard pilots were not part of this link at all – 'A' shop yard loco men and shunters were a separate group who only worked in the yard. The locos used here were selected by the 'A' shop yard foreman, Mr. Stan Morris, from the withdrawn locos coming into the factory. For many years they were Absorbed engines. They never went to the shed. Mr. Morris would change the locos periodically as other condensed engines became available. At weekends the locos used to park up either near the Barn, opposite the Reception Shed, or on one of the roads off the turntable, and there was usually a small heap of ashes alongside.

The west end of Swindon station, showing an up goods pulling out of the up loop and going out onto the main line to Paddington in 1948. In the foreground a pannier tank is seen working the 'A' Shop pilot duty and appears ready to collect the engines which are seen here waiting in what was known locally as the 'pool'.

A. C. STERNDALE

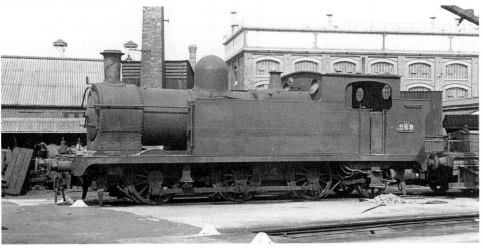

No. 269, a former Barry Railway 0–6–2T, was withdrawn in October 1949 and used as 'A' Shop pilot. It is seen here on a siding off the works turntable. To the left is the corrugated roof of the mess room which we used when working on the trial engines.

R. H. G. SIMPSON

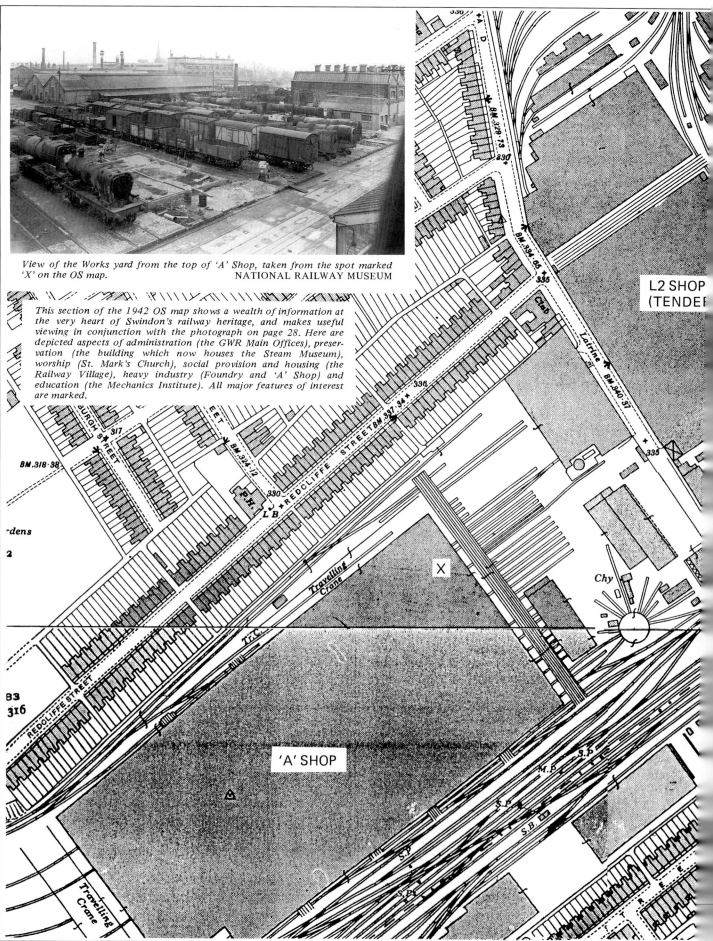

View of the Works yard from the top of 'A' Shop, taken from the spot marked 'X' on the OS map.
NATIONAL RAILWAY MUSEUM

This section of the 1942 OS map shows a wealth of information at the very heart of Swindon's railway heritage, and makes useful viewing in conjunction with the photograph on page 28. Here are depicted aspects of administration (the GWR Main Offices), preservation (the building which now houses the Steam Museum), worship (St. Mark's Church), social provision and housing (the Railway Village), heavy industry (Foundry and 'A' Shop) and education (the Mechanics Institute). All major features of interest are marked.

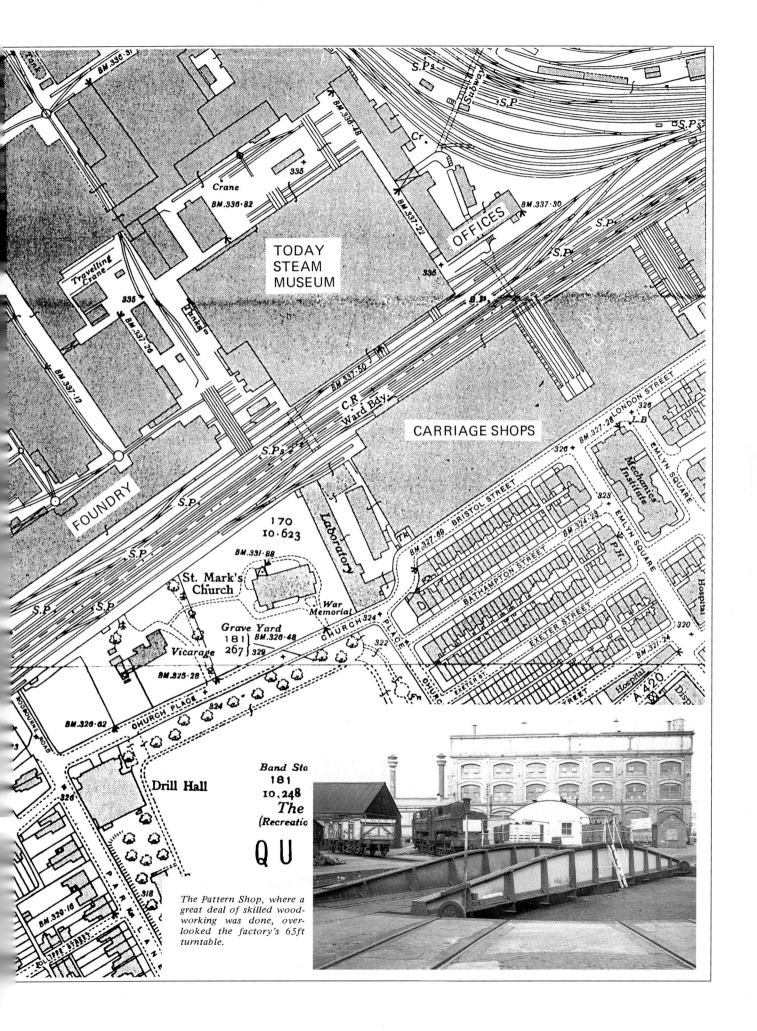

TODAY
STEAM
MUSEUM

OFFICES

CARRIAGE SHOPS

FOUNDRY

St. Mark's
Church

Laboratory

War
Memorial

Grave Yard

Vicarage

Drill Hall

CHURCH PLACE

Mechanics'
Institute

EMLYN SQUARE

Bristol Street

Bathampton Street

Exeter Street

London Street

Crane

Travelling
Crane

Band Sta
181
10,248
The
(Recreatio

Q U

The Pattern Shop, where a great deal of skilled woodworking was done, overlooked the factory's 65ft turntable.

GASWORKS PILOT

Down beyond Rodbourne, to the north of the running shed, was the GWR gasworks and the factory pilot's job was to shunt wagons of coal into the retort house siding, and push the empties up the other side of the building to receive coke after the gas had been extracted from the coal. I worked on this pilot occasionally, and clearly remember the smell of the gas – when you walked into the tunnel to enter the yard you were aware of it immediately. We had to take everything that was shunted out that had to go to the Transfer between 12.30 p.m. and 1.30 p.m. in the dinner hour, so on the gasworks pilot you always snatched your dinner break about noon, usually when you heard the shunter say "It's about 12, better have your grub, mate." Then at 12.30 you'd take a raft of wagons out of the gasworks, up round the side of the running shed, and up into the carriage shops, where the shunter would uncouple them and they'd go on their own under gravity until they came to a stop. The engine would come back down by the side of the wagons just shunted and into the gasworks. This happened every day at dinner. It was a fairly straightforward job on the gasworks, and the shunters on there were regulars. Coal went up to the top of the retorts by means of two endless bucket chains, after being tipped into a pit-hopper at rail level. Known as the continuous process retort, it made all the gas used in the Works and station, and they had enough left over to sell it to the Swindon Town Gasworks Company. You always saw mountains of coke from the gasworks by the side of the Gloucester line. The GWR gasworks supplied the gas for the shed, offices, station, factory and for trains.

Facing page: *An aerial view of the locomotive shed and gasworks area, looking south in 1954. Numbered locations are:*

1.   Engine shed and coal stage
2.   Stock shed
3.   Gasworks
4.   Iffley Road
5.   Main stores (worked by the brickyard pilot)
6.   GWR main offices
7.   Mason's yard (worked by the shed pilot)
8.   Paint testing shop
9.   GWR Bristol/Gloucester line junction
10.   Loco Yard sidings (worked by the loco yard pilot)
11.   Brickyard sidings (worked by the brickyard pilot)

SIMMONS AEROFILMS LTD.

This photo shows the area to the rear of the locomotive shed which was the territory worked by the gasworks pilot engine. The Gloucester branch features on the extreme right with the gasworks behind the camera. The area to the left was known as the pipe yard. The siding leading off the picture to the right served the stock shed, the other two being the principal sidings into the gasworks. The GWR gasworks dated from 1874 as the 1842 gasworks in the factory was proving inadequate for the extended needs of the Works, shed and station. The GWR Gasworks initially supplied 250,000 cubic feet of gas per day and the plant was later extended to become the largest private gasworks in the world. They closed in 1959, after which gas was supplied to the railway by South Western Gas, and closure did provide more space on this site for condemned engines in later years. '61XX' class 2–6–2 engines were a common sight here moving old locos.

NATIONAL RAILWAY MUSEUM

Wartime photo of Newburn shed, where the Newburn pilot engine worked, moving carriages in and out. This shed was built in 1938 to accommodate new stock from the Works, and was so called because it was erected on the site of the demolished Newburn House, the home of the GWR's Chief Mechanical Officer. The eastbound freight stuck in the Up loop was a typical sight in the war and note the engines standing awaiting attention in the factory. The long building to the right was the weighbridge. This picture was taken from the roof of 'A' Shop.

CTY. STEAM MUSEUM, SWINDON

NEWBURN PILOT

This was one of the pilot duties that involved an early job. The crew booked on at 4 a.m. and prepared a pannier tank or an 0–4–2T (No. 5800 for many years) to collect empty stock, usually a Bristol Division B-set, from Swindon Town station and take it to Cirencester Watermoor along the old Midland & South Western line to collect the workmen for the factory. This service would then work back to Swindon Town where its arrival would coincide with the arrival of a workmen's service from Chiseldon. The Cirencester contingent would all transfer to the Chiseldon which would come down to the Junction Station from where the men would walk to the Works. Meanwhile, the pilot crew would uncouple their coaches and leave them ready in the sidings at Town ready for the evening's return service, and would bring the engine down light and report to the Newburn siding where we waited for the shunters to arrive for 8 a.m. Very often you'd hear "Fit then?" from an arriving shunter and a typical rejoinder would be "Bloody fit, I'll say! We've done half a day's work already!"

At one time the service to Town had included a goods train which carried coal and other provisions for Old Town and which left Junction at 5.20 a.m. with two engines, a tank engine at the

Looking west at Swindon from the factory sidings, past the down side carriage shops, towards Rodbourne Lane signal box.

'517' class No. 1161 on the up main at Swindon, near the West box on a carriage works transfer trip. These 0–4–2 tank engines were thin on the ground after 1934 but this one, built in 1876, lasted until 1945 and is reported to have been at work on the Highworth branch during the war. Behind the water column we can see the carriage works and its sidings, the coaches visible being in the down branch line platform. R. H. G. SIMPSON

The west end of Swindon station with the wagon shop sidings to the extreme left, West box towards the centre, and the carriage shops to the right. The bike sheds here were for employees on this side of the line.
NATIONAL RAILWAY MUSEUM

Collett 0—4—2T No. 5805 on carriage side pilot duty, seen here near the coal wharf off No. 1 platform. This loco worked the final passenger service on the Malmesbury branch on 8th September 1951.
R. H. G. SIMPSON

Collett tank 0–4–2T No. 5800 setting back past Swindon West box down to the Gloucester line before going into the carriage works, at 11.0 a.m. on 25th July 1956, with a mixed bag of stock destined for the carriage and wagon works. The pannier behind, No. 3677 ex works, was on west end pilot duty.
R. H. G. SIMPSON

front, and another at the rear to provide banking up the steep gradient from Rushey Platt. The job was always booked as a 'banker-load' and we could be booked to drive either engine. At Town the first engine would drop into the goods yard while the banker stood clear at the platform. While the train engine was dispersing its train, the second loco was collecting coaches to form the workmen's service for Cirencester, then ran the 15 miles non-stop to there. The first engine, free of the goods wagons, would now pick up coaches and become the Chiseldon workmen's train and set off through Hodson Wood to collect its passengers. On the way in from Cirencester, workmen were also picked up at South Cerney and Cricklade, then the two trains joined forces as earlier described.

The Newburn shed was a carriage shed about a third of a mile long, stretching from 'A' shop right down to Rushey Platt Road, an asbestos-sheet construction at the far end of the Works on the down side, and so-called because it was built on the site of the demolished Newburn House, formerly the residence of the GWR Chief Mechanical Engineer. The shed was built as a stock shed to house spare coaches for excursion trains and during the War it was used for storing restaurant cars, out of use during hostilities because of restrictions caused by food-rationing. Later it was one of the main wagon repair shops, being used for re-roofing vans, and light repairs

of all kinds. There were eight roads inside the shed, with stop-blocks at the west end. Three shunters were required to work with the pilot engine at the shed, one right inside the building with hand-lamps in the gloom, one half-way in, and the third outside to repeat the hand-signals to the engine driver. With the early start, the crew would be relieved about midday.

The Carriage & Wagon Works, served by the Newburn pilot, was a long narrow section alongside the down main line, 'the Carriage Side'. In shunting terms it ran from alongside No. 1 Platform at the station, past Rodbourne Lane Signal Box, down to the Newburn shed, which stopped at the Wootton Bassett road, near Rushey Platt. Near the station was the site where platform trolleys and all sorts of barrows were repaired, a water tank, and the Sheppard Street coal depot, which was shunted by the loco here. Next westwards came No. 12 shop (Carpenters), followed by the factory of J. Compton, Sons & Webb Ltd, which made railway uniforms, and then Nos. 8, 7, 4 (carriage body shop), 3 and 2, which was the saw mill. There were traversers between 8 and 7, and 7 and 5 shops. Then came the Timber Yard (either side of Rodbourne Lane box) and then the Newburn carriage shed, which was painted with camouflage during the Second World War.

This area of sheds in the middle and foreground was known as the Masons Yard, I think because of its association with the bricks that were made there for the brick arches in the firebox.
NATIONAL RAILWAY MUSEUM

BRICKYARD PILOT

This pilot worked by Bullen's Bridge, Station Road to Ferndale Road, where the canal passed under the railway. The brickyard, nothing to do with bricks in my time, took its name from the brick arches for the fireboxes which were once made there. The name may well date back to when the factory was being built. The main function of this pilot was shunting in connection with the General Stores, close to the old brickyard, preparing loaded open wagons and box vans which were sent to depots and stations all over the system with items ranging from stationery, brushes and uniforms to tools for sheds, and even whitewash. It was like a station in the stores, with platforms, but more closed in. They would periodically have sales in there for the workforce – old uniforms, pickaxes, or maybe a shovel with a broken handle being sold off cheap, one that you could easily fix, maybe with a visit to 'Chippy' Humphries, the shed carpenter.

A rare look at the area behind the locomotive shed, this being the rear view of the 1908 extension to the original shed, housing the big turntable. It provides a glimpse of the crews' bike shed (labelled 'X') and the lean-to structure along the east wall, which served as mess-rooms for crews and cleaners. In the foreground is the pipe yard, and, in the left distance, the brickyard area worked by the brickyard pilot engine. NATIONAL RAILWAY MUSEUM

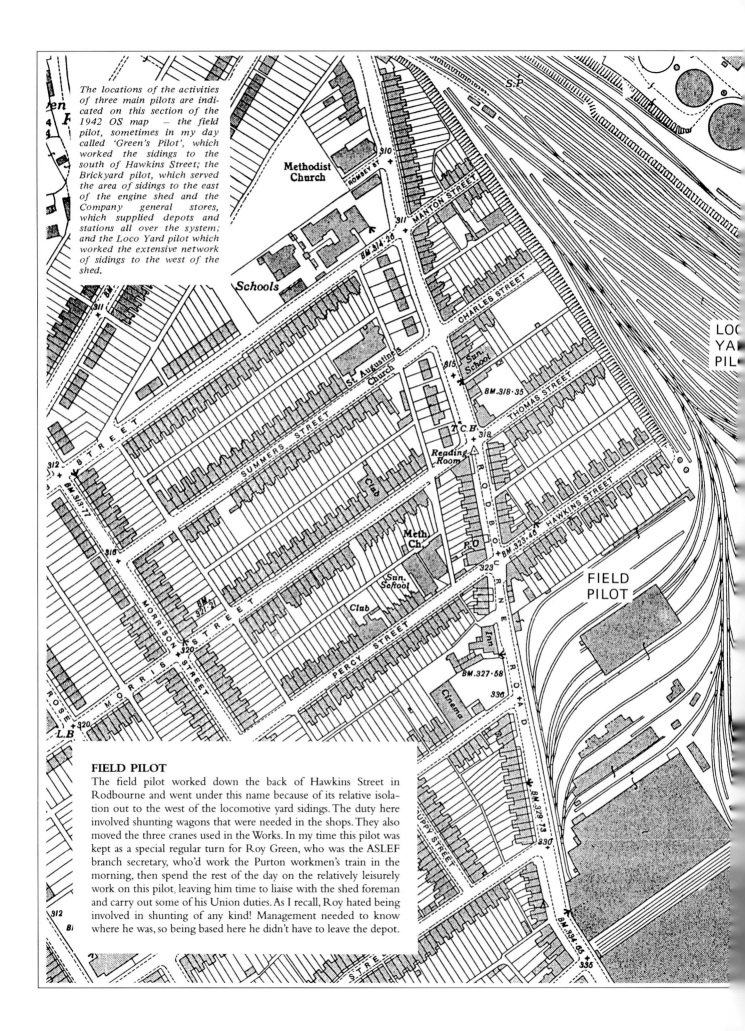

The locations of the activities of three main pilots are indicated on this section of the 1942 OS map — the field pilot, sometimes in my day called 'Green's Pilot', which worked the sidings to the south of Hawkins Street; the Brickyard pilot, which served the area of sidings to the east of the engine shed and the Company general stores, which supplied depots and stations all over the system; and the Loco Yard pilot which worked the extensive network of sidings to the west of the shed.

FIELD PILOT

The field pilot worked down the back of Hawkins Street in Rodbourne and went under this name because of its relative isolation out to the west of the locomotive yard sidings. The duty here involved shunting wagons that were needed in the shops. They also moved the three cranes used in the Works. In my time this pilot was kept as a special regular turn for Roy Green, who was the ASLEF branch secretary, who'd work the Purton workmen's train in the morning, then spend the rest of the day on the relatively leisurely work on this pilot, leaving him time to liaise with the shed foreman and carry out some of his Union duties. As I recall, Roy hated being involved in shunting of any kind! Management needed to know where he was, so being based here he didn't have to leave the depot.

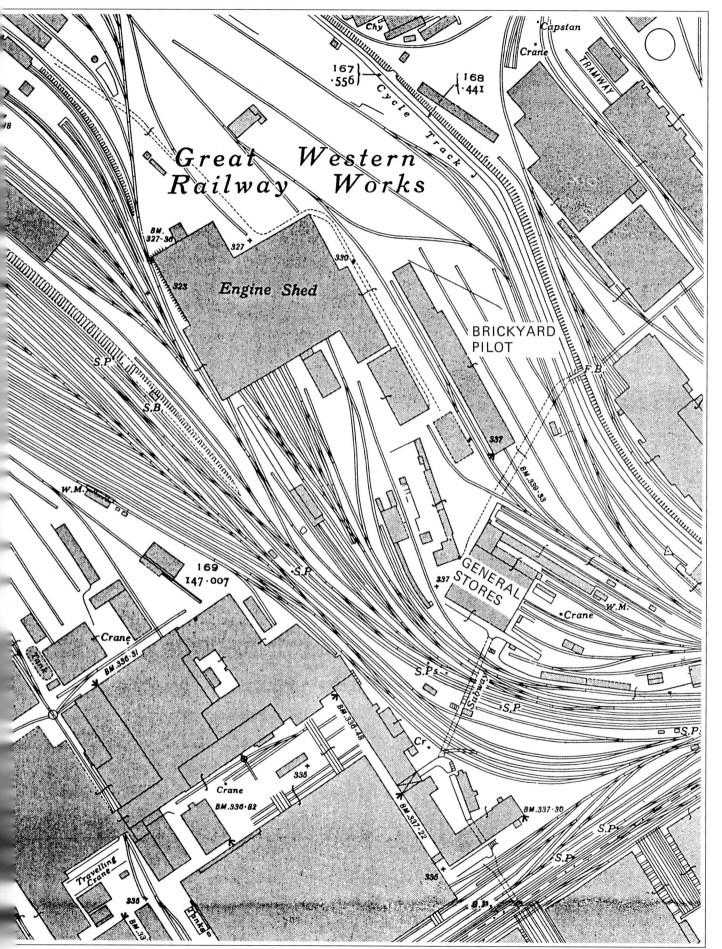

Great Western Works
Railway

Engine Shed

BRICKYARD
PILOT

GENERAL
STORES

An aerial view looking southwards across the Locomotive Yard Sidings (centre), with the GWR Gasworks (bottom right) and the main road artery in this part of Swindon, Rodbourne Road. The sidings which branched away to the right here, filling the angle between Hawkins Street and Rodbourne Road, was the area worked by the Field pilot, the main function of which was shunting rails and pointwork from 'X' shop. The Field pilot was often known as 'Greeny's pilot' on account of the Union rep driver who regularly worked here. The long, large building (marked 'A') was known locally as 'Crystal Palace' because of its rounded roofs with glass and its corrugated iron sides. It was a store (labelled 'machine spares' on plans) which contained spare machinery and goods from manufacturers not immediately required in the Works. The dark long strip seen running parallel to and below the 'Palace' was a wall built to shelter the residential streets here from some of the noise from the yard. The accompanying view on the left was taken in the yard marked 'B' on the main photo and the building at right was an iron store. At 'C' on the aerial view an old signal box was used as a base for the shunters. The upstairs area had an office for the head shunter, whilst below was the shunter's cabin and a room used by wagon shop signwriters. There was a weigh table directly in front of the building which the yard pilot would draw wagons slowly over. Other features on this view to assist readers are: D – Locomotive shed. E – Stock shed. F – GWR Main Offices. G – Pattern store.

Looking north over the Railway Village and the Gloucester branch junction, the carriage shops can be seen to the south of the main line, with the wagon shops in the centre of the photograph.

SIMMONS AEROFILMS LTD.

WAGON SHOP PILOTS (4)

This was a busy and fairly hazardous pilot duty involving pulling goods wagons out of the wagon shops, and over the four bridges at Whitehouse. With the sides and floor of these vehicles being wooden, they were often in need of repair, and would sometimes need sign-writers' attention to add the letters 'GW' to the side.

Taken from the roof of the machine shop (15), this busy view of the wagon shop sidings includes a glimpse of the smith's shop (14), top left, the electricity shop, centre top, where batteries, alternators and dynamos were produced for coaches, and the iron store (with the open door). The wheel shop (16) can be seen at right with rows of new wheels on the ground outside, and there is an unexpected view of the bunker of a normal pannier tank engine on the right, unusual because it was the short wheelbase '13' class tanks that normally worked the tight curves of these sidings.   NATIONAL RAILWAY MUSEUM

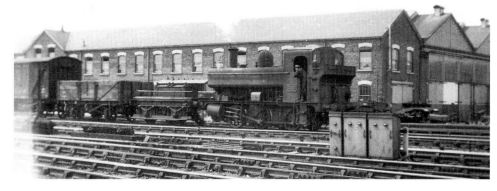

A '13XX' class tank engine shunting No. 15 shop (machine shop), seen from No. 8 platform, on the wagon shop pilot duty.   R. H. G. SIMPSON

This north-facing view over the east end of Swindon station and the carriage and wagon shops is useful for showing the positions of the three shunters referred to on page 75, when co-ordinating movements to assist pannier tank drivers moving carriages in and out of the carriage shops. The positions of each shunter are marked 'X'. There's also a good view of the Water Sidings just north of the passenger station.

SIMMONS AEROFILMS LTD.

A close-up of the carriage works with a multitude of new coaching stock in the sidings, with the wagon shops and attendant wagon sidings in the foreground.
NATIONAL RAILWAY MUSEUM

CARRIAGE SHOP PILOTS (3)

In the carriage shops at the Works there would be new carriages in different stages of construction or painting. Every day it was essential to move out the ones that were ready to go into traffic, so this meant that long rafts of carriages had to be pulled right out of the workshop, then those that were ready for service were shunted out, with the partly-finished ones being moved back in again. You would pull out as many as 12 at a time. These shops could hold a great many coaches in construction, and, as on the wagon shops pilot, when you pulled a line of coaches out your loco would be on top of Beatrice Street bridge, and the length of the train and the curvature of the track required a similar co-ordination with shunters as in the work at Newburn, which required three men. Carriages ready for service would be stood out on a siding and at the end of the day they would be shunted down to the station where they would be added to a train which used to run at 6.50 each night to Paddington – be they paper vans, milk vans, passenger stock, they all went to London. It was a tough job on those pilots because all the couplings on the stock were brand-new, of course, very stiff and newly-painted, and I've seen as many as twelve new vehicles on what we called 'The Bank' waiting to go into traffic.

One of the carriage shop pilots was assigned to the Highworth workmen's train, with a 4 a.m. booking-on time, then on return from Highworth it would leave the branch coaches in the east end bay platform and become the carriage shop pilot, known as 'The Royal'. We had to be in position by the dummy at West Box at 10 a.m., and at that time the signalman would pull off and we would go out of the siding with several coaches which had been picked up outside the down carriage shops sidings, then over the down line,

over the up main, over the Gloucester branch and into the carriage shops. This was such an important duty involving crossing the main lines that it was a diagrammed turn which appeared in the Working Timetable. We'd deliver them to the finishing shops where the other two carriage shop pilots would assume responsibility for them, their job being to be based here all day and shunt carriages in and out to make space in the Works. 'The Royal' was assigned to that 10 a.m. slot because it was a period of the day when it was easy to fit in the manoeuvre without interfering with main-line trains. At about 2.0 p.m. the procedure would be reversed; the first sign of the movement for anyone watching from the No. 4 station platform would be wagons and carriages being propelled into view. Another Carriage Works pilot was the loco that shunted past No. 15 (Machine) shop, whose side faced No. 5 Platform's west end and the West box, and went 'round the corner' to shunt No. 13 shop, the wagon frame shop. In the 1950s, this was almost always one of the '1366' class, usually 1369 or 1371. Nos. 1366 and 1365 might have been used very rarely. Finished carriages were moved out to The Bank to await being added to that 6.50 p.m. to London.

SPARE TURN

All links at Swindon had their spare turns where a crew simply booked on and waited to be assigned to a duty, depending on who hadn't turned up for whatever reason. Only the one spare turn was necessary in this link.

There were also two small links at this level which served the shed and yard which were on their own, not actually part of the main links.

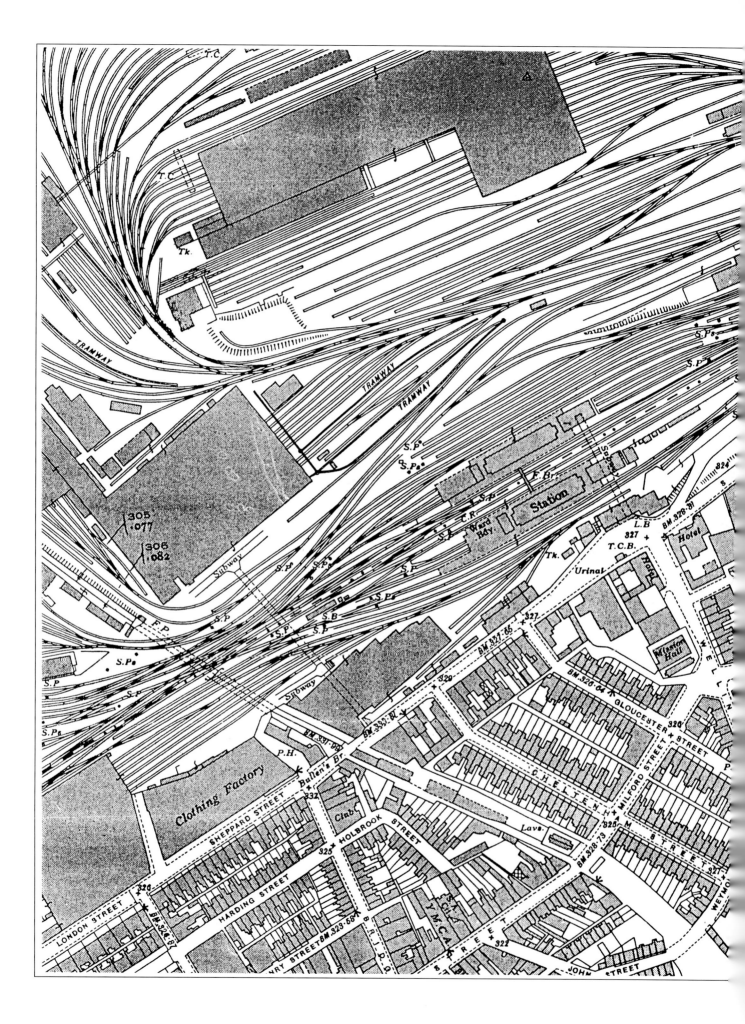

Swindon East signal box was built during 1910-11, superseding the former East box and branch line box at this end of the station. As built, East box had 69 levers with two spare and nine spaces. It measured internally 42ft x 12ft, with the floor 13ft above rail level. Additional brickwork was added to the lower part of the box during World War Two to make it better protected from bomb blast. Beyond the box on the right, in the centre distance, we can just make out the Station Road sidings which were used for stabling passenger carriages. The down side station pilot was to be found in these sidings and behind East box. The Cocklebury sidings on the opposite side of the running lines were worked by Transfer pilot No. 3. The boarded crossing at the end of the passenger platform was for staff only and not for public use.

COLIN MOUNTFORD

No. 6325 hauling a freight up the Gloucester line past Swindon's coal stage in 1948. The elevated road section visible here had a gradient of 1 in 125, easing to 1 in 200 at the north end. During the war years there were lengthy queues of locos at the coal stage, and main-line freight engine drivers in the loops at Swindon were frequently running short of coal. However, many of them found it easier and quicker for the signalman to give them a path to Rodbourne Lane where they could cross over into the Works and obtain their fuel there rather than add to the congestion at the shed. A. C. STERNDALE

Swindon Locomotive Yard Signal Box, which opened 27th January 1924. It replaced an earlier box of the same name (originally Swindon Box 'G' until 1909) which stood several yards along the line towards Gloucester. It had a three-bar vertical tappet with 4in centres, with 30 levers. The dimensions of the box were 27ft by 11ft by 8ft to operating floor. The box closed in 1968, when the Swindon panel extension towards Kemble with singling of the line took place and came into use on 28th July 1968. A Prairie tank loco, No. 4111, can be seen in the left background by the loco shed and to the right GW coal wagons on the elevated road of the coal stage.
CTY. SWINDON MUSEUM

The view from the top of the coal stage during the early '40s, with some very busy activity in the loco yard sidings. To the left of the Locomotive Yard signal box a '67XX' class pannier tank is seen at work on loco yard pilot duty, whilst the '28XX' class goods engine on the right was bringing a coal train up the Gloucester line from South Wales. The buildings by the box included an oil lamp hut, a ganger's hut and the drivers' relief cabin. A grindstone for sharpening tools is also visible at lower right. As I recall, there was a spiral staircase inside the coal stage to allow maintenance men (and photographers!) access to the top. CTY. COLIN TREMBLING

SHED PILOT

This was simply a tank engine that pottered about in the loco shed dealing with anything that wanted moving – wagons in the way or locos that couldn't move on their own. The engine was kept in steam and was on duty just during the day, working 8 a.m.–5 p.m. I remember there was a cantankerous bugger nicknamed 'Jumbo' who used to work this pilot regularly.

LOCOMOTIVE YARD PILOT

This had two functions. One was to form trains of wagons in the yard to the west of the Gloucester line, usually freights going in the Gloucester direction. The other was to come across to the coal stage road when required and ensure that the elevated road was kept full of loaded wagons so that coaling locos could be maintained round the clock. It was a rough old job on this pilot – my old pal Freddie Simpson used to say that the work here made him giddy! The loco yard at Swindon was the only yard of which I am aware in which the shunters used to signal the roads using bookies' ticktack signs to each other. At night the loco yard pilot was used as a fire engine pilot. There was a loco yard pilot on every turn so it covered the whole 24 hours, with booking-on times of 5.30 a.m., 1.30 p.m. and 9.30 p.m. At night it would also be involved forming the Bordesley Junction goods. Daytime work included shunting equipment coming in to stock the stores and assisting with taking new stock out of the factory up to the Transfer.

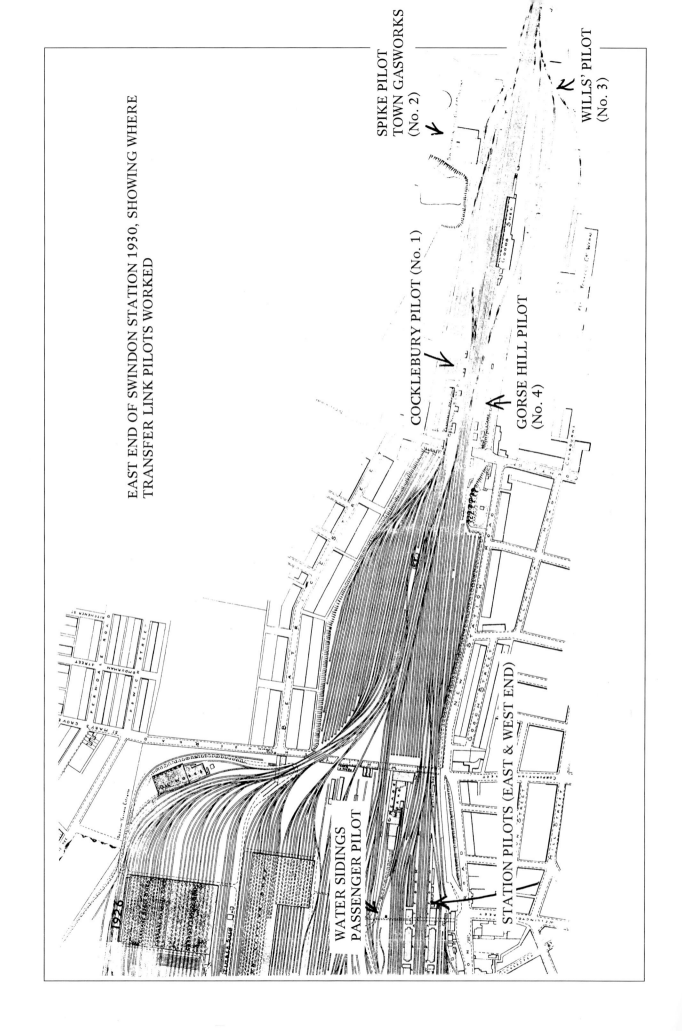

EAST END OF SWINDON STATION 1930, SHOWING WHERE
TRANSFER LINK PILOTS WORKED

SPIKE PILOT
TOWN GASWORKS
(No. 2)

WILLS' PILOT
(No. 3)

COCKLEBURY PILOT (No. 1)

GORSE HILL PILOT
(No. 4)

WATER SIDINGS
PASSENGER PILOT

STATION PILOTS (EAST & WEST END)

No. 10 THE TRANSFER LINK

The name for the link came from the association of its pilot engines with goods work in the Transfer Yard, the origin of the term 'transfer' coming from mixed gauge days on the GWR when it was necessary to transfer goods from one gauge to another at the east end goods yard, a costly and inconvenient procedure. The name also reflected the type of work done – in every turn of duty there would be a transfer of wagons from the down side to the up side or vice-versa. There were four pilot engines in this link, usually 57XX, 36XX or 74XX class tank engines, which were employed on goods shunting, and the link also included the three passenger or station pilots. There were three turns each day, booking on at 5.45 for a 6 a.m. start, at 1.45 p.m. for 2 p.m., and at 9.45 p.m. for 10 o'clock, and similarly for the station pilots with the exception of the Water Sidings pilot which was on two turns daily. There were 22 turns in this link including a spare turn and a relief engine, thus it took in excess of five months to work round the link. In earlier times crews work-

ing this link booked on and off at the shed, but in my day you booked on at a cabin by Gorse Hill bridge provided for the purpose of booking on crews and goods guards at the Transfer. When booking on had been at the shed, you were allowed 45 minutes to walk to the Transfer, and similarly for walking back, but clearly the GWR considered this a wasteful practice and abolished it. There was a specific route for walking, clearly defined, so there was no risk of injury or accident caused by taking a short cut. Periodically, the LDC representation would walk the route with management to check the timings to see that they were realistic, but it clearly made more sense to book on and off at the Transfer.

You never prepared an engine on this link because every pilot thus employed was kept continuously in steam, and there was a separate little turn at 8 a.m. each day in which a crew would book on and prepare a pannier tank as a spare pilot for the link, known as the 'Runabout' pilot which relieved the other pilot engines in the link in turn so they

The east end of Swindon station, seen from Swindon East signal box, with the Cocklebury sidings to the left and Station Road sidings to the right.
COLLECTION G. COOPER

could go to shed. A similar arrangement existed for the passenger pilots. The four pilots were arranged so that there were two engines working round the clock on each side of the main line.

The Transfer Yard used to extend from the bridges near Beatrice Street right up to where the Highworth branch left the main line, on the up side. On the down side the Transfer extended from Highworth Junction just as far as Gorse Hill bridge. It was usually very busy on the Transfer, the only slack time being a Saturday night when no freights were due in. Normally, as fast as you formed one train, another one would come in that would require shunting, with wagons needing to be removed and added to other trains. For example, a goods train would come in from Paddington and would contain wagons for Gloucester, Cardiff, Bristol, Westbury and the Midland & South Western line. The roads into which these various wagons were put was the responsibility of the shunter, but these roads varied – there were certain roads for brakevans but, unlike some yards elsewhere, no one road that was designated for, say, South Wales traffic. It depended on what was in the yard when the shunters came on duty, because sometimes the Transfer was so choked with traffic that you had to move wagons so as to have room to shunt. Sometimes you had wagons attached to your engine for the entire shift because you had nowhere to put them!

There were five pilot engines in the Transfer link, comprising a total of thirteen turns as four of them worked all three shifts over 24 hours. These engines all had local names according to the area of the yard that they worked, two of them operating on the down side and two on the up side. Their main task was forming goods trains ready to leave the yard, and dividing goods trains that came into Swindon. Four of them were numbered 1 to 4 but employees' recollections and reference to working timetables have shown that there was some variation in both the names and numbers accorded to these pilots over the years, so for the purposes of this account I shall base the information on the 1949 GWR Working Timetable.

NO. 1 PILOT ENGINE – Highworth Junction Down Side

This pilot worked continuously from 6 a.m. Monday morning through to 6 a.m. Sundays. It was sometimes known as the Wills pilot because it worked the siding provided for the tobacco firm H. O. Wills. Transfer Link men always used to like working this turn at Christmas because the tobacco company gave out 200 cigarettes to each man, presumably given away as Christmas presents if the recipient was a non-smoker! This pilot was also sent to Shrivenham at 9 a.m. daily to shunt the yard there for an hour. The work at Swindon's goods shed was a Transfer Link job, being undertaken by this pilot, its work on the Wills siding being on the same down side of the main line. The pilot engine used to place box vans in the goods shed for unloading, then we'd pull the empties back and put them in the yard for dispersal.

NO. 2 PILOT ENGINE – Transfer Down Yard

If there were wagons containing equipment for Chiseldon or Cirencester arriving on a down train, this pilot, sometimes known as the Gorse Hill, would shunt and split up the wagons for the appropriate destinations, and the traffic would be stationed in these down sidings. There would come a time in the day when this traf-fic would be transferred across the main line to the up side, because goods trains up to Old Town would leave from that side of the Transfer. Thus a lot of No. 2's work was transferring wagons to the Cocklebury side of the yard. Observer Colin Mountford recalls that one of the pilot movements occurred about 9.55 a.m.–10.00 a.m. each morning. After the Down 'Bristolian' had gone through, usually about 9.50 a.m., the East and West Box signals would be pulled off 'single peg' and then quickly 'double pegged', and at Rodbourne Lane box's signals too, giving the impression that another express was coming. Instead it was a pannier from the Transfer coming across on to the Down Main with the transfer freight for Swindon Town ('Old Town' to the residents). She really used to get up a good speed too. The loco was always a Swindon '8751' class pannier, often from among 9600, 9604 or 9605. If it was 9600, you could tell a mile off, as she rocked badly from side to side when at speed.

NO. 3 PILOT ENGINE – Transfer (Cocklebury) Up Side

The Cocklebury pilot worked continuously in 1949 except for the hours between 2 p.m. and 10 p.m. Sundays, working the Cocklebury and coal sidings. If a goods train from London had wagons for South Wales, and, say, Andover, it was the job of this pilot to perform the required shunting, in the up sidings that ran over Gorse Hill bridge. It would also sort and shunt wagons brought over by No. 2 pilot.

NO. 4 PILOT ENGINE – Highworth Junction Up Side

This engine worked continuously from 6 a.m. Mondays to 2 p.m. Sundays and was mainly responsible for the shunting of the Town Gasworks sidings. It was known locally as the 'Spike Pilot'. The main work was moving loaded coal wagons into the Gasworks and bringing coke out.

NO. 5 PILOT ENGINE – the 'Runabout'

As already mentioned, you never prepared an engine in this link because every pilot thus employed was kept continuously in steam as there was a separate turn Mondays to Saturdays in which No. 5 pilot worked 8 a.m.–4 p.m. to relieve the Transfer pilots, although there was a time when this shift ran 10 a.m. to 6 p.m. The so-called 'Runabout' would go to the Transfer to release a pilot and take on its work which would allow the engine to go to shed to be re-coaled and reconditioned for another day's service. The spare would successively change with all the Transfer pilots until they had all been relieved for attention at the shed. When the spare had completed its work, it would itself go to shed. I worked that turn many times. It was intended to allow two hours for a shed visit, so in theory all four engines would get shed time within an eight-hour shift, but of course it didn't always work out like that. Sometimes a pilot might be gone for three hours and you'd find your shift was up and all four engines had not been serviced, so the runabout crew had to stay on duty until the job was done. While on shed the pilot crew were liable to take their time – they weren't shunting the marshalling yard if they were on shed, after all! I think at one time this engine was used with a fresh crew after its Transfer duty to the Wootton Bassett workmen's evening train and also shunted the yard at Bassett until well into the evening and also did some banking work at Dauntsey.

The 'Runabout' also had an 'RR' duty (runs as required) in the Working timetable listed as a 6.30 p.m. trip light engine from Loco Yard to Swindon Transfer (6.38 arrival). This turn was for transferring rafts of wagons between the two points. For instance, if a freight came up from Gloucester it could be split up in the Loco Yard and wagons shunted out for the Bristol direction, and it was the job of the 'Runabout' to move this traffic to the Transfer.

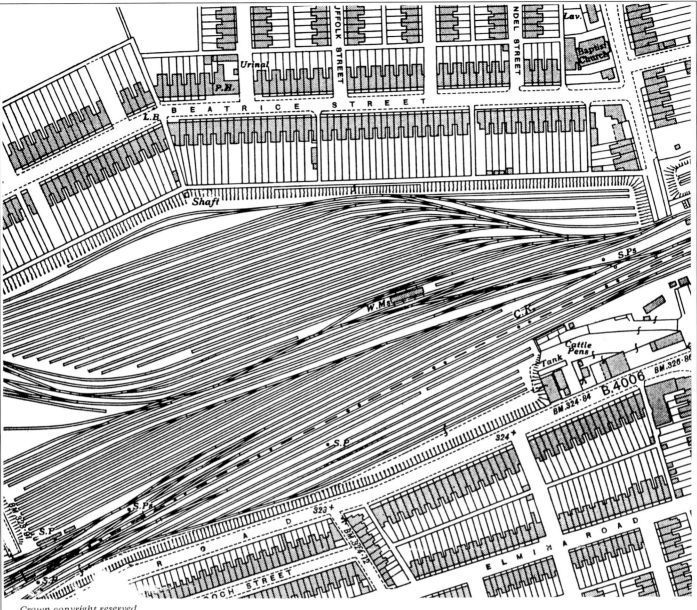

This '28XX' class goods loco was heading a down goods train through Swindon, seen from the down sidings along Station Road. Across the main line a transfer pilot pannier tank can be seen with a shunting truck, almost certainly the Cocklebury or No. 3 pilot engine. These extensive sidings were situated between the GWR main line and Beatrice Street. ROYE ENGLAND

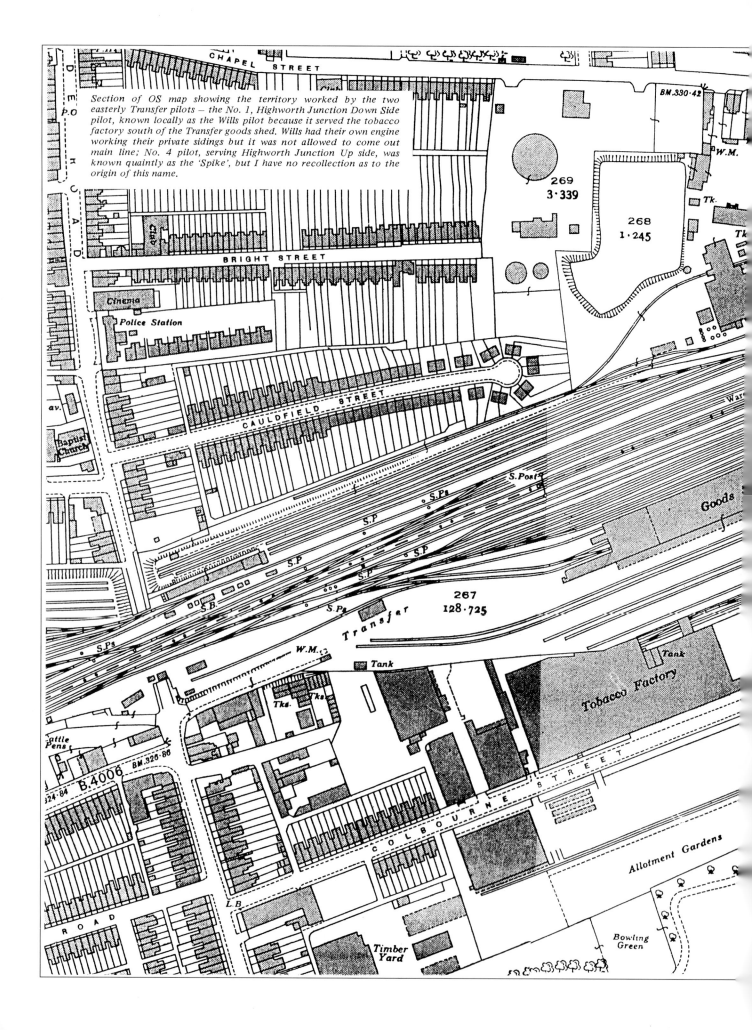

Section of OS map showing the territory worked by the two easterly Transfer pilots – the No. 1, Highworth Junction Down Side pilot, known locally as the Wills pilot because it served the tobacco factory south of the Transfer goods shed. Wills had their own engine working their private sidings but it was not allowed to come out main line; No. 4 pilot, serving Highworth Junction Up side, was known quaintly as the 'Spike', but I have no recollection as to the origin of this name.

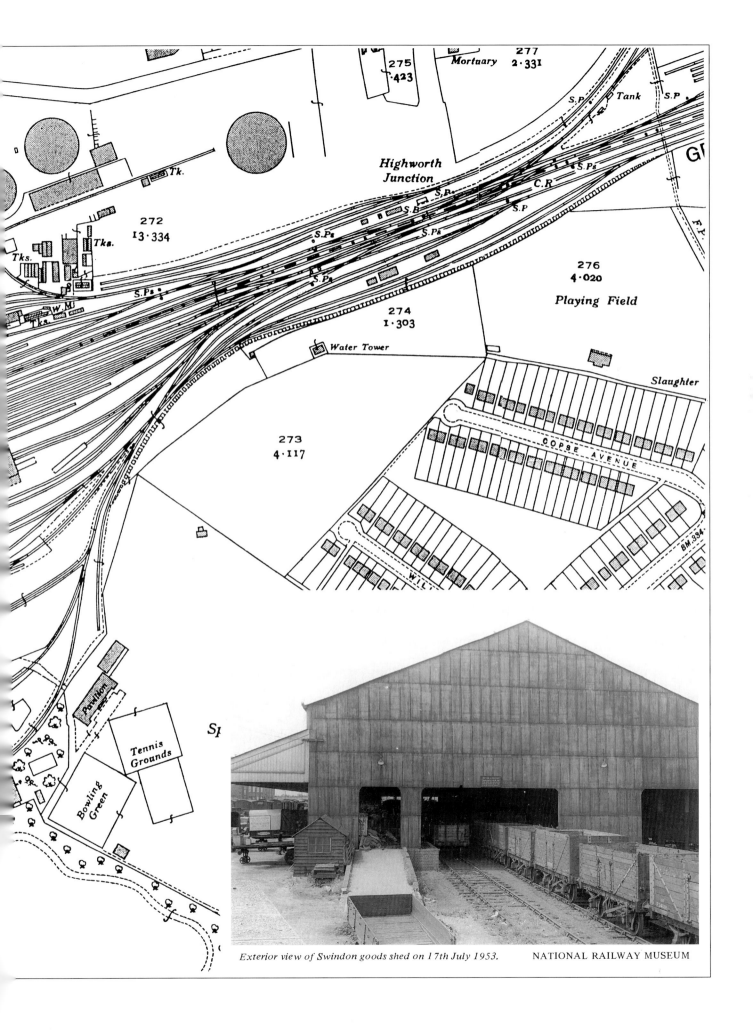

Exterior view of Swindon goods shed on 17th July 1953. NATIONAL RAILWAY MUSEUM

275
·423

Mortuary 277
2·331

S.P.   Tank   S.P.

Highworth
Junction

C.R

S.Ps

S.B

S.P

S.P

S.Ps

S.Ps

272
13·334

Tk.

Tks.

Tks.

W.M

Tks.

S.Ps

S.Ps

276
4·020

Playing Field

274
1·303

Water Tower

273
4·117

Slaughter

COPSE   AVENUE

BM 334·

W.I

GR

F.P.

SP

Pavilion

Tennis
Grounds

Bowling
Green

More views of Swindon goods shed.

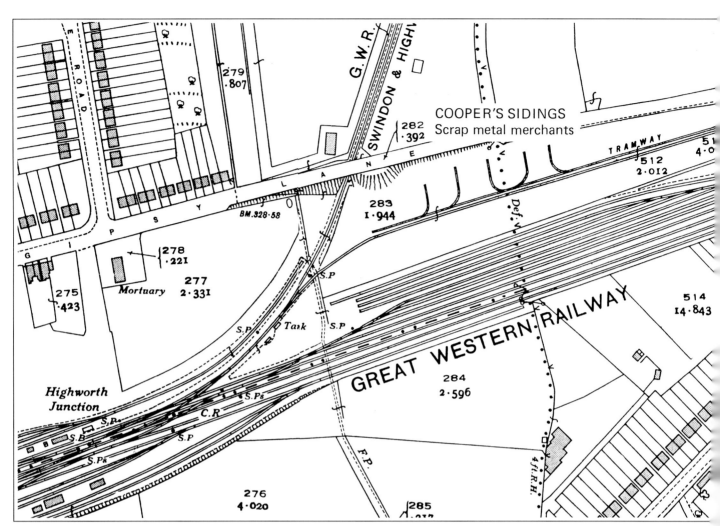

G.W.R.

SWINDON & HIGHW

COOPER'S SIDINGS
Scrap metal merchants

279
.807

282
.392

283
1.944

TRAMWAY

512
2.012

51
4.0

BM.328.58

278
.221

Mortuary

277
2.331

275
.423

S.P.

S.P.

S.P.

Tank

S.P.

Def. V

GREAT WESTERN RAILWAY

514
14.843

284
2.596

4 ft. R.H.

Highworth
Junction

S.P.

C.R

S.P's

S.B

S.B

B

S.P's

S.P

F.P.

276
4.020

285

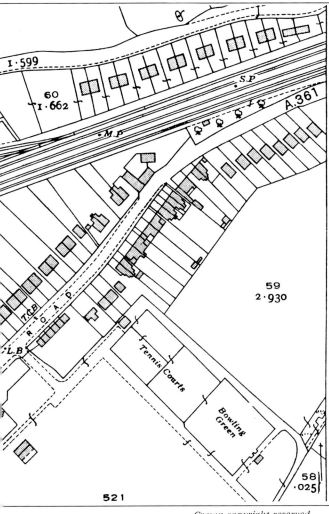

Crown copyright reserved.

MARSTON SIDINGS PILOT

Otherwise known as the South Marston pilot, this was a single night turn in which a tank engine was sent up to Marston Sidings to shunt the fish traffic that had come down from Hull and Grimsby via the Banbury fish train. When I worked it as a fireman during the War, I remember it as an 8.40 start on this duty, although the 1949 Working Timetable shows it as an 11.30 p.m. to 5.45 a.m. turn. During that time it would leave Swindon shed after being prepared and called at the Transfer to attach a goods brake van and two Eastern Region brakevans for use on the 5.45 a.m. Marston Sidings to Cardiff and the 5.30 a.m. to Bristol Temple Meads. The shunters at Marston would put all the West of England fish traffic on one road, the South Wales on another, with the vans in order according to their destination – for South Wales, the Newport traffic would be at the front of the train, the Cardiff would be next, and the Swansea last. I worked this pilot many times, and when the traffic warranted it, this locomotive would be used to assist the Old Town goods train at 5.15 next morning. It was usually described as banking the train but in fact was normally used to double-head on the front of the train.

I well remember one character associated with this pilot who was nicknamed 'Fagin', a loveable rogue whom everyone on the railway knew! He used to love that job, and he'd come up the relief line as he took the engine up to South Marston and shout to the Inspector at the Transfer, "Don't forget I'm ready to bank the Old Town in the morning!", a job that would guarantee him 12 hours with some overtime. If the Inspector replied "I don't think I've got enough traffic!", Fagin would be heard to shout "*You* put some more on and I'll bring the buggers back!" He'd expect a few extra wagons to be added to make a load so he could work that extra time! He was always after overtime, but would never push anyone out of the way to get it. He had a reputation as something of a scavenger – he would go in the drivers' cabin and check the hotplate where we boiled our teacans. Men used to put a penny on there to help it boil quicker, and if there was a coin left on there he'd pocket it! He gloried in his jackdaw image. He was habitually scruffy and was once apprehended by the Transport Police in Cardiff who refused to believe he was a driver! At his funeral I recall his brother telling the tale of how Fagin used to complain during the War, "The Germans got better food than us, better uniforms, better guns – we're on the wrong bloody side!"

Facing page: On 24th March 1949 a Highworth branch goods is seen coming off the branch at Highworth Junction hauled by Collett 0–4–2 tank engine No. 5804, an engine regularly allocated to passenger and mixed work on the Malmesbury branch. I remember there was a Highworth turn where you booked on at 12 noon and worked a 1.0 p.m. goods. There was never much at Stanton but at Hannington and the terminus we handled a lot of coal, cattle feed, potatoes and carpets from the factory in Highworth. We had two guards on that turn because of the steep gradients on that line. The OS section above illustrates the layout where the branch joined the main line, and I recall that the sidings to the east of the junction were known as Cooper's Sidings, named after the scrap metal business that used them. The public footbridge beyond the signal gantry on the photo evokes a happy childhood memory – in the late 1920s a couple of our neighbours in Havelock Street, a Mrs. Lanesbury and a Mrs. Townsend, used to take me and their children across the fields from the Shrivenham Road to this bridge, where we'd wait to see the 3.55 ex-Swindon, the 'Cheltenham Flyer', leave for Paddington.

S. C. L. PHILLIPS

Swindon station, looking east in June 1951, with Collett 0–4–2 tank No. 5804 standing on the centre up road. Here we see the carriage shed referred to on page 91 where the West End station pilot awaited duties.
L. B. LAPPER

A similar view through the station with one of the passenger pilots pulling a rake of coaches into the platform on 4th April 1946. The signals were off for a main-line express coming through.
H. C. CASSERLEY

WEST END STATION PILOT

There was a small three-road carriage shed abutting the end of the station, between Nos. 5 and 8 platforms, though the roof was probably not long enough to cover more than one coach. Very occasionally the pilot engine would stand inside. Like its eastern neighbour, it covered station duties round the clock, and its job was to tail up trains. It waited in the sidings opposite West Signal Box and if a train came in with a horsebox that needed removing, the West End pilot would do it, along with a variety of topping and tailing, putting on an additional coach or an ENPARTS van or a Siphon C, or taking similar off. Three hours were allowed for the station pilot to be relieved, and it would go to shed daily between 1.30 and 4.30 p.m. and then return to its duty. In earlier years this pilot was known to assist slip coaches into the station.

EAST END STATION PILOT

This pilot covered the three turns daily and waited on the down side by East Box. Its main function was shunting parcels vans. It would be used to form parcels trains. The busiest times for the pilots were when the fish trains came in, or when the 2.20 Paddington parcels came down in the afternoon, as the 5.22 Swindon to Bristol parcels had to be formed from this train and the down side pilot literally had to tear the Paddington to pieces in order to form the 5.22. The only time we prepared a pilot would be on a Monday morning, with only one pilot being on duty on a Sunday, then we would take it up to the station. At all other times we booked on and walked to the station.

When on down side duties, the West End passenger pilot tended to wait in the open between jobs, on the down branch sidings at right, near the old parcels office. These bay platforms usually contained coaching stock for the Old Town MSWJ services.
LENS OF SUTTON

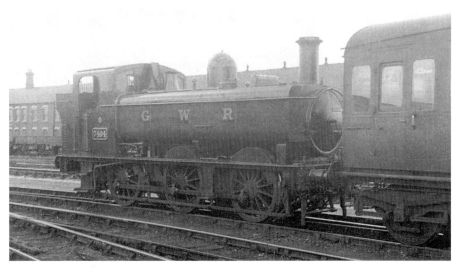

Pannier tank 0–6–0 No. 7404 on West End pilot duty just off the end of No. 5 platform.   R. H. G. SIMPSON

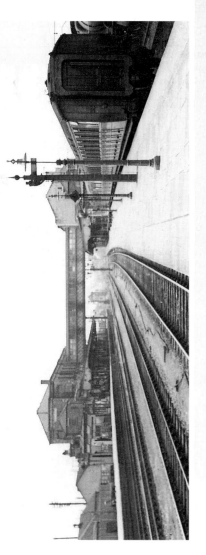

The east end of Swindon station with LNER stock in the branch bay on 7th June 1949.
L. B. LAPPER

The view from East box, with an up express passing on the main line. The Water Sidings to the right on the north side of the station were full of coaching stock.
E. J. M. HAYWARD

WATER SIDINGS PILOT

This pilot covered only the 6 a.m. to 2 p.m. and the 2 p.m. to 10 p.m. turns. The name of the location was derived from the former existence of a reservoir on this site, from which in earlier times the depot, station and Works took a large part of its water supply. The engine on the early turn would first go with empty stock to Kemble at 6.35 and run as a passenger and workmen's service. I had an engine failure with a hotbox once on that run. Returning to Swindon for 7.40, the loco would resume as a station pilot and shunt coaches in these sidings north of the station. I don't recall this as a very busy job. In fact, I fired for one driver on that duty who used to clear off to the pub and leave me alone on the footplate ("You'll be alright, kid!") and return to fill the cab with the stench of stale ale!

Judging by the position of the wagon shops in the distance, this Collett tank 0–4–2 No. 5802 was on pilot duty in the Water Sidings. This locomotive was allocated to Malmesbury shed in July 1933 when the junction for the Malmesbury branch was altered from Dauntsey to Little Somerford, thus heading the last train on the old line and the first service on the new shortened branch there.
R. S. CARPENTER

Another view of the east end of the station, looking towards London with a passenger coach on the left in the Water Sidings. An Aberdare '26XX' class goods engine is seen on its way to shed after leaving a freight in the Swindon Transfer on 4th April 1946. This was the only class of engine I ever experienced on which steam was used to assist in the reversing motion of the engine.
H. C. CASSERLEY

This view of the coal stage with the Loco Yard sidings beyond shows the line right below the coal stage where I was on a loco alone as a young fireman and was taken off by Shift Foreman Holder for being too inexperienced (page 97). My driver had left me alone on the footplate with a 'King' class engine, No. 6003 King George IV, a really heavy engine! You can see a line of coal trucks waiting to be moved by the Loco Yard pilot, a line of empty trucks on the ash-loading road waiting to be loaded, and, on the incoming road, a Prairie locomotive with a firedropper at work.

SHED AND COAL STAGE LINK

An undated view of the coal stage and its elevated road seen from the Loco Yard. The old broad-gauge shed is visible to the left behind the signal post. As on the page opposite, the line of coal trucks in the holding sidings were waiting to be shunted up to the coal stage. There were always loaded coal trucks here and even if the coal stage ran out in the middle of the night, there was a night turn for the Loco Yard pilot to deal with it. NATIONAL RAILWAY MUSEUM

This was a small, separate, unnumbered link between the Transfer and the Van links in which six sets of men were employed on a round-the-clock provision, three sets on the shed, one crew per shift, and three similarly on the coal stage. It was a progressive link for firemen but not for drivers. The loco men were employees who had been fetched off the main-line work, mostly because of eyesight problems, to undertake relatively light duties, and they would remain on the link until such time as their eyesight improved or they retired. For firemen, if there was a big promotion push under way at any given time, many might miss this link altogether as clearly there would only be a limited number of vacancies available in this link.

At the coal stage the main duty was for the rostered crew to bring the locomotives down from the firedropper's pit and put them under the coal tip where they would be coaled by the coalman. This crew was also expected to monitor the situation outside the coal stage road when engines were out beyond the yard waiting to come in for coaling. In fact, I've known times during a late afternoon or early evening when there were so many of them they stretched back past West Box into the station opposite the refreshment rooms on the incoming road. The problem here was to check each one to ensure that there was enough steam up to move them into position when the time came, but not so much fire that it would make life difficult for the firedropper. We used to couple them up together ourselves, take off each handbrake and move them in one go with the leading engine. This was against the rules but far more efficient. Of course, once coaled, they would be moved individually with their remaining steam onto the shed roads or big turntable roads according to their next duty. On a really busy job here, the shift foreman might detail someone from the spare turns on the other links to come and assist us – there were no spare turns in this link.

The shedman would have taken the numbers of all the engines off the duty sheets, and information about where they were going on their next turn of duty, and walk up the coal rank road and chalk on the side of the tender or cab the number of the road where he wanted that engine put, and it was the shed crew on this link that would deal with this manoeuvre. If the engine was facing the wrong way round for its next turn, he would chalk 'BT' on it to indicate that it had to go to the big turntable shed for turning. If there was

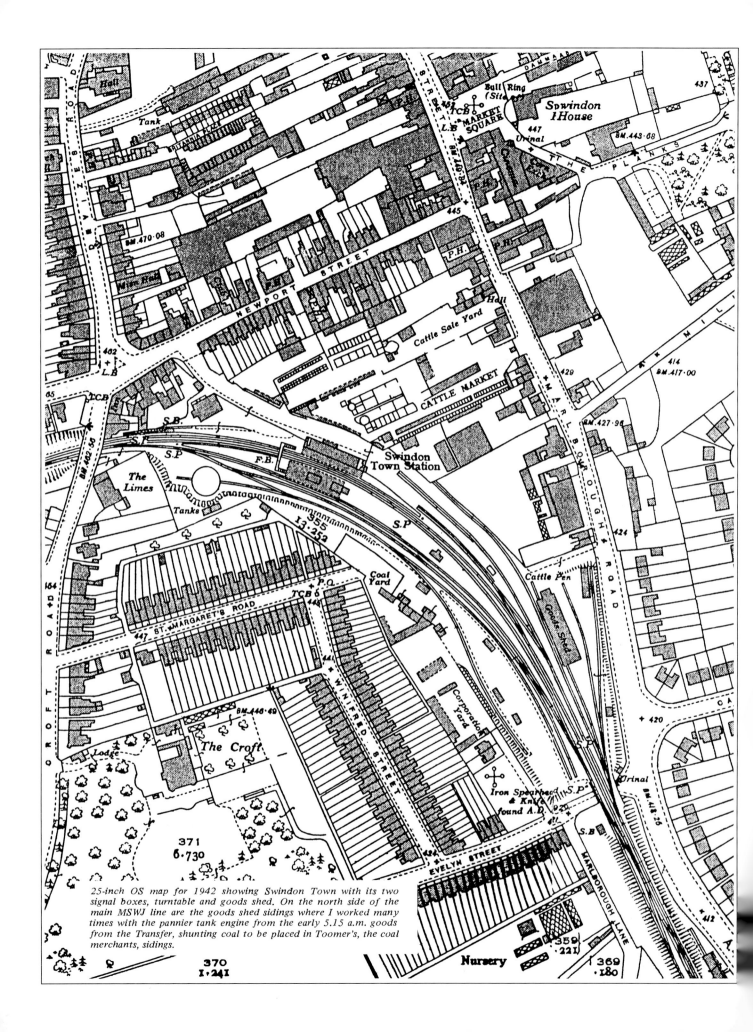

25-inch OS map for 1942 showing Swindon Town with its two signal boxes, turntable and goods shed. On the north side of the main MSWJ line are the goods shed sidings where I worked many times with the pannier tank engine from the early 5.15 a.m. goods from the Transfer, shunting coal to be placed in Toomer's, the coal merchants, sidings.

room around the turntable, it would be left there, but if room was restricted, it would be turned there and then left on one of the straight roads, now facing in the direction required. They didn't bother with the chalking with the tank engines which were, just put in the small turntable shed or wherever they could be accommodated.

I was up on the coal stage one night just before the War as a young fireman, and I was on a loco on my own about to move it when I was spotted by the shift foreman. There were supposed to be two men on the footplate, of course, but it was common for there just to be the one in these situations, otherwise the work would simply not get done. I was suddenly aware that I was under scrutiny;

"'Ow long you bin firing, m'son?"

"Just started, guv'nor. 'Bout six months."

"Well you won't be 'ere tomorrow night. I'm sending you to the Transfer!"

And that's where I went the night after. That's how strict they were. It just wasn't considered safe for a young fireman to be moving an engine on his own.

NO. 9 THE OLD TOWN LINK

Swindon Town station on 9th June 1951, with the 11.13 from Swindon Junction arriving behind pannier tank No. 5772. This was the service that for some obscure reason was known as the 'Dodger'.
R. C. RILEY

Just under the Van Link was this small link of men, about six crews as I recall, who did regular work on the services usually associated with the connection between Swindon Junction and Swindon Town, and services on the old Midland & South Western Junction Railway. This was not a major link in that, like the Shed and Coal Stage, it was only a link for promotion for firemen, and with only a small number of vacancies at any given time, if there were more firemen up for a move up the ladder from the Transfer than there were places available, it was another situation where they missed out this link altogether. Again the drivers were mainly men who remained in the link who had come off the main line through failing eyesight or health. Talking with former colleagues about this link, we think that there were normally about six turns in it, which matches up with the recollections of there being six crews. There were no spare turns in it, so when men were off work, ill or on holiday, a crew from the Control Link would normally fill in.

SWINDON JUNCTION TO SWINDON TOWN, two turns

I remember some of the old boys who used to run the little connecting service between the GWR station and the MSWJR station in Old Town. There were normally three return trips on each turn, and I used to use one of them, the 11.7 'Dodger', to travel up to Town to relieve the crew from the early morning goods who had been shunting the yard there. This little shuttle dated from about 1923 and was provided mainly as a connecting service between the GWR and the Cheltenham-Andover trains on the MSWJR – I don't think many people beyond railway enthusiasts actually used it to get from one side of town to the other. Observer Colin Mountford recalls that the morning passenger service ran at 11.07 (certainly in the 1950s). It comprised two non-corridor coaches, which were always there in No. 3 bay platform when he arrived at the station about 8.45 a.m. About 9.30 the carriage cleaner would come and wash all the windows on both sides with a brush that exactly fitted the width of the windows, and then about 10.45 a loco would come off shed, cross over the main lines and back into No. 3 to head the train. He often used to travel on this train on a Wednesday, in order to see the locos on the 'Triangle' outside the works offices, and in the Con Yard, because you weren't taken to see these on the Wednesday afternoon trips around the Factory.

MARLBOROUGH – SAVERNAKE BRANCH SERVICE, two turns

The Marlborough train started out each day as an empty train of passenger stock, usually a 'B' set of two Bristol Division coaches, hauled by a 45XX class tank engine, which went up to Swindon

Town around 6 a.m. and formed the first branch train of the day to Savernake, the engine remaining throughout the day through both turns until the last train in the early evening. In between trips along the branch the yard at Marlborough was shunted, and this sometimes involved a run up to the old GWR 'High Level' station which was then a goods station rented out to the West of England sack contractors as a depot, and we would deliver or collect several box vans. The Marlborough branch was also worked from Swindon shed and provided three trains each way on each turn, morning and afternoon, between the Low Level MSWJR station in Marlborough and the Savernake High Level station down on the Berks and Hants.

It was always very unhurried work on this railway backwater. The maximum speed over the MSWJR was 35 m.p.h., yet I do remember one driver who once came down from Chiseldon to Junction in 3½ minutes on a Tidworth Tattoo Special, the prescribed running time for that section being ten minutes! They took him off for that! Other old workmates have recalled that this link also provided a service at peak times involving runs to Patney & Chirton for schoolchildren, but my time on the Old Town was short and I have no recollection of working this.

HIGHWORTH BRANCH

At about the level of the Old Town Link, and sometimes remembered as part of this link but in fact being a separate little link on its own, was the work on the Highworth branch. Two turns daily accounted for the work with 35XX and 48XX class tanks, and my old colleague Freddie Simpson recalled that on late turns there was a passenger guard on the branch who was booked to do the uncoupling at Highworth. Not wishing to get his uniform dirty, he used to give Fred a bar of chocolate to do the job for him!

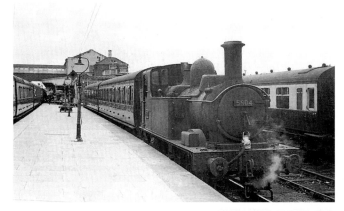

A Collett '58XX' class 0–4–2 standing in the bay platform at Swindon with the evening Highworth workmen's train.
COLLECTION COLIN MOUNTFORD

Facing page: A wartime scene at Highworth, with George Watts and Austin Palmer in charge of the Highworth branch train. They were looking out from the footplate in the direction of Fairford, and my old colleague George recalled that when this photograph was taken they were in fact discussing the proposals which were once afoot to build a link between the East Gloucestershire Railway at Fairford and the Highworth line. CTY. GEORGE WATTS

Collett 0–4–2 engine No. 5800 seen in Highworth station having worked bunker-first with an evening passenger service, in August 1950. T. J. EDGINGTON

NO. 8 THE VAN LINK

The Van Link is always remembered with some affection at Swindon as a popular duty, its turns always local, and with hours that were far better for your social life than say, working on the goods link where you never knew when you were going to get off. Mark Wilkins remembered it as "a lovely little link." The apparently odd name arose from the fact that many of the jobs in it had a van attached, although this was clearly not so with the light engine trials which made up four of the turns in the link. Basically, therefore, No. 8 comprised trial runs on engines which had just come out of the factory after a repair, and the early morning and late afternoon workmen's services which conveyed men between their homes in surrounding towns and villages and the GWR Works. The most turns I ever recall in this link was 24, so if you remained on the link for a year you would expect to work most turns twice in that time.

LIGHT ENGINE TRIALS

The turns on engine trials were always very enjoyable, partly because of the respectable starting time, and it was a different and very interesting job. There was also the possibility of getting off early! We had four turns on the trials and always booked on at 7.40 a.m. at the factory, although the four weekly turns would not be consecutive weeks in the link. Long-time colleague George Watts remembered it as "our night in bed". The trials always involved

tender engines, freight or passenger, and usually we ran to Dauntsey and back – occasionally there might be a run to Kemble, but Dauntsey was always the recognised run for the trials, as there was a signal box there and a convenient siding where you could check the engine before running back. Tank engines, such as panniers, were just tested up and down the factory sidings, from the weighbridge up to the main offices. There were four sets of men on trials work each week, and there could be four locos to test each day, sometimes three, sometimes five, it depended on the Works.

The engines were brought out of the 'A' shop on the traverser and left outside for a factory pilot to collect and haul away to the reception shed which stood at the eastern end of the 'A' shop alongside the running lines. The tenders were also brought here from 'B' shop and joined up with their engine by yard labourers and some coal added. So basic preparation was done by Works enginemen and then, usually the day after, the engine was towed to the weighbridge, the next building westwards of the reception shed, and here was where the Van link men took over. The loco could be facing in either direction, towards London or towards Bristol – it didn't matter, and just depended on how the loco was assembled and how it came out of the workshop on the traverser. The weighbridge was a two-road shed, one road being a dead-end with stop-blocks just outside the Locomotive Inspector's office, the other being a through-road which passed over the weigh-table itself. The Loco Inspector would be there, Roy Leonard, and Chargeman Drinkwater, and whatever locos were coming out of the shops he would detail the crew for the job. The trial engine would be moved into the

A 'Hall' class 4–6–0 inside the Works. After it was completed it would have a trial Van link run down to Dauntsey.   LENS OF SUTTON

This view, looking west from the top of the Pattern Shop, contains a wealth of activity and interest in the factory sidings. The sidings running between the 'A' erecting shop at right and the open-sided shed at left were the holding sidings for locomotives awaiting admission to the Works or disposal for trials in the Van link. Visible in the distance is the weighbridge where we collected our engines for trials after they were left there by the 'A' Shop pilot. The open-sided shed, its one closed side facing the main line, was used for coupling engines and tenders and for coaling. This was the location used often during the war for coaling engines when there was congestion at the coal stage at the locomotive shed. Several of the 'Castles' and 'Kings' here were already linked up with their tenders. Rodbourne Lane signal box is visible on the left with the 65ft Works turntable in the right foreground. The building with the open doors in the shadow of 'A' Shop was the test house, which was used to send in locos that required a quick specific check — they could be put on rollers which could simulate loads and speed.
NATIONAL RAILWAY MUSEUM

4-6-0 No. 4942 Maindy Hall *having just had her tender added in the open-sided shed was awaiting the lighter-up prior to trials down to Dauntsey next day — it would take eight or nine hours to prepare a stone-cold engine. 4th July 1947.*
H. C. CASSERLEY

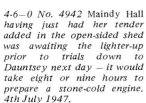
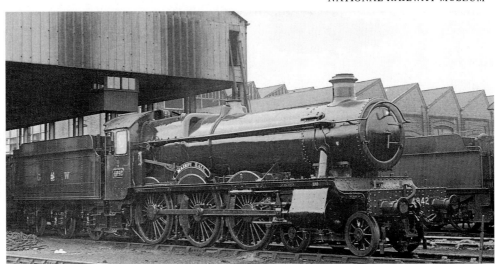

From left to right, the Works buildings seen here were the wheel shop, 'A' shop and the machine shop. The dark area on the front of 'A' shop was the access opening to the traverser, the moving section of electrically-operated track which moved engines in and out of the Works. This is a pre-war view prior to the building of Newburn shed for coaching stock. Newburn House was still in place, the residence of the GWR's Chief Mechanical Engineer. The other prominent building in front of the Works was the weighbridge.

NATIONAL RAILWAY MUSEUM

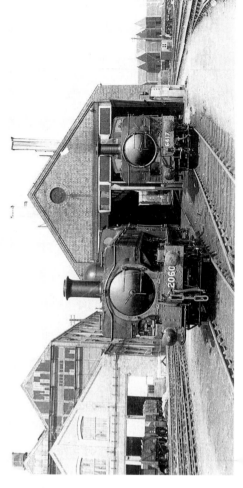

Pannier tanks Nos. 2060 and 6417 standing outside the weighbridge on light engine trials. Tank engines such as these would not be taken out on long main-line tests but would simply be tested up and down the engine line outside the factory. 4th April 1946.

H. C. CASSERLEY

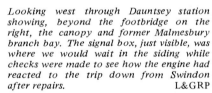

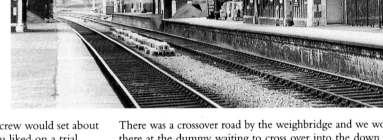

Looking west through Dauntsey station showing, beyond the footbridge on the right, the canopy and former Malmesbury branch bay. The signal box, just visible, was where we would wait in the siding while checks were made to see how the engine had reacted to the trip down from Swindon after repairs. L&GRP

weighbridge on the dead-end road where the crew would set about preparing it. You could have as much oil as you liked on a trial.

The fireman's duty included removing the brass covers of tender axle-boxes, filling the keeps with oil, and replacing the covers. As every oil-pot was dry and all trimmings had to be replaced, this was a good time for drivers to instruct their firemen in the art of making trimmings. You'd also have to raise steam and clean the footplate. Once sufficient steam had been raised to move the loco, it was run outside and onto the other road so it could come back in on the weigh-table. Each pair of wheels was weighed separately, the weights being recorded on huge dials inside the office. Two fitters, Charlie and Reg, I remember, with huge spanners, would crawl around, and under the engine, tightening or loosening up the nuts to adjust the amount of the loco's weight carried by each axle according to the official diagrams. With the weighing completed, the engine was then moved outside, the tender topped up with water and more steam raised, while the Inspector kept an eye on things. He had to be informed when the engine was near its 'blowing-off' point, so that he could check the pressure on the clock when the safety-valve actually lifted. Our job was purely to get the loco ready for light running, and when all was ready we told the Inspector and he contacted Rodbourne Lane Signal Box to ask for the road to Dauntsey.

There was a crossover road by the weighbridge and we would stand there at the dummy waiting to cross over into the down sidings to wait for the right of way. The Inspector came with us and two fitters also rode on the front of the loco, just clinging to the handrail, something that would not be allowed today.

If the bearings were tight anywhere it would show up on the run and we'd take the engine gently on the 12 miles down to Dauntsey at about 35 m.p.h., so our passengers on the buffer-beam were quite safe! At Dauntsey we'd go through the station on the down main, through the crossover road onto the up main, then drop back into the siding by the signal box, where the Malmesbury line used to come round years before. There we would check every bearing, oil-pot, rod and gland, and you'd check your engine for hot-boxes, the Inspector going round with you. Boiler pressure was very important and, if the engine was blowing off, it needed to be doing so on the set figure for the safety valves to operate. If the bearings were tight, like the straps on the slidebars, the fitter could slacken the straps that held the slidebars together if he found they were a bit warm. We might have to wait for the road back to Swindon, especially if a slow freight had gone up Dauntsey Bank ahead of us and, once under way, the bank itself would prove to be a good test of a newly-outshopped engine. If we had come down head-first, we'd now be going tender-first back to Swindon. On return to the weighbridge, everything would be checked again – the smoke-box was opened and inspected, the firebox checked and if everything was in order we'd take her to the 65ft turntable in the Works and the Inspector would declare her safe and sign the form which transferred the engine from the responsibility of the Works to the Traffic Department. We'd take in it turns to go to shed, and we used to like that because we were booked for an extra hour's overtime until 6.30 but we could do the job in well under the hour, have her signed for by the shed foreman and leave her by the coal stage and get off home early.

They never put more than five tons of coal on the tender of an engine that had just come out of the Works. Of course, we could get as much as ten tons onto a tender as long as it wasn't above the height of the cab. At some point these newly-tested engines would be selected by the shed foreman to go on trial jobs, 'running-in' turns, on stopping trains in No. 2 Link. Some thousand locos a year came out of the Works after heavy and light repairs, which works out at about four per day and providing the appropriate work for the four crews.

The view from the foot-plate, a 'Castle' class 4–6–0 locomotive on trial, working tender first from Swindon. The view looks back towards Swindon and is a little misleading – you simply have to remember that this light engine was running backwards, not running 'wrong line'! I have heard it said that the trials engines always worked in a certain direction, say, always tender first to Dauntsey as here, but this was not so it simply depended on which way the engine came out of the factory on the traverser. You always had to work tender-first in one direction as there was no turntable at Dauntsey. On the up main you can see an ATC ramp for Dauntsey Incline signal box distant signal.
CTY. MARK WILKINS

A July 1937 view of No. 5067 St. Fagans Castle being turned on the Works timetable, resplendent in new paintwork. The driver is seen lifting the locking lever to lock the turntable for access to the running line.   *B. ECCLESTON*

A '45XX' class tank approaching Cirencester Watermoor with a workmen's service from Swindon in July 1950. In the pre-Grouping days before 1923, the Midland & South Western Junction's Works were at Cirencester and when the GWR absorbed its smaller neighbour, the Works were closed and the employees were transferred to Swindon Works. The GWR were therefore obliged to provide workmen's trains to convey its inherited workforce from Cirencester, South Cerney and Cricklade to and from Swindon, Monday to Saturday. Over the years this number dwindled to a handful by the 1950s, but the service remained until the final closure of the Cheltenham to Andover services in 1961.
COLLECTION M. P. BARNSLEY

WORKMEN'S TRAINS

Since the last years of the 19th century, the GWR had provided workmen's train services to convey the factory workforce to and from their homes in surrounding towns and villages. In my day, there were six of these – Highworth, Shrivenham, Purton, Wootton Bassett, Cirencester Watermoor and Chiseldon. Because their duties were only at peak times, the diagrammed working of the locomotives ensured that all of them had booked work to do during the day and much reference has already been made to these arrangements in the Factory Link section. Booking-on time for these early duties was normally 5.30 a.m., although the more complicated arrangements and longer journey involved with the Cirencester required a 4.10 a.m. booking-on. The '13XX' class tank engines that worked on the four wagon shops did not normally do the workmen's trains, although they might occasionally be pressed into service for them.

The Highworth service coaches were kept in the east end bay at Swindon Junction station and, as I recall, the workmen's train called at all stations in both directions – Stratton, Stanton, Hannington and Highworth, and regular passengers could also use these trains if they wished, although they didn't ride on free passes, of course, as the workforce did. Payment could be made to the guard – they had lady guards on there during the War, and a lady in the signal box at Highworth. I recall that the workmen all had a very firm routine on those trains – they were all positioned on the same part of the platform each morning and they expected you to stop exactly where they needed to be for *their* compartment. If you were a couple of feet out you'd know it! I always remember over-running the platform at Stanton one morning and a voice called out "What's the matter this morning, driver?" I retorted, "I got a dining car on!"

There was also a 6.35 to Kemble which was used by workmen but this was a timetabled passenger service, the engine becoming the Water Sidings pilot at the station. I really have little recollection as to what the Shrivenham workmen's loco did after its early morning stint. It may have had some east end pilot duties but I can't be sure. George Watts recalled that the Van Link was a link he badly wanted to get in but he missed it as a fireman because of two years away at Old Oak Common. I was never keen to leave Swindon and was content to wait for promotion – it came quickly enough anyway with the War. George always reckoned that there were good jobs in the Van Link – local, interesting, leisurely, good day turns, and a chance to lie in a little if you were on the trials!

The Purton and Wootton Bassett workmen's trains are a story unto themselves. They used to race each other to be first into the platforms at Swindon Junction as whoever finished second had to deal with putting both trains away, moving two pairs of B-sets away into the Water Sidings ready for the evening. Workmen on the Purton used to complain about Roy Green, the Union man, who used to run that train so fast they hadn't got time to open their papers, never mind read them! Green and his fireman 'Hammer' Hayward used to be the regular pair on the Purton, but Greeny, a law unto himself, couldn't get off the footplate fast enough. They say he used to go home to breakfast before returning to join his fireman on the field pilot, but the bulk of his day was spent on doing Union work.

UFFINGTON-FARINGDON BRANCH SERVICE, two turns

As far as I can recall, and confirmed by Mark Wilkins, the Van Link included the Faringdon branch service. Faringdon engine shed was long closed in my day, and the service worked from Swindon shed. There was an early booking-on time of 4.10 a.m. and we took a '58XX' class 0-4-2 tankie out through the Water Sidings to the Transfer to collect the goods wagons and a single passenger coach to work the branch as a mixed train. We always left the Transfer from the down side for Faringdon. We left the goods wagons at Uffington and worked the early morning passenger train with the lone coach which was more than enough for the branch's needs. We shunted out the empty wagons from Faringdon that had to come back to Swindon and left the coach at Uffington at the back of the station ready for the afternoon turn men, then took the goods wagons to Swindon Transfer. I recall working the early turn but never the later one. The p.m. turn began with a fresh engine from Swindon. One colleague of mine recalled that he used to fire on the Faringdon branch with a driver who used to bring a shotgun with him. Halfway along the branch he would stop the train, alight and go off into the fields while the fireman took the branch train into Faringdon alone. On the return trip to Uffington the said driver would re-appear at the set-down point, usually with a couple of freshly-bagged pheasants!

A down goods near Badminton hauled by No. 2813, photographed on 10th May 1935. Swindon to Stoke Gifford was our local pick-up goods on this line (page 119).

L&GRP

No. 7 CONTROL RELIEF LINK

This was a relief link in which men were under the jurisdiction of the Controller responsible for trains, as opposed to the spare turns in each link, in which the crews were under the orders of the shed foreman. The main requirement was a good knowledge of routes – for instance, Swindon to Reading, to South Wales, or short trips out to the branches at Calne, Cirencester, Highworth or Faringdon. Control Link men would book on duty at the locomotive shed, then walk up to the Control Relief cabin and report to the Train Controller, then wait there until called upon, at such time as a train calling at Swindon required relief. The Controller might be up at the Transfer or elsewhere, and he would ring up the relief cabin and ask for a driver by name, instructing him to report to the Transfer for working a train to the West, or to report to the Rodbourne sidings for a train in the London direction, these being the two relieving points. Men in this link booked on every day at the same time for a week, and would let the Controller know they were there – "We're the 7.15 control set," and the Controller would know which men had the best road knowledge of a particular route. Sometimes you might sit there for five hours in that cabin before you received a call telling you that you had a train to work. There were occasions when you were never called at all, and were sent home after seven hours on shift with no jobs expected.

During the War I recall that this link had 76 turns in it that went right round the year, the largest link at Swindon, and you never booked on at the same time twice because the booking-on times varied from every 15 minutes at busy times to every two hours at quiet periods. It was divided into three sections, one large one and two smaller sub-links, and in a 12-month period it was possible to book on but never cover the same turn on duty. If I booked on at 3.15 a.m. for a week, the Link was so large that I wouldn't come in at that same time for over a year! There was one booking-on time that was a debatable point among our men but we couldn't do anything about it as it was within the rules – we used to book on Monday morning at one minute past midnight, and then book on again at 11.50 Monday night, therefore booking on twice in one day. If the Monday morning booking-on time had been before midnight it would have counted as a Sunday turn, an extra turn to the driver and more money, so the GWR saved money in this way!

Control Relief was principally for freight work, but if there was an emergency with a crew for a passenger train, a control crew could be claimed by the shift foreman. After many years firing you would be expected to have good road knowledge, and the moment you became a driver you were expected to sign the 'knowledge of road' card – the route cards were kept in the office for reference. You were entitled after three months to ask for a revision of any particular route where you felt you needed an update and, when you went on knowledge of road trips, you were a third man on the footplate. Once you'd looked over the route in question, you

were then obliged to sign the card to acknowledge that you were qualified to work trains over it as you had full knowledge of the signals on that route, in any conditions, day or night. Usually the road knowledge revision would be on a daytime journey, but it wasn't always possible. The Swindon-Leicester run, for instance, was a night run, so if a driver was liable to work this route he would be given about a fortnight to arrange daylight familiarisation before riding on that job overnight.

You might report to the cabin and find six sets of men ahead of you, but if a train came in requiring relief and those men already there had not the required knowledge of road, then you might be used immediately if you had the necessary familiarity. The Controller would only ask you to work a train over a route for which you had signed the card. The cabin was a spartan affair, an old horsebox in corrugated iron, with benches, a table, stove with gas ring and the phone on the wall, and during the fallow periods we told stories, played cards, or got our heads down and slept.

The requirement for the relief was occasioned mainly by the arrival of a train on which the crew had been on a very long duty and were coming to the end of their eight-hour shift, or maybe did not have the knowledge of road beyond Swindon. It was possible for a Control Link crew to be pinched by the shift foreman, and during the War, with only 12 turns for each of the four passenger links, at peak periods the Control was very stretched and this situation occurred frequently. If the shed had no appropriate crew available on a spare turn to cover a sickness absence, the foreman would telephone the Controller with "I'm going to have to take your 2 p.m. Control set." Thus the factors that governed how far you could travel as a Control Link crew were how far you had road knowledge and how long you'd been on duty. It might be that a crew would work a train to Gloucester from Swindon but when they reached Gloucester they'd been on six hours after station stops and yard shunts had been completed, so the Controller at Gloucester would relieve them with a Gloucester Control crew, and have the Swindon men travel back to Swindon. If there was no train available for them to work, they would travel back 'on the cushions' which would get them back to their depot within their hours. This is what the Controllers were for.

In peacetime the GWR would ensure that a crew did not make excessive overtime, and this was also the Controller's responsibility. If a driver and fireman worked over twelve hours, as you never quite knew how long your duty was going to be on a freight, the shift foreman had to write out a report stating why they had been on such a long turn. If I'd booked on at 6 a.m. and worked until 8 p.m., a 14-hour turn, I could not be booked on again until 8 a.m. next morning because Board of Trade regulations stipulated that there must be a rest period of 12 hours. If I'd done 14 hours the day before, it meant that I couldn't catch my turn of duty at 6 a.m. next day. Normally on Control Link you'd only be

A superb view of Swindon Junction in the 1950s, seen from the parapet of the roof of 'B' Shop. There is a wealth of interest here. This parapet was extended from the printhouse to 'B' Shop and I spent a lot of time up here during my breaks just watching the railway activity when I first worked for the GWR in the printhouse in 1936. Numbered features seen are (1) The Main Office block with the drawing offices and the broad gauge stone reliefs (from the original broad gauge shed) on the wall. (2) The Paint Shop, where paint testing was carried out. (3) The Carriage Shop Sidings. (4) Water Sidings, originally the site of reservoirs providing water supply in Brunel's day. (5) Town Gasworks in the distance, where the 'Spike' pilot worked. (6) Swindon Junction Station. (7) Relief cabin where crews would wait for orders to relieve trains. (8) Swindon West Signal Box. (9) Down Side Carriage Shops. The steps in the bottom left corner led to the tunnel from the Bristol Street Works entrance. The open-cab Pannier Tank with the shunters truck in the right foreground was on 'B' Shop pilot duty whilst the '13XX' in the sidings on the left was another Factory pilot on wagon shop duty. (10) Dummy or ground disc signal which authorised the movement of coaches being taken from the carriage siding — from down main to up side carriages shop (see notes on 'The Royal'). The engines in the centre were fresh from trials and waiting to go to shed. CTY. SWINDON LIBRARIES

A 1941 view of Swindon, with the coal stage and locomotive shed prominent, and the buildings of the Masons yard at right. The two London, Midland & Scottish locomotives here, class '8F' Nos. 8290 and 8291, were on loan from the LMS and are seen in the holding siding waiting to be coaled at the coal stage. These engines spent a lot of time during their loan period at Ebbw Junction shed. Control relief men would have handled them during normal freight work. You can see a line of well wagons on the outer Loco Yard siding. COLLECTION PETER TIMMS

likely to get in one return trip. If you booked on and were required immediately for a freight to Gloucester, you could work that train and it might take, say, four hours with shunting all stations, then you would be available under the jurisdiction of the Gloucester Controller to work a freight back to Swindon and therefore accomplish the two jobs in eight hours. A longer outward journey and the booked work would very likely be just one way. More than two jobs on a shift was very rare.

One freight that I worked a great deal during the War years was the Didcot pick-up goods. This was nominally a Didcot shed job but during that time I worked it a lot on Control. We booked on at 1.10 p.m. and prepared a locomotive to take to the Transfer to collect the traffic for all stations to Didcot. Drivers would carry their Working timetables on the road and they had every train in there. They'd say "If we can get to Knighton by such and such a time, the Up South Wales is due there then, so they'll have to put us inside for him to go by." They would run their trains knowing they'd be held there for half-an-hour or more, which was using up their time. I also remember long hours on the Didcot pick-up and many times hearing a signalman lean out of his box and call "Got to put you inside, mate, got the passenger about!" You would always let a helpful signalman have a large lump of coal for their fire – there was no coal allocated to signal boxes, but management knew how they obtained it.

My old colleague Bill Hinder was one driver who would never refuse a signalman a lump of coal. Booked arrival in Didcot was 7.45 p.m., rarely achieved, of course, so you were frequently over your hours and would travel home 'on the cushions'.

One Control Link job that I did several times was the '11.50 Neath', a vacuum-fitted night train from Paddington to Carmarthen goods, which was expected through Swindon at 3.12 a.m. However, there was no one at Swindon shed specifically booked for it because it was a Control job dependent on what time it arrived as to who worked it. The train, normally worked by a '49XX' class 4–6–0, ran via Stoke Gifford and Severn Tunnel Junction. I can still hear the Controller's voice on the phone saying "Come up the Transfer and have the 11.50 Neath." Whether you had a return working or not depended on how many hours you had left on your shift – if there were not enough then it was home 'on the cushions'.

Booked freight jobs in Nos. 5 and 6 goods links at Swindon could revert to the Control Link if they were running very late. Another big job that was always under Control was the 3.20 a.m. Rogerstone, due in Swindon just after 9 a.m. I relieved her many times at Loco Yard sidings as she came via Gloucester. It was rare for Swindon men to work it beyond Reading.

A '28XX' class 2–8–0 standard goods class heading a freight from Gloucester into Swindon in 1945 with 43 loco coal wagons for Old Oak Common. An old Swindon landmark, the gasometer appears to the right, whilst to the left we see the locomotive yard sidings – the signal was the loco yard starter. The dummy signal in the centre served as a subsidiary signal for entry into the loco yard sidings.
CTY. STEAM MUSEUM, SWINDON

On occasions there could be a lot of friction between drivers and the Controller. Sometimes he would ring up for a specific driver who might say "Don't know the road, mate." Some drivers could be awkward if they hadn't been over a particular route for four or five months and would request a revision, whereas another man might go for years without working a route and he'd take the train over it when the other man refused. There might be awkwardness over drivers saying "If we can get up to Reading, mate, we can catch the so-an-so back to Swindon well within our hours and be on our way home." But of course, it didn't always work out as simple as that, as the freight might be caught up in a loop or siding, especially during the War years. This was the big difference between working in the Control link and working in the passenger links, because the latter knew reasonably well what time they'd be booking off, because it would be a scheduled service. Barring a serious mishap, passenger men knew when they'd be off duty, whereas Control men never knew when they'd be booking off. The Control Link rose to about 70 crews during World War II and even so the demands on the link during hostilities were very strenuous. In total, as a fireman about 1942, and as driver in the late 50s, I spent about five years in Control.

No. 5/6 GOODS LINKS

A '28XX' class freight engine, No. 2863, on a pick-up goods near Wantage Road.   H. E. S. SIMMONS

At Swindon shed the bulk of the work for the crews was relieving through freights – there were not many goods trains that actually started from Swindon. Although the work was evenly spread through both links, the main difference was that No. 5, the senior of the two, had more vacuum-fitted goods trains in it than No. 6, and No. 6 had more of the local pick-up goods trains. Believe it or not, before the War the goods links had double-home jobs in them to Bristol and Cheltenham. This occurred because if a crew worked a pick-up goods shunting at every station, by the time the full job had been completed, your eight hours would be almost up, or on certain busy days you would be well over your hours, so you would book off and spend twelve hours in lodgings, then resume next day on a pick-up goods back to Swindon.

Double-home working ceased with the War, with ASLEF being against it. There were twelve turns in each goods link – if you had 13, with 52 weeks in a year, you would be on the same turn every Christmas.

The goods links were where the good money was, with a lot of overtime. If you were assigned to jobs through the Severn Tunnel you were in the money, especially during the War when freights spent long hours stopped at signals and being held in processions in loops. The 28XX class engines were mostly employed through the tunnel, and you had to 'sign the road' to indicate your willingness and ability to work it. To some men the thought of going through the tunnel on a goods was frightening, even hardened Swindon veterans regarding it with awe and respect.

Knighton loop line is seen here, looking towards Swindon. This up loop could hold as many as five long freight trains when necessary. Below is the Crossing signal box. I spent many hours in this loop during the war. Signalman Nelson used to loan crewmen his bike so that they could cycle to a local pub in Shrivenham when they were certain they'd be in the loop a long time! I can still picture that bicycle, by the crossing gates leaning against the box steps.

ROYE ENGLAND

KNIGHTON CROSSING SIGNAL BOX

The vacuum goods trains had a continuous brake throughout, so they could run at faster speeds (50–60mph) because there were no loose-couplings and they could therefore stop in a shorter distance. An ordinary loose-coupled freight train could run at speeds of 20–30 miles an hour. The higher speed was important for perishable traffic which required fast delivery. There was one I recall, mentioned earlier, that ran at 11.50 every night through to Neath, carrying many goods for export, and early one morning this train derailed at Wootton Bassett with No. 6907 at its head, when the points were not set quite shut for the South Wales line. She went over on her side and I remember it well because I was coming down with a train just behind it. When the breakdown gang arrived to put her back, they found a lot of the traffic spilt out onto the tracks – sweets, cigarettes, bottles of sauce, teddy bears and chests of tea burst open. The men were allowed to use anything they picked up from the tracks but they daren't take anything away!

Because the vacuum freights could go faster, they could travel further in a shorter time, which really put drivers in the money with mileage payments. Before the War, I remember the 4.07 to Exeter was a double-home job, with 18–20 hours off before working back. This train was part vacuum brake, part loose-coupled. Where you weren't fully vacuum braked, the jobs were maximum 35mph runs with a lot of sidetracking into loops to clear the way for the fast passenger expresses. You might leave Swindon going east and only get as far as Knighton and the signalman would divert you into Knighton loop, so it took a long time to go a short distance. You might be in there for a fast train from Temple Meads or South Wales, perhaps several trains, then you were out again, as far as Challow, then limp up the relief line as far as Wantage Road, so you could easily go over your eight hours just going from Swindon to Didcot. Many a time I worked a freight to Didcot where I was relieved by Didcot or Reading men, and you'd report to the Controller at Didcot and he'd say, "Alright Swindon, it's back home on the cushions for you!" So you'd travel back to Swindon in a passenger compartment because your shift was up. But there were days when your freight went well over the shift and, like working on the Control Link, you sometimes just had no idea when you were going to finish your turn of duty. In modern times most of the freights run at night because the 125 High Speed trains literally saturate the track space.

After all these years, it is difficult to be precise, as my time in the goods links was very short with the rapid promotions, and my experience in those days on the vacuum-fitted trains nil, but I recall working the following freights in No. 6 Link:

THE 8.50 p.m. WESTBURY PICK-UP
We booked on about 8.30 p.m., a '72XX' or a '51XX' class tank engine having been prepared for us, which we took up to the Transfer. We shunted everywhere at night on the down trip – Wootton Bassett, Dauntsey, Chippenham, turning south at Thingley Junction, then calling at Melksham, Holt Junction and Trowbridge. Coming back you would pick up again at every station the wagons you'd previously knocked out to bring back to Swindon. We were booked to leave Westbury at 12.15 a.m. and we were usually back in

Swindon about 4 a.m., but of course during the War years when I did that run you never knew what time you'd be back, or how long you'd be in the yards on the way down. Traffic was commonly coal, farm machinery and implements, and foodstuffs for livestock, and you would work at every station as required. On those occasions when we were on time, we would book off around 4.30 a.m.after disposing of the loco and the driver writing up his daily record.

An interesting memory of the night Westbury concerns one George Benfield, a crafty workmate of mine who once used to play football for Swindon Town. On the Westbury he knew that if he ensured his train got behind the 'Up Waker', a night train from Penzance, it would slow him down sufficiently to allow him to get 12 hours in by the time he reached Swindon Transfer. Coming off the Westbury line at Thingley Junction, knowing he was in front of the Penzance, he needed a delay at Dauntsey. So as the signalman there tried to hurry him on, he'd stop his train on the pretext of not knowing what the signalman was trying to communicate. "Let's see what he wants, I couldn't hear him properly!" he'd say to his fireman, by which time he'd created enough of a delay to hear the words he wanted to hear from the box – "Right, get back inside!" whereupon the train would be shunted back into Dauntsey sidings to allow the 'Up Waker' to pass.

2.30 a.m. BORDESLEY JUNCTION EMPTIES
This train of empties from the Town Gasworks was prepared at Spike. We would book on at 1.15 a.m. and take the locomotive up to the Transfer to collect the train and would normally take it as far as Gloucester where we were relieved by a crew from the shed there. Bordesley Junction was a goods depot serving the Birmingham area, and this was a slow, loose-coupled night train running at about 25 mph.

THE 9.10 p.m. TIDWORTH GOODS
Working timetables show this as 'RR', runs as required, but when I was on it it ran every night, Saturdays as well. It was a 'K' headcode and ran non-stop from Swindon Town to Ludgershall, where we ran round the train for the trip into Tidworth along the branch. We had tank trains and military traffic into Tidworth but not so much on that train. Our loco would be a '78XX' class or '68XX' Grange, the heaviest allowed on the MSWJ line. After we'd shunted Tidworth we were scheduled to leave at five minutes after midnight with a 3.23 arrival back in Swindon, but it rarely worked out like that, of course. You couldn't run straight into Tidworth from Swindon – you had to run round your train at Ludgershall and go in bunker-first.

THE 8.15 a.m. GLOUCESTER GOODS
My main experience of the goods links was on the local pick-up goods to Gloucester. We'd book on at 7.30 a.m. to prepare the locomotive and leave Swindon Transfer about 9 a.m. with the first call at Purton. The actual train that left Swindon was prepared in order by the shunter, and any traffic for Purton, Minety and Kemble was close to the engine for easy shunting. It was normal practice to shunt out all the empties from the previous day on the down trip and leave them out ready to be picked up when you made the return trip later in the day. On these trains you'd shunt every station with farming equipment, foodstuffs and coal forming a large part of the traffic. Every local station had a coal merchant with a dump in the yard. There would be stalls to store deliveries of coal, as at Purton, and the local coal merchant would be there with his lorry, and he'd weigh and bag the coal, then deliver it around the village. You were always shunting the coal out, and picking up empties on the up trip to take back to the collieries. We might be ninety minutes shunting at a single station. At Kemble there was the historic

Stroud goods yard, looking towards Gloucester. On the Gloucester pick-up goods we spent the longest time shunting here, although, of course, we often didn't get this far, changing footplates with a Gloucester crew at Coates, near Kemble.

L. E. COPELAND

branch to Cirencester which provided a great deal of goods business. We'd normally work that line with '45XX' or '55XX' class tanks and after uncoupling at Cirencester Town there was never enough time to fit in all the manoeuvres required – we never had a minute on that branch. Drivers' wives in Swindon often used to travel to Cirencester on their privilege tickets to shop there.

The Down Gloucester pick-up was worked by Swindon men and Gloucester men would work it in the other direction. The intention was to meet half-way and change footplates, and as a rule this would be at Coates, just north of Kemble. If you reached Coates and the Up was nowhere in sight, some men used to get quite annoyed about it. I was on that turn many times and had to continue down as far as Stonehouse before we met the Gloucester men but by that time the Swindon men wouldn't change over as they'd worked the bulk of the run, and so they'd simply work on through to Gloucester and travel home 'on the cushions'. The Gloucester men might say "We had to wait for an engine" and we'd reply "Can't

help that, mate, I'm going on to Gloucester as booked." That happened many times, working most of the route and refusing to change over – why should we have done, when we'd done most of the job already? It could be slow going on that line – you could finish your shunting and be ready to move but the signalman would not let you out because of an expected main-line train. If the passenger was a stopper, such as the Chalford railcar, which called at all the halts along the Stroud Valley as well as the main stations, it could take a lot of time to get you back on the road. In ideal circumstances, and I experienced the changeover many times, if the Gloucester left on time and everyone was playing the game, the old goods station at Coates was the best place to switch footplates, so the Gloucester crew would have worked Stonehouse, Stroud, Brimscombe and Chalford, and we'd have shunted Purton, Minety and Kemble. The busiest work was at Stroud, where the famous old goods shed still exists. When we reached Coates, we'd shout to the signalman;

Stroud station, looking east. I always thought Stroud was a very picturesque station, especially when they had their hanging baskets up. J. H. RUSSELL

Stroud's most famous railway building, the still-surviving goods shed with its lettering advertising express goods services. I always felt a great sense of history on the run to Gloucester.
J. H. RUSSELL

A tranquil evening scene at Brimscombe, 10th October 1948, with Brimscombe East signal box visible in the distance to the left of the goods yard crane. This box was built principally for working the goods yard, dating from 1898, but in my day its opening as required was governed by the hours of the porter signalman who only came on at lunchtime, so if we called in the morning with the down pick-up, our movements in and out of the yard would be controlled from East Box on the up platform on the station.

L. E. COPELAND

Brimscombe shed, where two banking engines were stabled to assist heavy trains up the steep gradient through the Golden Valley and the Sapperton tunnels. Here we see a large Prairie 2–6–2, No. 4123, taking water while waiting for an assignment.

R. S. CARPENTER

"Where's the Up pick-up?"

"Oh he's down at Brimscombe!"

"Great! We'll have a bit o'grub and wait for him to come up."

You had to fit in a lunch-break when you could, so when things worked to plan there'd be time for tea in a billy can and a delicious fry-up on the shovel in the firebox.

Working up from Gloucester, one of the Brimscombe bankers would assist us through Sapperton Tunnel if we had a heavy train. We'd pull up over the points at Brimscombe and the guard would give the banker driver the load and he would know how many wagons you were over the authorised limit. If you had six wagons over, he was responsible for giving you enough support to deal with them. Those banker drivers on their '61XX' class locos were very skilled and would never push you any more than they had to. There were a lot of tricks. If we knew a banker wasn't giving us enough and pushing like he should, when we went through the tunnel we'd pull the smoke plate out, chuck it in the tender, then piddle on it! All the fumes would waft back down the tunnel to the banker men to let them know they should be 'pushing' their weight! The bankers would drop off just by Sapperton Sidings Signal Box at the east end of the tunnel.

At the end of the shift back at Swindon, by the time you'd got back to the Transfer and left your train in its siding for the pilot to take over, taken your loco to shed and booked off, you'd normally filled the eight hours easily. If it was short of eight the foreman would usually let you off early. If you were over the eight, as it often was, you'd get time and a quarter pay.

THE 10 a.m. STOKE GIFFORD LOCAL GOODS

This was another job that had once been double-home working before the War. Some colleagues have recalled it as a job on which crews changed footplates but when I was on it we worked through to the large goods depot at Stoke Gifford, then into Bristol St. Philip's Marsh, then we'd walk to Temple Meads and travel back 'on the cushions' as there was no back-working. We booked on at 9 a.m. and prepared a Standard Dean Goods or a '28XX' class, any freight engine that was available. First call was at Wootton Bassett where over ninety minutes was allowed for shunting the yard. The calls at Brinkworth and Little Somerford were briefer but there was generous shunting time allowed at Hullavington and Badminton. Half an hour each usually accounted for the work at Chipping Sodbury and Coalpit Heath, with a scheduled arrival at Stoke Gifford at 5.21 p.m.

5.15 a.m. SWINDON TRANSFER TO SWINDON TOWN

At 5.15 each morning a goods train left Swindon Transfer with general goods and coal for stations along the old Tiddley Dyke. However, according to a local agreement with residents, no shunt-

Brimscombe station from the west, seen from the top of the home signal. The Gothic-style goods shed was very similar to the one at Stroud, except that this one no longer exists, swept away as was virtually every trace of Brimscombe station when it closed in 1964. To the right is the now rather overgrown Thames & Severn Canal, crossed by a footbridge to the right of the down side station buildings. Clearly visible are the lamp hut, the valanced awning over the forecourt, the covered footbridge, and the water tank surmounting the banker shed. An interesting feature here was the electric gong on the end of the goods shed which sounded three times to warn engines shunting at the west end of the station into the goods yard to keep clear of the up line as a main-line train was expected.

L. E. COPELAND

An up freight at Kennington Junction on the 'Hinksey' run, headed by an Austerity '28XX' class 2–8–0 goods engine. R. H. G. SIMPSON

ing could take place at Town until 7 a.m. because of the excessive noise. A lot of the bigwigs from the Works lived up there, so shunter Bill Morse was not booked to start until 7.0, whereupon the traffic for stations to Cirencester and Cheltenham would be shunted across to the down side, with the Marlborough direction traffic retained on the up. A great deal of the work involved shunting Wilmers' coal. It is my recollection that this goods service was part of the Old Town Link, but for how long and how that fitted in with the composition of the rest of the link now escapes me. The train engine from the freight remained here.

11 p.m. ROGERSTONE TO OLD OAK COMMON LOCO COAL, the 'Roggy'

We booked on at 8.40 p.m. and walked to the station to relieve a '59XX' locomotive which was prepared for us and it was attached to the front of the 'Red Dragon' to Newport. There we uncoupled and went to Ebbw shed, then worked to Rogerstone where we picked up the locomotive coal train, some 60 wagons, to Old Oak Common. We ran via Severn Tunnel Junction and Badminton to Swindon Rodbourne Lane Military Sidings, where we were relieved by Swindon men at a scheduled 3.50 a.m. They would work to Old Oak Common and return light engine to Swindon. We would try to arrive nearer 6 o'clock if we could and thus get twelve hours in. Every twelve weeks that was your big money. Rogerstone jobs were known as the 'Roggy'. Some of these came round via Gloucester and, if you didn't require relief there, it was an absolute money-spinner. The train would be banked up Sapperton through the tunnel with one of the banking engines from Brimscombe. Each depot fought for the jobs they thought were good for their men. Being a mileage run and an all-night turn, the 'Roggy' was a prestigious job, and it also employed a Swindon guard, a skilled goods guard who made sure the train stayed in one piece. All Rogerstone turns involved travelling down there on the cushions and working back. We also worked coal empties trains down to South Wales and invariably on these turns we had relief at the tunnel and Severn Tunnel Junction men took over from there.

11.34 p.m. CARDIFF TO SWINDON, 'The Long Dyke'

We booked on at the shed at 8.45 p.m. and walked to the station and rode passenger on the 9.15 Swindon to Cardiff train. At Cardiff we

walked to Canton shed and picked up a loco that had been prepared for us, usually a '59XX' class 4–6–0 and took it to the Long Dyke freight sidings to collect a train of mostly box-vans and sheeted wagons, part of the 6.35 p.m. Carmarthen-Paddington goods. Scheduled arrival into Swindon was just after 2 a.m.

The No. 5 Link, the more senior of the two goods links, had more part-vacuum and fully vacuum-fitted freights in it. Booked jobs in this link in the late 40s included:

THE 8 a.m. 'TAUNTON VACUUM'

We relieved this train at Highworth Junction and took it on to Banbury, mainly boxvans with a 'D' headcode on the engine, a '49XX' or '59XX' class. If running to time, we would return with the 2.20 ex-Banbury to Bristol East Depot, a train of some 60 boxvans.

THE 1.05 a.m. to OXFORD, the 'Hinksey'

We booked on at the shed at 12.15 a.m. and walked up to the Transfer, for which we were allowed 45 minutes, and relieved the 10.05 Bristol East Depot to Banbury at Highworth Junction. The locomotive was usually a 'Hall' or 'Castle' and it was a part vacuum train of general goods. At Oxford we were relieved and walked to the shed to prepare a '28XX' class engine to take to Hinksey sidings to relieve the 9.45 p.m. Oxley Sidings to Westbury at 5.25 a.m. Booked arrival back in Swindon, rarely achieved, was at 7.07 a.m. We booked off at the Transfer.

THE 11.12 p.m. to ACTON

This was a train of mixed freight, part-vacuum-fitted, which we relieved at West loop just by the junction of the Gloucester line. This was the 7.50 p.m. Alexandra Dock Junction to Acton, booked to arrive at 2.37 a.m. The loco was usually a '28XX' or '49XX' class and we would normally work it as far as Reading. Only if right on time would we work it to its destination, and it was always a trip home 'on the cushions'.

LIGHT ENGINE DISPOSAL LINK

This was a small separate Swindon link that was just below No. 4 Link for promotional purposes, between the freight links and the passenger links, and was peculiar to Swindon shed, primarily because of the location of the Works and the presence of the stock shed nearby. When a locomotive had passed its trials, it would be returned to Swindon shed for its running-in period, firstly on stopping trains, then semi-fasts and eventually on fast expresses if appropriate, until it was considered 'run in'. It would then be allocated to any depot that required that particular class of loco for its diagrammed work. For instance, if it was a 'King' class, whatever shed had work commensurate with that type of engine and required a replacement because one of theirs was going into the Works for repairs, then that would be where the loco was sent. This despatching of engine stock would be undertaken by the men of Swindon shed's Light Engine Disposal Link.

There were two sets of men working this link, one set working the 6 a.m.–2 p.m. shift, the other doing the 2 p.m.–10 p.m. turn. Their sole duty was to take locomotives from the stock shed to another depot, hence disposing of a light engine that was required elsewhere. These men would require good knowledge of road, as a driver would never go anywhere if he hadn't signed up for knowledge of road for a specific route. Every three months we had to sign up to show that we knew all the signals for a particular line. If you hadn't been over a certain road for a considerable time, you could go to the roster clerk and ask for a day looking over the Old Town road, the Cardiff, whatever you needed. It was then the responsibility of the clerk to book you to ride on the footplate of a train that was going that way.

I only recall the Light Engine Disposal for a couple of years before World War II, because with the outbreak of the War, locomotives were needed so urgently that none ever went into the stock shed, as they would come out of the factory and be required and allocated immediately. Men were never in the link for very long. The stock shed was used for a time to store old engines waiting to be cut up, with old coaches and railcars, but certainly from 1939 there never were any surplus engines. The stock shed did not come under the jurisdiction of the running shed – built in the 1880s, it was owned and operated by the Works.

4–6–0 No. 6964 Thornbridge Hall *in Swindon stock shed. Locomotives would be stored in this shed, located to the rear of the loco shed near the Gasworks, until such time as they were required. The stock shed booked crew would take an engine to whatever depot needed it, usually returning with a similar loco needing attention. This disposal worked all over the system – if a loco was to be sent to Plymouth, for example, Swindon men would take it as far as Bristol or Taunton. Everything eventually came to Swindon for heavy repairs – there were workshops at Wolverhampton, Old Oak Common and Bristol, but big heavy repairs needed Swindon attention. Over twelve months more than a thousand locos would pass through Swindon shops, then out into service again via the stock shed.*   H. C. CASSERLEY

No. 2840 near Stratton Green Bridge on its way into Swindon with a pick-up goods c.1938.

H. E. S. SIMMONS

In 1940 there were 139 locomotives based at Swindon motive power depot for diagrammed work, covering shunting, freight and passenger duties. There were 250 drivers, 250 firemen and 60 engine cleaners, three shift foremen (one for each shift, 6 a.m. to 2 p.m. / 2 p.m. to 10 p.m. / 10 p.m. to 6 a.m.), and one shed master on duty from 8 a.m. to 5 p.m.

During 1940 I clearly recall firing on many of the well-known named locomotives. These included:

4089	*Donnington Castle*	7014	*Cathays Castle*
5009	*Shrewsbury Castle*	7015	*Carn Brea Castle*
5067	*St. Fagan's Castle*	7037	*Swindon*
5068	*Beverston Castle*	4062	*Malmesbury Abbey*
5083	*Bath Abbey*	4056	*Princess Margaret*
4015	*Knight of St. John*	4948	*Northwick Hall*
5900	*Hinderton Hall*	5932	*Haydon Hall*
2902	*Lady of the Lake*	2908	*Lady of Quality*
2934	*Butleigh Court*	2940	*Dorney Castle*
2950	*Taplow Court*	2971	*Albion*
2933	*Bibury Court*	2947	*Madresfield Court*
2978	*Charles J. Hambro*		

During early summer of 1940, when I was on a spare turn in the Factory or Transfer links, I arrived at the shed to find that I'd been assigned to driver Bill Basing the following day to work an evacuee train from London. This was very exciting for me and I really felt that I was making a real contribution to the War effort. Bill was quite heavy-handed as a driver, I recall – tough on the locomotives but a good mate all the same. He was one of those rare drivers who thought nothing of going off to organise the tea for him and his fireman!

After booking on, we walked up to the station and relieved Old Oak men and worked the train forward to Cardiff, where we in turn were relieved, and returned home 'on the cushions'. I don't remember the final destination of the train but clearly many of those young Londoners were bound for sanctuary from the dangers of the South East of England. The children were a pitiful sight, peering anxiously out of the carriage windows when the train came into Swindon Junction, with their name labels a reminder of the drastic situation in which they and the whole country found themselves. I've often thought what a terrible ordeal it was for many of them, separated from their parents and friends and headed for apparent safety, but also to uncertainty, home-sickness and often to domestic arrangements which simply did not work well.

One of the biggest effects of the war on the GWR was the amount of time it took for a freight train to complete a run. This was partly because they were continually held in various goods loops along the route to allow expresses and higher-priority traffic to pass and partly because of the number of times they'd have to run slowly or stop completely because of air raid alerts. My old colleague Norman Wiltshire told me a tale of one particular wartime run with driver Frank Blackmore when running a goods between Swindon and Didcot. They'd booked on at 7.15 on a Friday night and were held all night in the goods loop between Ashbury Crossing and Knighton Crossing behind four other up freights, all held back because of bombing in London. After

eventual arrival at Didcot, they found they weren't able to get a passenger service back to Swindon until about 1.30 p.m. Saturday afternoon when they caught a stopping passenger from the bay platform. They'd missed the earlier fast train because they hadn't got relief in time. Didcot is only 30-something miles from Swindon, but by the time they'd booked off Saturday afternoon, it was nearly 4 p.m. – they'd taken 20 hours to work a goods to Didcot. I identified very strongly with Norman's tale as many times I'd been stopped at Shrivenham, then crawled up along the goods loop to Knighton Crossing. Before you went into the loop, the signal was pulled off and the signalman would call out, "There's two up there already, driver." I've been in Knighton loop so long, gradually moving up one by one, that there were occasions I was actually relieved there. A relief crew would be sent to Shrivenham on a stopping passenger on the cushions and they'd walk down from the station to relieve you. I've even gone back to Knighton the next day and relieved the *same* train that was now standing first in line instead of fifth when I had left it!

I recall one Barry Smith at Swindon shed who once did a 42-hour duty in these circumstances. When he eventually was relieved, he walked to the bottom of Victoria Hill and there, dog-tired after his extended stint on the footplate, he decided to catch a bus up to his home in Old Town. As he tried to board the first bus, the conductress put her hand up and informed him "Sorry, essential war workers only!" He had to stand aside and let all the rest of the queue on after he'd been on duty 42 hours!

I was on duty for 36½ hours on one occasion just running a freight to Didcot. I also served some protracted duties, especially during the runs down to Southampton Docks during those times when we were dispersing shiploads of cargo. This was a time when the old Midland & South Western line really proved its worth, as indeed it had in World War I. Just outside Marlborough, on the way to Southampton, there was a tunnel and it was decided during the war that it wasn't completely safe, so it would require re-lining. The Americans wanted to blow it up and make that section into a cutting, but the land above belonged to someone who owned Savernake Forest so the tunnel remained.

Often you had no food with you. Freight trains just ambled along and got there when they could. It was a very frustrating job in these circumstances. There were times when we were stopped in sidings with no imminent prospect of progress, when I've got off the locomotive and climbed over a fence into a field to see if any potatoes had been left on top of the dirt by the farmer. If I was successful I'd bring them back and put them on top of the firebox and that was your actual jacket potato! No butter, of course, but just some quick nourishment inside you. Many times when stopped in snow, I've melted snow to make a can of tea. I had terrible carbuncles break out on my wrists and the doctor said it was because I wasn't getting the proper food. Excuse the pun, but an Oxo cube really was a square meal! As fireman you could get closer to the firebox on your side of the cab so you tended to be warmer than the driver, who'd be huddled up in his corner in his great overcoat trying to stay away from the icy blasts of wind that would roar through the upper sections of the cab. Your biggest worry was that if you were going to be stationary for several hours, you had to keep the fire going but be careful not to run out of water. If that happened, the next thing was you'd have to shovel your fire out, before the water got too low. As industrial workers, we received a ration of eight ounces of cheese a week compared to two for the rest of the population. My Mum used to shop at Liptons and get our rations there, but such were the shortages during the war that if you were up the town and saw a queue, you joined it, in order to get whatever limited supplies were available. You had coupons for clothes, for furniture, as well as food.

One serious problem caused by the long hours spent by freight trains in congested loops was that the loco boiler was in steam for many hours without the locomotive accruing mileage. Boiler washouts, essential for cleaning out accumulated scale and dirt, were therefore not carried out with the correct regularity during this time, partly owing to shortage of labour and also because of irregular working of engines which did not return to their home depots at their appointed times and were therefore not available for attention according to schedule. The normal procedure was for locomotives fresh from Works attention to be sent to the running shed for trips on timetabled services as trials. The initials of the home depot to which they were allotted were stencilled on the out side footplating and when they had been tried, they were sent there on a train which would get them to, or at least in the direction of, the depot. Unfortunately, in the general shortage of locos, engines put on trains to somewhere near their home shed didn't necessarily make it but were worked away on any train for which such a locomotive was required. As a result, engines were finding themselves all over the system and it might be several weeks before they reached their home depot. With no attention during such periods, the boilers got into a terrible state, congested with scale and, with copper sideplates burnt, they could require a heavy boiler repair after a couple of months instead of the customary five years. Much attention was therefore accorded to boiler washing, and those responsible for maintenance at engine sheds came up with a plan based on the last digit of a loco's number, which ensured that there would be no more than ten days between washouts. It was decreed that at whatever sheds engine were on the 1st, 11th and 21st of a month, each engine whose number ended in '1' in that depot, had to receive a washout irrespective of whether a loco belonged to that depot or not, and so on for '2', '3', etc. It was still not ideal but it did improve the situation and we all had to make the best of things.

With the advent of radar, we were fortunately able to know when enemy aircraft were leaving France. When it was evident what part of the Channel the Luftwaffe were crossing and it was clear what part of the railway network was likely to be affected, that section was alerted and all trains in that area would be brought to a stand. You'd see the signalman lean out of his window and call "Air raid red, driver!"

That meant that we would proceed with the train at about 15 mph, because if any bombs were dropped in front of the train and the track destroyed, coming off the rails at that speed was not as serious as if we'd been travelling at normal rate. We would remain creeping along at the 15 mph until we reached another signal box where we'd be stopped and then hear "All clear, driver!" Then we would resume normal speed. That was the system to which we worked.

Our GWR Works at Swindon contributed much to the war effort. All the major railways were approached by government to assist by carrying out munitions work in their factories. I can recall seeing 15-inch diameter battleship guns for the Royal Navy in the engine pits in 'A' Shop. Huge orders were undertaken for the military Railway Operating Department in preparing a hundred Dean Goods 0–6–0 locomotives for service overseas, and there was manufacture of heavy bombs (the heaviest being 2000 lbs), Hurricane fighter parts, motor landing craft and bullet-proof plating for armoured cars. Further wartime locomotive construction included more 'Hall' class 4–6–0s and class 28XX 2–8–0 goods engines. However, probably the greatest contributions of all at Swindon came from the Tool Shop, in the production of high-precision thread taps, milling cutters and jigs to be supplied to aircraft builders, and from the Wheel Shop, where some 15,000 4-inch diameter turret rings were manufactured for tanks. Altogether, the value of war work undertaken at the Swindon factory totalled some £27 million.

During the war we had machine guns based at Swindon station, one battery on top of the station building and the other atop the coal stage on the water tower. The only time I heard either of them used was one lunchtime when I was walking towards the shed to book on for the 2 p.m. turn. A German plan flew over very low and they let fly at it from the top of the coal stage, but they inflicted no damage that I recall. We did have fatalities in Swindon from air raids. One at 6.40 a.m. on 27th July 1942 left bomb craters in fields near Rodbourne. Considering the strategic importance of the works, it seems incredible they were never hit. A lot of damage was caused in Beatrice Street and Ipswich Street in December 1940, and an August 1942 raid saw 15 deaths in Ferndale Road and 9 killed in Kembrey Street, with 35 people injured and 20 houses demolished. You can see brickwork in Ferndale Road today where the differences in the building clearly show where houses were restored after the bombing. My pal Freddie Simpson recalled that raid because he was close to the loco shed at the time, waiting to start work, and many of the crews ducked under tables in the messroom when the bomb hit. The ground was shaking, Freddie recalled, and when they emerged they noticed that the huge beams that held up the roof of the cabin had shifted about half an inch. They'd lifted when the bomb exploded and then resettled. Freddie also tells the tale of the German bomber strafing his street while he was talking with a neighbour at the end of the front garden. Luckily, they weren't hit but Freddie picked up one of the bullets and still has it! Due

The anti-aircraft machine gun battery on top of Swindon station on 3rd March 1941. There appears to have been some accommodation provided on the station roof for the soldiers, a relief area built of the same materials as the battery above. Taken looking north, the photographer had his back to the town and parcels office. The platform seen here was the one known as the Down branch, and at this time the walls still contained an array of enamel signs advertising tea, cough cures, oil engines and something called Turog, this last being partially obscured by a Swindon Junction nameboard hanging askew. The destination board fixed to the column directed passengers to 'Kemble, Stroud, Gloucester and Cheltenham Spa'.

CTY. STEAM MUSEUM, SWINDON

Blast damage in Drove Road, Swindon, 29th August 1942.
WILTSHIRE NEWSPAPERS

Damage in Beatrice Street, Swindon, 19th December 1940, seen from Cockle-bury sidings. Incredibly, no railway installations were damaged.
PUBLIC RECORD OFFICE

Some of the bomb damage of 14th August 1942 in Ferndale Road.
WILTSHIRE NEWSPAPERS

A wartime view of a famous Swindon store, McIlroys, with not a person or a vehicle in sight, and Havelock Street off to the right. It was a very classy shop with a wonderful staircase and its landmark clock tower with its three faces. They'd have a toy bazaar at Christmas there and we'd stand there goggle-eyed after school!
CTY. SWINDON LIBRARIES

Female labour was a great help during the war. We had girls at the shed working on boiler washing, a procedure which was under great pressure during hostilities. Each girl on this job would work assisting one of the regular boiler washers in a pair. I think there was some feeling initially that girls couldn't and shouldn't be doing men's work, but this was gradually overcome by the attitude, determination and sheer good work undertaken by the ladies. We also had girls working in the Stores issuing oil waste and uniforms, and I remember there was one lady named Rosie working in the office where they booked crews on and off, who later married one of our shift foremen. There was also a large female workforce in the Works where they assisted in the reception and despatching of locomotives, on boiler repairs, and even operating overhead gantry cranes in the shops.

'Castle' class No. 4096 Highclere Castle *seen at Swindon during the war with its anti-glare screen in position. It could be rolled back by the crews during daylight but if we heard 'Air raid red, driver!' from the signalmen, it would be pulled over the cab to hide the sight of the fire from enemy aircraft. When down, the tarpaulin made operating conditions very difficult, especially in summer, with a hot and intensely stuffy footplate and little room in which to manipulate larger tools such as the pricker.*
PUBLIC RECORD OFFICE

to government restrictions, no direct mention was made in the local papers. Swindon was always referred to as 'a town in the south of England'. A further blast that August killed 8 people in Drove Road.

I can remember clearly the night when Coventry was bombed. I was firing a freight train from Reading and we were stopped at Shrivenham signal box and heard the air-raid alert. It was my duty as fireman to go up into the signalbox and sign in the register for what they called Rule 55, to remind the signalman that we were stationary on the running line. The signalman would initial it, to acknowledge that I was stood outside his box with the signals at danger. As I climbed down from the locomotive on that occasion I stepped on something soft, and when I peered down through the darkness I could just discern that it was a cat that had been killed by a train. It was a bright moonlit night and as I looked skyward I could see dozens of white vapour trails of the German bombers across the face of the moon as they headed for the Midlands. I didn't know they were going to bomb Coventry, of course, but I realised the next day. There were also occasions when we were stopped at Reading by an alert and we could see the flak exploding in the sky over London, 36 miles away.

It was in the early part of the war that I had my biggest scare of all. I was well up on German aircraft because at that time you had posters of German uniform and profiles of German fighter planes plastered all over the town to aid recognition, I was working with driver Bill Heath on a west-bound goods down Dauntsey Bank, approaching Dauntsey station, and looking back along the train, I saw a German aeroplane coming down towards us. I immediately recognised the feared Heinkel 1–11, the biggest fighter plane the Germans had. I knew that the Luftwaffe were then 'train-busting' in France with their Fokke Wulf 19s and Messerschmidt 109s, cannon-firing warplanes, diving down onto trains in attempts to burst the locomotive's boiler with cannon shells. Success would mean the engine would explode and the train would pile up behind it, and this was now our greatest fear. We were a sitting target, high upon the embankment with open fields on either side, and the aircraft passed low and close to us; we could see the iron cross on the fuselage and the swastika on the tail. I was surprised to see an audacious wave from the pilot. He banked and disappeared up into the clouds and we waited in fear as we expected him to return and try to explode our boiler. To our great relief, we never saw him again – maybe he was already out of ammunition, or maybe he just decided to let us live, I'll never know. The only thing I am sure about is that I didn't require a laxative for a fortnight!

I witnessed another scary episode down at Southampton Terminus station, although the danger this time was not to me personally. I'd relieved a troop train at Swindon Town with driver 'Kitch' Townsend working down over the MSWJ and I observed an angry situation as a platoon of disgruntled American soldiers threatened to rebel, throwing their rifles down onto the track in the station. I'd done this trip many times, the Terminus being the major point for the troops to board their ships. It was always a recognised thing that upon arrival in Southampton the fireman would get off the engine and go back through the train as it was emptying, and the guard would come in the opposite direction, going into the compartments to pick up anything you could, because those Americans left everything bar their rifles – there'd be boxes of chocolates, magazines, packets of Camel and Lucky Strike, all just thrown on the floor. They were such a wasteful nation. I'd been to Southampton with other troop trains and been standing on the dockside as the train was being unloaded, and seen gas stoves all lined up on the platform. It was a recognised thing, legitimate pickings. It had always been that way with the morning trains into Paddington, especially retrieving the newspapers. Well, on this occasion, the guard and I had armfuls of spoils, and we headed towards the engine to

GREAT WESTERN RAILWAY.

Circular No. 3508.
G.1/A.R.P.

General Manager's Office,
Paddington Station,
London, W.2.

September 20th, 1938.

Air Raid Precautions.

It is considered desirable that, purely as a precautionary measure, the staff should be acquainted with the procedure which they should adopt in the event of an air raid.

The following instructions are, therefore, being issued as a general guide to the staff and where necessary will be amplified in detail to individual members of the staff by the Company's Officers as quickly as possible.

Organisation.

The Company's system will be divided into a number of areas, each of which will be under the charge of a Local Air Raid Precautions Officer. The areas will be sub-divided into sections according to local conditions, each section being placed under the charge of an Air Raid Warden.

The Local Air Raid Precautions Officers, who will be appointed by the Company's Officers, will be responsible for the training, control and equipment of the necessary first aid, fire-fighting, decontamination and rescue and clearance squads in their areas; also for the restriction of lighting during raids.

Air Raid Warning.

Warning of an impending air raid affecting any particular area will be received at the Paddington Telephone Exchange from the general railway Headquarters in London, and the Superintendent of the Line's Telegraph Department will be responsible for the immediate despatch of the warning to all stations, depots, etc., in the area affected.

Nature of Warning.

The responsible officer will at once advise the staff under his control by a pre-arranged signal, i.e. klaxon horn, fire hooter, whistle, or other convenient means. Generally this signal should be a succession of intermittent blasts, each of about five seconds' duration, with an interval of three seconds, the whole signal lasting two minutes.

Action to be taken by staff on receipt of warning.

1. *Staff required for A.R.P. duties.*

   Members of fire, first aid, decontamination and rescue clearance parties should proceed at once to the posts allotted to them by the Company's Local Air Raid Precautions Officer.

   Air Raid Wardens in charge of posts will be responsible for the issue of all necessary material and equipment to the squads under their control and will advise the Local Air Raid Precautions Officer when the arrangements have been completed.

2. *Staff required for essential railway service.*

   Certain members of the staff will be advised that they will be required for essential railway services during air-raids. These men should remain at their posts until enemy aircraft approach, when they should take shelter in the nearest convenient place until the raiders have passed.

3. *Staff not required for essential railway duties or A.R.P. work.*

   These members of the staff should proceed at once to the nearest shelter, details of which will be advised by the appropriate officers. Gas masks—which will be distributed by the Municipal Authorities in the event of emergency—must be carried by every individual and put on as directed by the Warden in charge of the shelter.

Operation of Services during Air Raids.

On receipt of an air raid warning, passenger trains should, except where other instructions have been given by the Superintendent of the Line, be stopped at the first station, where passengers should be warned and given an opportunity of alighting. The trains should then proceed cautiously at a speed not exceeding 15 miles per hour, subject to the proper observance of fixed signals.

Freight trains should be stopped at the first signal box and the drivers warned to proceed cautiously at a speed not exceeding 10 miles per hour, subject to the proper observance of fixed signals.

Detailed instructions will be issued by the officers concerned to the locomotive and traffic department staff.

Drivers of Horse and Motor Vehicles in streets when alarm is given.

Drivers of horse vehicles should return with them to the stables, if practicable. If not, they should secure their horses and place a tarpaulin over them, after which the drivers should take cover in the nearest shelter.

Drivers of motor vehicles should drive to the nearest side turning, stop their engines, turn out all lights, protect load and seat with tarpaulin cover and take shelter.

The ambulance train in the sidings at Shrivenham in June 1945, with No. 6965 Thirlestaine Hall. CTY. MARK WILKINS

sort and share it all out, when I saw this group of soldiers tossing their rifles onto the track, whereupon a man, whom I assumed was their commander, came up with a sub-machine gun on his shoulder, looked the men full in the face, then barked "You, you and you, follow me!" He walked them towards the engine and I was walking behind them. The guard and I climbed upon the footplate, and the lieutenant, or whatever he was, lined those fellows up against the side of the boiler, stepped back about fifteen yards, and turned to the platoon on the platform and coolly instructed "Pick up your rifles, or I'll drop these three here and now!" I believe he would have done it too, within his rights, because it was a mutiny. Fortunately, the soldiers clambered down and retrieved their weapons, but it was a frightening incident while it lasted.

Ambulance trains were stabled at Shrivenham until required. These were hauled by LNER engines and crewed by LNER men who would stay with the locos for a week at a time, sleeping in the train. Our engines would be added to give extra power if there was an excessive load. Two special sidings were constructed there for the reception of American casualties. A 14-coach ambulance train maintenance unit was constructed by the GWR and stabled at Swindon. I worked on ambulance trains and can remember receiving messages from the on-board surgeons via the guard, instructing us to slow down to 15 mph while they were performing operations. I made many runs to and from Southampton Terminus collecting injured soldiers. I saw many awful sights on Swindon Town station, which is where we'd usually be sent to work a train. There were German prisoners, some walking

about and some laid out on stretchers, and all wearing the original bandages that were put on when they were first landed on the beaches in Normandy. I think they were being taken to a hospital in Cirencester and there was one boy, I recall, no more than 16 or 17 years old, who was lying on a stretcher. There was a blanket over his chest as far as his waist, and then there was nothing, the blanket was flat. He had no legs, and at one end of the stretcher were his jackboots. I often wonder what happened to him.

One of the greatest accomplishments of the war was the Dunkirk evacuation – to have moved as many men from the continent as they did in such a short time was a great achievement, using just about anything that would float. As a young fireman, I remember working a train from Southampton Docks to Swindon Junction and relieving other trains at Junction, which were filled with weary, dispir-ited but very relieved servicemen of many nationalities – Belgian, Polish, French – I can still picture them laying list-lessly in the corridors when the trains came into Swindon, and the local branch of the Women's Voluntary Service set up operations on the platform dispensing cups of tea to the men.

I believe that at one point, wounded soldiers were being flown into Wroughton Aerodrome from Normandy, then they were transported in lorries up to Swindon Town station, I always remember the station up into Newport Street being cordoned off by the police and no one was allowed in that area, although, of course, my driver and myself would be allowed through in our uniforms to relieve the train crew there. We were allowed 45 minutes' walking time from Swindon shed, but we could catch the bus up Victoria Hill for tuppence and often did – if I was working with Alfie Guyatt, we'd always ride the bus up as he wanted to spend the time saved in the pub, the Royal Oak on the top of Croft Road bridge!

Another direct effect of the war was the end of double-home working, the practice of crews working a train one way, staying in lodgings overnight, then working the run in reverse next day. This was a common practice before the war, even between locations as close together as Swindon, Bristol and Gloucester, but the food shortage caused by the war heralded its abolition. The unfortunate part about it was that the London men stated that they wouldn't mind doing passenger work double-home, which caused a lot of anger as the feeling was that the cessation of the practice should be consistent, right across the board. London to Plymouth with double-home was a good job, overnight with the lodging allowance, and I remember Old Oak men coming to Swindon to discuss it, but in the end common sense and consistency prevailed.

At Bristol Temple Meads they had deep air-raid shelters and if the sirens sounded, you just followed everyone else down under the station at the western end of the platform. I called them 'dungeons' where passengers, crews and station staff all huddled until the 'all clear'. Bristol itself took a terrific pounding from the bombing, and I have vivid memories of numerous hosepipes all over the streets as the fire services sought to contain blazes which broke out after the Luftwaffe had dropped their deadly load. Bath was attacked too, and I've heard it said that the Germans had targeted Bath as a reprisal for Allied attacks on Germany's historic cities, although I have also heard the theory that the Royal Navy had a depot there and that this was the reason for the city being hit. Up in the main street in Bath, next to where Woolworth's used to be was a big church, and when I worked a train down there the night after an air raid, I saw the damage caused by a bomb which had struck the top of the bell tower. The bell had fallen right down the inside of the tower and had burst open the front doors of the church with the force of its landing. You could see the doors hanging off their hinges and the bell standing upright inside.

Many railwaymen were not so lucky as I was – locomotives were blown off the tracks by raids and some crews were killed, because, of course, disruption of the transport network was a prime purpose of an aggressor. The Up line near Bath took a direct hit on the viaduct just outside the station and it was 18 months before it was repaired, so it was single-line working during the time, right through to Oldfield Park. Railwaymen were at risk every day but the attitude was "We never close. We will get you there." The work of the railway had to go on.

No. 4 PASSENGER LINK

I was promoted to No. 4 passenger link during the last months of the War in 1945 and fired for driver Arthur Taylor, although my time in the link was short and my memories of the turns are somewhat blurred. Broadly they can be summarised as local passenger work, 'B' headlight trains, on stopping services. Former colleague Colin Hawkins recalled that there was some London work in No. 4, a night parcels train to Paddington, then returning with a West London parcels departing at 5.30 a.m., which bears out roster clerk Danny Williams' recollections that there was London work in all of the passenger links to keep the links balanced and help the crews maintain knowledge of road.

My driver, who schooled me through my first months of passenger firing, was Arthur Taylor, who was born in Gloucestershire in 1891 and was a veteran of the original Midland & South Western Junction Railway, starting as a cleaner at Andoversford in 1913. At the Grouping he was based at Gloucester shed as a fireman and his '20s experience included firing on the Chalford railcar. I remember him telling me that times were so rough on the impoverished old MSWJR that the men did not get paid every week. Like a lot of the men, after his move to Swindon in 1931 he kept an allotment off the Pinehurst Road, from which he kept his family self-sufficient in vegetables. He retired in 1956 and passed away in 1977.

The following reconstruction of No. 4 Link is not intended to be exhaustive nor fixed precisely in time but it is

My first passenger link driver, Arthur Taylor, seen about to leave his home in Wheeler Avenue, off Cricklade Road, to report to shed. I remember Arthur humorously saying "When we're 70, they ought to shoot us!" Arthur's son, who took this photograph, used to refer to this family photo as '12.45 off shed'.

ANTHONY TAYLOR

known that at various times the link included the following services in a 12-turn rotation. The list includes ten turns, with the other two being the a.m. and p.m. spare turns.

2.51 p.m. TO PADDINGTON

The engine was prepared for us on this turn. We booked on at 2.30 p.m. and walked to the station to run this stopping passenger service. The locomotive was usually a '73XX' class 2–6–0 and this was the main Paddington trip in the link in my time, which was to ensure consistent knowledge of road to Paddington through all the passenger links. This train ran all stations to Slough, then fast for 5.30 p.m. arrival at Paddington. The engine was turned at Ranelagh bridge and backed into Paddington for the 7 p.m. departure which ran fast to Maidenhead, then all stations to Swindon. At Didcot we

cut off and went over into the bay and took on another set of coaches, and waited some considerable time for a connection from Oxford. This was a full and tiring turn, with arrival in Swindon after 10 p.m. and booking off about 10.45 p.m.

11.55 a.m. TO DIDCOT

In the 40s these trains were frequently used for Swindon engines on running-in turns after Works trials in the Van Link. These could be anything – 'Halls', 'Kings', 'Castles' or any 4–6–0 passenger engine. The midday train to Didcot was a stopping service calling at the wayside stations at Shrivenham, Challow, Uffington, Wantage Road and Steventon, with a 12.42 arrival at Didcot. Broadly, there were four trains in each direction on the morning turn, three in the afternoon/evening, the jobs shared with Didcot crews, but the midday

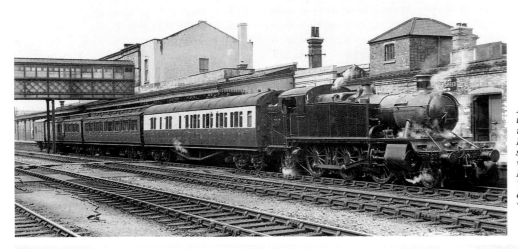

A Swindon–Didcot local in No. 4 link, a four-coach train hauled by a large Prairie 2–6–2 No. 6106, seen at Swindon station with the 4.2 p.m. to Didcot on 22nd May 1939. We used to call the old clerestory-roofed stock 'pigeon-lofts'.

L. R. LAPPER

The single headlamp denotes another stopping train, a 'Castle' class 4–6–0 No. 7007 Ogmore Castle, seen here brand new at the head of a two-coach train on a running-in turn into Steventon, the last stop before Didcot. Steventon used to sit right on the dividing line between the London and Bristol Divisions. 5th July 1946.

E. JOHNSON

A '55XX' class 2–6–2 small Prairie locomotive about to leave Marlborough MSWJ station with a two-coach passenger train for Swindon. There was a refreshment room on the station here which was also much used by the townsfolk as well as rail passengers. We would go in there for hot water for our tea and I remember the fellow who served you was also a bookie's runner, so crews with an interest in horses could place bets with him.
P. J. GARLAND

A goods train on the Midland & South Western proceeding cautiously down the bank from Swindon Town to Rushey Platt sometime in 1947.
COLLECTION M. P. BARNSLEY

A '43XX' class Mogul 2–6–0 hauling a two-coach 'B-set' past the iron foundry on a Swindon–Bristol stopper in No. 4 link, the 11.30 a.m. calling at all stations to Temple Meads along the South Wales Direct.
DAVE 'BRINKWORTH' JONES

train was always a Swindon turn in my time. Old colleagues report this loco being used during the afternoon on station pilot duties at Didcot, before returning at 6.08 p.m. with the stopping train known as 'Paddy's Mail' which was allowed 51 minutes for the journey to Swindon.

12.45 p.m. TO LUDGERSHALL

The Christmas Day turn chronicled in Chapter 4 was a No. 4 job, normally a Sunday afternoon turn. MSWJR turns from Swindon in No. 4 were south-inclined, those in the northerly direction being normally worked from Cheltenham. The jobs in the Swindon area itself tended to be undertaken by the Van and Old Town links, but those farther afield in the Southampton direction came under No. 4 passenger. The 12.45 was a job where we used to go down to Ludgershall and connect with the branch train from Tidworth. On one occasion I was firing the 6.08 out of the bay to Tidworth with a '45XX' and a B-set and there was a local resident who lived close to the station who used to take your photograph and make a fuss if you were making too much smoke. On this particular day I had put a bit round the fire and was producing some smoke and this bloke came down his garden shouting, "Put your blower on!" Arthur, my driver, was round the other side of the engine oiling, and he heard the commotion and came round to investigate.

"What's the matter?" he enquired.

"All this bloody smoke!" complained the local.

"Well you've got a solution ?" opined Arthur, and he firmly suggested that the man move house to solve the problem!

3.10 SWINDON TOWN TO SOUTHAMPTON

On this job we booked on at 2.15 p.m. and were allowed 45 minutes walking time up to Old Town where we travelled 'on the cushions' as far as Andover. There we relieved the Andover men on a '43XX' class Mogul 2–6–0, who had worked the train from Cheltenham and took it on into Southampton. We then worked the 4.36 p.m. goods out of Southampton Central and arrived back in Swindon at 7.6 p.m. where we were relieved by Cheltenham men. I remember seeing buzz-bomb damage to thatched cottages somewhere between Romsey and Andover when working that service.

Arthur Taylor, my driver in No. 4 link, with (left) fireman Eddie Lewis.
KENNETH LEECH

11.30 a.m. TO BRISTOL

This turn was part of the somewhat sparse passenger service provided on the South Wales Direct line of 1903, via Badminton. We booked on at 10.30 a.m. and prepared a '63XX' or 'Hall' class locomotive, and hooked up to usually four coaches in Swindon station. Station stops were made at Wootton Bassett, Brinkworth, Little Somerford (with connection for Malmesbury until 1951), Hullavington, Badminton, Chipping Sodbury, Coalpit Heath, Winterbourne, Filton Junction, Horfield, Ashley Hill, Stapleton

Pannier tank No. 8779 on a mixed train at Kemble for Cirencester Town on 1st September 1952. H. C. CASSERLEY

Road, Lawrence Hill and Temple Meads, where arrival was around 1 p.m. Passenger use of this service was rarely substantial. We went to shed at Bristol and the return working from Temple Meads did not leave until 5.45 p.m., arriving back in Swindon at 7.22 p.m.

1.58 p.m. TO CIRENCESTER TOWN
We booked on at 12.50 p.m. and prepared a '46XX' 0–6–0 pannier tank engine to run all stations to Cirencester, calling at Purton, Minety & Ashton Keynes, Oaksey Halt and Kemble. We remained on the branch to work three return services on the branch, the 3.10 3.50 and 4.40 from Cirencester and the 3.35, 4.25 and 5 p.m. from Kemble. We had very limited time at Town and in my day a shunter was employed there to uncouple and recouple the locomotive. We returned to Swindon with the 5.15 p.m. from Cirencester and arrived back at 5.56 p.m., booking off at shed at 6.25 p.m.

10.20 a.m. TO READING
This was normally with an engine out of the Works, on a 'running-in' turn. We booked on at 8.20 a.m., and had two hours to prepare the engine which, just off trials, would need a lot of oiling and checking over. Also at Reading shed there would be a fitter available for any attention required to the engine. The train was a stopping service calling at all stations to Reading – Stratton Park Halt, Shrivenham, Uffington, Challow, Wantage Road, Steventon, Didcot, Cholsey & Moulsford, Goring & Streatley, Pangbourne, Tilehurst and Reading. After time on shed, we worked the 2.40 p.m. back to Swindon, arriving at 4.27 p.m. Before booking off, the driver would make a list of anything that required to be done to the locomotive, and we'd book off at 5 p.m.

LIGHT ENGINE TO CHIPPENHAM/BANKING AT DAUNTSEY
After running the evening workmen's train to Wootton Bassett, the coaches would be left there in a siding and we ran the engine light to Chippenham, where we took it on shed and returned with an engine that was due to come to Swindon for boiler washing. We ran light to Dauntsey where the signalman would put us into an up siding to wait for the 'Up Cocoa' to come through. This was a goods train prepared at Bristol which departed from there at 9.20 p.m. and was scheduled to get into Paddington at 1.20 a.m. Invariably its load would necessitate assistance up Dauntsey bank, and we would provide the banking then run on light to Swindon shed and book off.

2.57 a.m. TO SOUTHALL
We booked on at 2.30 a.m. and walked to the station to relieve the Whitland to Kensington milk train. We cut off at Southall and ran light to Ranelagh bridge, where we turned the engine ready to work the 9.15 a.m. Paddington–Taunton as far as Swindon.

At the end of the war we were glad it was over, but as railwaymen we knew it was going to be a long time before we got ourselves right again. Locomotives and rolling stock were in terrible condition, and to do your job, with the state of the locomotives and the railway itself, required more than the normal call of duty. The old cleaning routines in the shed had lapsed and maintenance of stock had suffered. In the years before 1939 there were situations where they'd never send a locomotive out, but during and after the war every loco had

IDENTIFICATION CARD
GREAT WESTERN RAILWAY

No. 72905

The undermentioned person is authorised to be on the Lines and Premises on the Great Western Railway Company while in the execution of his duty. This card is valid until cancelled or withdrawn.

NAME IN FULL *Brown R.K.*

DEPARTMENT *C.M.E.*

GRADE *FIREMAN*

STATIONED AT *SWINDON*

SIGNATURE OF HOLDER *R.K. Brown*

This Identification Card must be signed in ink by the holder immediately he receives it, and be carried by him until further notice when engaged in work on the Railway. It must be produced at any time on request, and the holder must, if required, sign his name as a proof of his identity.

Signature of
Issuing Officer

C.L. Swit

General Manager.

A photograph featured in the GWR Magazine in October 1945, with Swindon driver Chris Brown on the right on No. 1000 County of Middlesex, *built in 1945, the first of its class, at Paddington. The dignatories being photographed were (from left to right) F. W. Hawksworth, the GWR's Chief Mechanical Engineer; Sir James Milne, GWR Manager; and Viscount Portal, the GWR Chairman.* GWR MAGAZINE

to be used as there were no replacements. You had to do the best you could with what you had. If a loco was in fairly good nick, even on an express, it wasn't excessively hard work to shovel the coal; it would be a satisfying experience to work it and reasonably easy to keep the boiler pressure up. Where there was less time and fewer men to maintain the locos, firing became that much harder. A well-maintained engine was always easier to work because you lost less power, but if the maintenance was poor, then the crew had to somehow compensate for the deficiencies themselves.

Looking back on the period of conflict now from sixty years on, I remember one of the worst privations and source of discomfort suffered by the engine crews was the stifling heat on the footplate when working at night under the tarpaulins required during the black-out, especially in the summer months. We were so gateful when the end of the war brought that great inconvenience to an end. It was also good to go out on a train again free from the fear of being attacked by the Luftwaffe, and, of course, there was no more reporting for duty at the shed carrying a tin helmet and gas mask. Anyone forgetting these appendages would be summarily despatched home to fetch them! And still today, whenever I think about the dietary limitations caused by the war, I remember so vividly the taste of Spam and dried eggs – the meat was produced from pork leftovers and the eggs were in powdered form and when cooked resembled an omelette.

A VE Day party in Havelock Street in 1945. Oddly, I am unable to recognise anyone in this photograph, even though I was living there at the time. Our house is in the centre of this view, No. 50. The windows indicated by the arrows were the front bedroom, which ran the entire width of the house facing onto the street, with two more bedrooms at the rear. In winter time Mum would open the right-hand sash window and reach out and shovel snow off the top of the bay windows below as she was worried about leakage into the front room. It was in this room behind the bay window that the incident of the half-crown, the cat and the candle took place! In those days this was a typical town street of terraced houses, with a corner shop at each end. Today it is almost completely business premises, with our old home a busy cafe. Each house had a narrow garden in front enclosed by iron railings until the metal was removed in the early 1940s for the war effort. Our front door had a distinctive diamond in the porch visible here. COLLECTION PETER SHELDON

CHAPTER FOUR
CHRISTMAS DAY ON THE MSWJ

I worked many Christmas Day turns during my years at Swindon shed. I can't say that I ever really enjoyed going out on the footplate at the height of the festive season but that was your lot as a GWR man in those days. You see, it was a recognised thing at Swindon that whatever turn you worked on the Sunday prior to Christmas Day, then you would have to work that same turn on Christmas Day itself – that was the rule. Most of those public holiday workings have long since faded into the recesses of my memory, but I have never forgotten the frustrations of one particular duty, 25th December 1945, when I was booked to fire the return evening working between Swindon Junction and Andover over the old Midland and South Western line.

Christmas Day in the forties had a simple ritual to it in our family – we usually spent the 25th at my Dad's parents' house and Boxing Day with my mother's parents in North Street. It would be chicken for Christmas dinner in those days, not turkey, and there'd be King George's somewhat hesitant speech on the Home Service on the wireless in the afternoon. There'd be an evening singalong around the piano, then there'd be the expected family party games like Poor Pussy, in which you were blindfolded and had to guess the identity of the person upon whose lap you were sat!

My driver that memorable Christmas Day was Freddie Browning, long since gone, a lovely fellow to work with. I was a 24 year old fireman just two years away from promotion into the top link and still living at home with my parents at 54 Havelock Street, Swindon – I didn't leave home until 1955 when I married. In those days there were two Christmas Day runs over the old 'Tiddley Dyke', as we used to call the old MSWJ route. The 10.10 from Swindon arrived in Andover Junction at 11.45, and returned from there at 12.30, arriving back in Swindon just after 2 p.m. The other train, the one we worked that day, was the 4.45 afternoon train, due to make Andover at 6.30, the return departure leaving there at 8.5 with arrival back in Swindon at 9.47. It began quite uneventfully – I had a full Christmas dinner inside me and cycled my regular route to work – down Commercial Road into Milton Road, past Emlyn Square and down through the tunnel, the main works entrance in Bristol Street – to the shed where Freddie and I took charge of a 44XX class Prairie tank around 3.30 p.m. I was in No. 4 Link at the time, that section of the Swindon roster that provided men for the engines coming out of the factory on trials after a refit, and also for the local stopping services such as all stations to Didcot and, of course, the 'Tiddley Dyke'.

I loved the old Midland and South Western line – it was a quite historic railway, and had the character of a railway in a garden. Everyone seemed to know everyone else and it was full of characters, the plate-layers, the signalmen, the porters. Or course, all the signal boxes had to be open all the time we were on that Christmas Day working, just for those two round-trip services. They used to do all sorts in those boxes – cut blokes' hair, grow tomatoes, and they'd have well-tended allotments round the back and plenty of time to care for them while on duty! You could obtain broiler chickens from a porter or signalman, or maybe fresh vegetables, and there was an altogether slower pace of life evident along the line in those days. There was a maximum speed of 35 m.p.h. imposed on all trains working over it.

One humorous memory of the MSWJ concerns the Bishop of Bristol, who once came to talk to the railwaymen at Swindon. He had been born in Old Town and was talking about the old 'Tiddley Dyke'. He was a down-to-earth character and despite his religious standing you could talk to him like you could one of your workmates. All the same, I told him, just a little hesitantly, that the MSWJ was also known under another name.

"What was that?" the Bishop enquired, very interested.

"Well, sir, it was the Piss and Vinegar Railway!"

It was a relief to see a smile on the Bishop's face. "How did it get that name, driver?" he laughed.

"Well, sir, during the First World War, the soldiers at Tidworth barracks used to come into Swindon on a Saturday night to go to the Empire Theatre for a night out. When they came out they went on the booze, of course, then bought fish'n'chips. Then they'd return to Old Town station to catch their late train back to barracks. You had a horde of young soldiers on a night out, you can imagine what it was like! There were no toilets on the train, so if they needed to answer a call of nature, full as they were of an evening's drinking, they'd drop the leather strap, open the window and just relieve themselves out into the night! So that's where the name came from, soldiers needing to relieve themselves in a hurry and the vinegar on the fish'n'chips. And if the wind was in the wrong direction when they had the window down, they got their own back in a hurry!"

Well, the Bishop roared his socks off – "I've never heard that before, driver!"

As I said, working a Christmas Day was nothing new for me. There was even one occasion when I was on duty twice on a 25th December getting home from a trip 3.30 a.m. Christmas morning and going back on duty at 7.25 p.m. Christmas night. However, what made the 1945 turn different was the way things turned out after working a train that needn't have run and nobody would have been any worse off.

Having prepared the Prairie, we came off shed, crossed over onto the Gloucester branch, then ran back across the main line and round the back of West Box and onto our two coaches, a Bristol Division 'B-set' in the downside bay. As we left the station on time at 4.45 p.m., there were just three people on the train – myself, Freddie, and our guard, whose name I cannot now recall. We branched off at Rushey Platt, where we took the electric tablet from the signalman at the Midland & South West token station and climbed out over

Cheltenham Spa, Swindon, and Andover Junction—continued.

Down Trains. — **Week Days.** — **Sundays.**

STATIONS.	B Pass.	K 8.30 p.m. Tidworth Goods.	B Pass.		B Passenger.		B Passenger. SO	B Pass.	D C'ches.	B Pass. and Milk.	B Excursion.		B Pass.	B Passenger and Milk.	B Excursion.
	dep.	arr. dep.	dep.		arr. dep.		dep. SO	dep.	dep.	dep.	arr. dep.		dep.	arr. dep.	arr. dep.
	p.m.	p.m. p.m.	p.m.		p.m. p.m.		p.m.	p.m.	a.m.	a.m.	p.m. p.m.		p.m.	p.m. p.m.	p.m. p.m.
Cheltenham Spa (High St.)	...	...	...		... ...		...	...	...	...	... ...		...	... ...	... ...
CHELTENHAM SPA (L'down)	...	...	...		— 7 20		...	...	...	...	... ...		...	... ...	... ...
Lansdown Junction	...	...	...		7 21		...	...	...	...	... ...		...	... ...	... ...
Gloucester Loop Junction	...	...	...		7 26		...	...	...	...	... ...		...	... ...	... ...
Cheltenham S. & L'hampton	...	...	...		7 31		...	...	...	...	... ...		...	... ...	... ...
Charlton Kings	...	...	...		7 39 7 41		...	...	...	...	... ...		...	... ...	... ...
Andoversford	M	...	...		7 46 X7 48		...	...	...	...	... ...		...	... ...	July 2nd only
Withington	...	...	...		7 57		...	...	...	...	... ...		...	... ...	
Chedworth	...	...	...		8 1		...	...	...	...	... ...		...	... ...	
Foss Cross	7 8	...	...		8 11 8 14		...	10 55	...	...	... ...		...	... ...	
CIRENCESTER (Watermoor)	X7 18	...	...		8 20 8 21		...	11X 2	...	...	... ...		...	... ...	
South Cerney	7 28	...	...		8 28 8 30		...	11 10	...	...	... ...		...	... ...	
Cricklade	—	...	...				...		...	...	2 38		4 45	... ...	7 20
Blunsdon	—	...	8 20				...		10†10	...	CS		CS	... ...	CS
Moredon Halt	7 45	...	8 24		C8 41 S		CS	11 25	10†18	10 30	2 47		4 53	... ...	7 28 7 29
Swindon (G.W.)		...	8 28		8 45 X8 51		11 5			10 39	2 56			5 18 5 20	7 38
Rushey Platt		...	SO		X9 4		X1118			10 43	2 59			5 24	7 41
SWINDON TOWN		...			9 8		11 21			10 49	3 7			5 29 5 30	7 47
Chiseldon		...			9 13 X9 15		11 26 11 27	D		10 59	3 16			5 39 5 41	7 56
Chiseldon Camp		...			9 24 X9 27		11 36 X1137	C'ches.							
Ogbourne		...			9 37 9 39		9 40†			11 9				5 50 5 52	
MARLBOROUGH		...			9 40†									5 57 5 58	
Savernake (Low Level)		...			9 42†		11 47 11 48							6 4	
Wolfhall Junction		8Y 40	R		9 44† 9 45		11 53 Sat.			11 15				6 9	
Savernake (High Level)		10 50	10 40		9 51†		11 58 night			11 20				6 14 6 15	
Grafton South Junction		11 10	11 0		9 54† 9 55†		12 7			11 24				6 22 6 23	
Grafton			—		10 1 10 3		12 6 12 11	12†32		11 30				6 30	
Collingbourne Kingston					C S		CS	12†44		11 38					
Collingbourne					10 16 —					11 45					
LUDGERSHALL															
Weyhill															
ANDOVER JUNCTION															
Stockbridge															
Kimbridge Junction															
Romsey															
Redbridge															
Southampton Central															
SOUTHAMPTON															

Notes for Down Trains:
- **M**—South Cerney arrive 7.14 Cricklade arrive 7.25.
- M—South Cerney arrive 7.14. Cricklade arrive 7.25.
- **R**—When 10.5 p.m. Passenger Train Ludgershall to Tidworth does not run, the 8.30 p.m. Goods ex Tidworth will leave Ludgershall at 10.0 p.m. and run earlier to Andover Junction.
- **SO** also runs Dec. 26th and 27th, and April 10th and 11th, and May 29th and 30th.
- Forms 11.5 p.m.
- **Y—SX** Tidworth to Ludgershall.
- **SO** Commences June 4th. July 2nd only. To Tidworth due at 12.19 a.m.

Andover Junction, Swindon, and Cheltenham Spa—continued.

Up Trains. — **Week Days.** — **Sundays.**

STATIONS.	J Goods.	F Goods.	G Engine	E Perishables. RR	B Pass. and Milk Empties.	B Pass.	B Excursion.	B Excursion.	B Passenger.
	arr. dep.	arr. dep.	dep.	arr. dep.	arr. dep.	dep.		dep.	arr. dep.
	p.m.	p.m.	p.m.	p.m. W	p.m.	p.m.		p.m.	p.m.
SOUTHAMPTON		7R12 7 26		10 0					
Southampton Central		7 35		10 8					
Redbridge		§7 42		10 14					
Romsey		C7 55 R		10 33					
Kimbridge Junction		8 2		10 40					
Stockbridge									
ANDOVER JUNCTION	— 7 50	8 36 N8 49		1126E 0†135		12 20			8 22
Weyhill	C S	C S		p.m. p.m.	12 28 12 30	12 37 12 39	Commences June 4th.	July 2nd only	8 29 8 30
LUDGERSHALL	8 15 8 35	9 11		9.45 p.m. South- ampton Docks	12 44 12 45			8 37 9 6
Collingbourne	—	—	SO		12 50			9 11 9 16
Collingbourne Kingston	—	—		—	12 54 12 59			9 19
Grafton	—	—		—	1 4 1 6			9 25 9 27
Grafton South Junction	—	—		—				9 32 9 33
Savernake (High Level)								
Wolfhall Junction								
Savernake (Low Level)								
MARLBOROUGH	9 17 X9 33	C9 47 S		C12 10 S	1 16 1 25	— 3 25	8 15 9 42 9 45	
Ogbourne	C S	C S		a.m. a.m.	1 34 1 35	3 35	8 25 9 54 9 56	
Chiseldon Camp	—	—			1 40	3 40 8 30	10 1	
Chiseldon	C S	C S		12 55 1 5	1 43 1 45	3 44 8 34 10 8		
SWINDON TOWN	10 6 X10 40	10 16 10 31	11†120	C11 10 S	1 53	2 15 3 52 3 53	8 44 10 15 10 20	
Rushey Platt	10 46 *11 5	C10 35 S	C S	C S		CS	CS CS	
Swindon (G.W.)	11 15	—	11†130	—		2 25 4 0	8 52 10 27	
Moredon Halt								
Blunsdon								
Cricklade		C S		C S				
South Cerney		MC10 X67 S		C S				
CIRENCESTER (Watermoor)		C11 4 S		C11 19 S				
Foss Cross		C S		C S				
Chedworth		—		—				
Withington		C S		C S				
Andoversford		C C		C S				
Stop Board		11 42 11 P45		2 18 P2 21				
Charlton Kings		—		—				
Cheltenham S. & L'hampton		—		—				
Gloucester Loop Junction		12 2 P12 5		2 38 P2 41				
Lansdown Junction		12 6		2 42				
CHELTENHAM SPA (L'down)		12 11 —		2 47				
Cheltenham Spa (High St.)								

Notes for Up Trains:
- **M**—On Saturdays South Cerney 10.57X11.3, and thence 6 minutes later to Cheltenham.
- **N**—Assisted Andover Junction to Swindon Town on Saturdays.
- **R**—Leaves Southampton Docks at 7.5 p.m.
- **W**—Runs during New Potato Season.
- **§**—Will stop specially at Redbridge as required to attach Live Stock Traffic for stations beyond Andover Junction.

Our Christmas Day trip in 1945 was run as a Sunday service, shown above in the working timetable for that period. Our passengerless train was the 4.45 p.m. from Swindon Junction with a return from Andover shown here as the 8.22 p.m. departure.

Swindon Town station in 1935, with 'A' Signal Box and Sam Fay's old MSWJR offices on the bank behind. Town station represents my first memory of being on a railway station as a young child.
C. L. MOWAT
CTY. W. R. BURTON

the canal, so we now had authority to travel that road up as far as Swindon Town. Of course, that electric token was your key to the railway, and as long as you were in possession of that, no other train could enter that section from either end. The gradient from Rushey Platt to Town was a 1 in 75 – you knew you were going uphill, of course, but with a Prairie hauling only two 29-ton coaches, your locomotive was just as strong at the top of the gradient as at the bottom. What you did lose over such a climb was the momentum of your train. You handed in the token at Town 'A' Box as you came into Swindon Town station, where the moustached George Whitbread took it in with his customary "Rightcha be, lad!", then picked up another from 'B' Box on Evelyn Street bridge, which gave you the road as far as Chiseldon. You always used to shout out "Correct staff!" and that was one thing the drivers used to emphasise – when the signalman handed you the key, always look at it, to check that it was for the correct section. Swindon Town won many prizes over the years for its well-kept gardens, mostly looked-after by the signalmen at the Rushey Platt end of the station by 'A' Box. As mentioned in Chapter One, I remember Town station clearly from my first visit there as a five-year-old when we went to pick up that puppy, and the hinges on the smokebox door showing up brilliant white in the fading light as the evening train from Cheltenham came under the Croft Road bridge. This Christmas Day at Town, the story was exactly the same as at Junction – we were not pestered by a single passenger!

Over the more or less flat course to Chiseldon, the MSWJ route took you through Hodson Woods round the back of Coate Reservoir. On this day, as on many other turns through here, I had time to look across to Coate Water and recall that it was there I undertook my first remunerated employment

during 1935–6, as a 10/6d a week gate attendant while waiting to be called by the GWR. My last job there each night would be to lock the back gate and there were many times I'd walk across the park and look across the reservoir thinking, "Who the hell would want to pinch all this bloody water?" The key, which I had to hand in at the boathouse before I clocked off, was attached to about 18 inches of an old oar, to make sure you didn't take it home with you!

At Chiseldon the complete lack of passenger activity repeated itself, and similarly at Chiseldon Camp, a halt used by local military, although it was rare to see passengers there anyway. At Ogbourne, as we looked over the deserted platforms, I remarked to Freddie about a time during the war when I was firing the 9.10 p.m. Swindon–Tidworth with driver Alfie Guyatt, and Ogbourne station was a hive of activity, not with folk intending to ride the train but with locally-based American soldiers trying to break into the signalbox to reach the local signalwoman, known as Queenie. She'd locked them out, and rung the police, who'd contacted the military police to deal with the situation. As Alfie and I brought the train into the station, I had the staff ready but couldn't see her. I alighted from the cab and as I climbed the steps to the box, I saw the last of the miscreants being loaded quite brutally into this lorry. I can still see them, these army police, with 'M. P.' on their armbands. Remarkably, as I recall, that signal box had only been built during the war years, and by American troops! Queenie was always very concerned about the welfare of the engine crews – I remember one occasion as I handed over the staff during a heavy shower of rain, she scolded me with "Where's your coat?"

Ten minutes from Ogbourne we took a slight rise over the Kennett and Avon Canal, then eased into Marlborough at

5.39, where the old terminus of the Marlborough GWR branch, known as Marlborough High Level, overlooked the MSWJ line and was still in use as a goods station at this time. Serving a town of reasonable size, one might have expected some patronage here, but looking back, even before the days of ritualised television viewing at Christmas, who would be likely to want to spend their precious holiday on a draughty Wiltshire platform waiting for a stopping train to Andover? Even the platform refreshment room, in those days used by the Marlborough townsfolk as their 'local', was quiet and uninviting. For me, Marlborough MSWJ station held memories of Sunday school outings in the 20s, when the journey on the train from Town for me was the highlight of the day, and we'd walk into the Savernake Forest and scramble for boiled humbugs!

Once through the tunnel and onto the falling gradient down to the old High Level station at Savernake and thence to Wolfhall Junction, Freddie shut off the regulator to conserve steam, then we crossed the Berks and Hants line at Grafton South Junction. The GWR used to issue all the farmers, whose land bordered the MSWJ line down here with working timetables, because of the lack of under-line cattle creeps and the necessity of moving cattle across the track. Only several months before, the need for farmers to know the timetable had been forcibly brought home to me while travelling passenger for a back-working turn from Andover. Driver Harry Bishop and I were due to back-work the 4.37 ex-Andover for Swindon Town, at which point we would be relieved by Cheltenham men, and as we approached Collingbourne we heard an awful crash. We looked out of the carriage window and saw a farmer sat in the seat of his tractor, legs dangling, with the chassis of his vehicle gone, severed by the engine! Incredibly, the farmer was unhurt, if rather shaken, and the glass had been broken in the front right eyeglass of the locomotive by the impact.

Predictably, on our Christmas trip, the small stations at Grafton and Collingbourne, and the tiny halt at Collingbourne Kingston with its sleeper-built platforms, failed to realise any local interest and we continued south towards Ludgershall with a passenger loading that would not even have troubled our footplate!

During our couple of minutes at Ludgershall station, I had time to reflect on busier times there during the war, when I'd worked trains with Sherman tanks aboard and had often taken a Swindon-based engine on the branch service into Tidworth. There was what we used to refer to as the 'Callgirl Train', which brought London lasses in from Andover to service the needs of the Americans based in Tidworth Camp, and would return them along the branch at a late hour so they could make the last train from Andover to London. A brief but unnecessary stop at Weyhill, a brief halt at the signal at Red Post Junction, then we were on old LSWR territory as we coasted into Andover Junction's island platform at 6.30 p.m., where we had ninety minutes in which to take our engine to the turntable and turn it around ready for the journey back to Swindon, and rest and enjoy our sandwiches. Not all crews would bother to turn the locomotive on this

working, as you could run a Prairie bunker-first just as easily as you could work forwards, but we usually turned it to make better operating conditions for the fireman, especially in inclement weather. As we enjoyed our tea and cheese sandwiches in the cab, I noticed in my lunch tin that my regular onion or shallot which I would eat with the sandwiches had been replaced with a slice of moist Christmas cake, a reassuring festive touch on the part of my mother. The onion would not have been advisable on this occasion, as I had planned to do some courting when I got back to Swindon!

It's strange that I cannot recall the name of our guard that day, as I can still picture the many times we looked out over the side of the cab to see him standing forlornly on the platform looking for the custom that never came. It seems hard to believe, looking back, that not one passenger boarded our train on that entire round-trip, and it felt like a totally wasted effort as we brought our train to a stand in Swindon Junction station at 9.47 that Christmas night. Our frustrations, however, were only just beginning.

Officially, our shift was 3.30 to 11.30, but a considerate shed foreman would usually sign you off when your main run was completed, unless he needed you for an emergency or to prepare another engine for another crew, so that night it was our intention to get off shed as quickly as possible and be home before 10.30. I had a date with my then girlfriend Marianne, who lived up in Old Town – shame Freddie couldn't have dropped me there on the way through! However, as we ran into the platform at Junction, there was a Station Inspector waiting there, Mr. Charlie Pullen, and his first words were just what we had dreaded hearing.

"Don't go to shed, Fred. We've got no shunting engine up here, it being Christmas Day, and the Up Taunton is due with a horsebox that needs removing. You tail her and get that box off and put her in the siding, then you can go to shed."

"Well now, how long we got to wait?" enquired Freddie, and you could feel his impatience rising.

"When the Taunton gets here."

"Well, that's all very well, Charlie, but we've done our booked job and I was hoping to get off home, it being Christmas an'all. Now we've got to wait around to do this."

"I'm sorry, Fred," replied the Inspector, soothingly, "but there's nothing we can do about it. There's no other engine available."

As you can imagine, my driver was in something of a temper over this. To tail an Up train at Swindon, you had to stand outside West Box, where there was a section of track that had a catch point at each end. A shunting engine could stand in between those two catch points, then when the Taunton came in to the platform, the signalman in West Box would close the points and give you the ground signal, or 'dummy' as we called it, and you'd go up behind the rear of the train. So the signalman shouted to Freddie, "Wait for the Taunton! Stand back in the trap!" The 'trap' was what we called that section between the points. Now the signalman hadn't shut the points at the opposite end, because there was plenty of room in there for our loco, but Freddie went back so fast, so cross was he at the enforced delay, that he went right through the open catch point and all our wheels ended up on the ballast! I always remember Freddie saying to me that he'd had a premonition that something like this was going to happen, whereupon I told him that I wished he'd told me and I might've stayed home!

Well, this was great, because now call boys, or whoever was available, had to be sent out to summon the breakdown gang and they weren't going to be thrilled to be called out on Christmas night. Had this incident taken place on a normal working day, it would have been less of a problem, as these men, shed fitters, would just leave their regular work and go to a derailment as required, but this was Christmas, they were all home, and there were few telephones around in 1945. The men were paid extra to be 'on call' for such emergencies, and having received the summons, they would have gathered at the shed to be briefed by the foreman as to what was required, then assembled in the breakdown van and a loco found to take them to the station. As I recall, the Taunton eventually came in and they cut the horsebox off and just left it in the station at the mainline platform until we were able to use the engine that brought the breakdown van to shift it. I don't remember if the Taunton had much in the way of passengers.

Of course, Freddie and I couldn't do anything except stay there with our engine while the fitters used traversers to jack her up and slew her round and back onto the track. If only one pair of wheels were off the road then it wasn't too serious a job, but this was all of them on a 2–6–2 – ten wheels!

We got back to shed at 4 a.m. Boxing Day! Then we had to write reports, and Freddie had to admit that he'd gone back through the points too fast, misjudged his brake application and couldn't stop in time. It was bad enough that we had to hang around for the Taunton and come off the road – all after making a trip to Andover and back for really no reason whatsoever!

Worst of all, from my point of view, I'd stood up my date! I'd told her that I didn't expect to see her much before eleven, and Marianne was an understanding girl who knew about the situation with the footplate, but even so, to not turn up at all! I went out with her for six years and I remember early on, her Dad gave me a right rollicking one night when I had her out until after 10.30 p.m., and we'd only been to the Regent to see Bud Abbott and Lou Costello. On the Boxing Day I was not booked on, so after I'd slept off our exertions of the previous day, I went to see Marianne, to timidly explain my non-appearance.

"What on earth happened last night?" she enquired, just a little testily.

"We was derailed!" I replied, trying to sound impressive.

"You was nearly divorced!" came her rejoinder.

I still maintain touch with Marianne today – she and her husband and my wife and I have often met up, and we still have a laugh about the time I stood her up because I was marooned with my engine. I never had any time for Beeching, but perhaps it was no bad thing that he hastened the end of Christmas Day working on the railways!

'59XX' class 4–6–0 locomotive heading an up passenger express through the mist by Swindon West signal box. It seemed that there were more catchpoints in the siding by West box than anywhere else. This shows the exact spot, the trap referred to in the story above, where we derailed on Christmas Day. You can see the dummy signal on the ground that protected the catchpoint, and the gap in the rail where we came off is marked with an 'X'. DAVE 'BRINKWORTH' JONES

Ted Veary ('Dusty Ted'), my gaffer on No. 3 link, seen here with fireman Jack Lawes, in the cab of 'Saint' class 4—6—0 No. 2927 St. Patrick. Ted is leaning on the handle of the reverser. In front of them you can see the water scoop handle, which allowed us to obtain 3,000 gallons of water in 15 seconds while travelling at high speed. The letter 'C' on the cabside denoted routes on which the engine was allowed to run, related to its weight on bridges.

KENNETH LEECH

CHAPTER FIVE

POSTWAR AUSTERITY

MY memories of the end of the war are quite hazy – I think I must have been hard at work on some anti-social turns, for although there was a great deal of local work in No. 4 Link, I was often detailed to do firing turns which ranged further afield when spare. All I can dimly recall is seeing one or two street parties on VE Day, and they don't even include the one held in Havelock Street where I lived! Old colleague Mark Wilkins recalled finding a ten-shilling note – quite a prize in those days – underneath a park bench in the GWR park on Faringdon Road! In the immediate postwar years, the use of ration books and a feeling of austerity continued for some time. Gradually you became aware that things were appearing in the shops again, and one obvious difference I remember is that you didn't see queues any more like you had done during 1940–45, although Titchener's was a quality baker in Regent Street where they sold the best bread in Swindon, and there would always be a long line outside there, it seemed.

After the war, in addition to working with engines that had been worked so hard with poor maintenance and cleaning, we had problems with the coal. We didn't have the high-grade South Wales coal that the engines were designed to burn, being supplied instead with cheaper Belgian and German coal. Later we had the awful briquettes, which was coal mixed with cement dust, a ruse to use up small coal. You needed quick combustion in the firebox on an express, and, of course, the briquettes would take time to get alight and they didn't give as much heat as proper coal. Anthracite fuel was also used and was the greatest curse of all to firemen because slow-combustion fuel meant falling boiler pressure, which in turn made the engine weaker, resulting in loss of running time.

Mundane locomotives like the 0–6–0 pannier tanks suffered even more from the lack of good maintenance during the war. Freddie Simpson used to talk about how the clinker would build up in their fireboxes, preventing air getting

A '59XX' No. 5939 Tangley Hall *on 'C' headlights with a train of milk tanks passing Denchworth, near Wantage Road, on 23rd June 1938.*

H. E. SIMMONS

'Star' class 4—6—0 No. 4015 Knight of St. John *passing Twyford with a parcels train c.1947.*

J. H. RUSSELL

through to allow the coal to burn properly. On some jobs, a relieving crew coming on duty would be greeted by the sight of clinker virtually hanging out of the firebox door. We were provided with a bar to break it up but we really needed the engine back on shed where the redoubtable firedropper could do a more thorough job.

At Swindon shed, the rapid promotions through the links occasioned by the conflict in Europe began to slow down, but I'd already reached the passenger links and during 1946 I was promoted from No. 4 to No. 3 Link where my driver was Ted Veary, known at the shed as 'Dusty Ted'. My time in this link was again fairly short and my memories of it somewhat blurred. Ted Veary was a native of Oxfordshire where he'd been born in 1895, and his first GWR experience had been at Oxford shed, transferring to Swindon in 1935. It is my recollection that he died in the early 1950s without reaching

retirement. Ted always took his teeth out to eat his sandwiches on the footplate, and during the winter it appeared that he sat up there in the cab always wrapped up in his old overcoat, which seemed to remain upon him until the summer timetable came in!

For my reconstruction of this link, sixty years on, I am indebted to the memories of my old colleague Mark Wilkins, who spent four years on No. 3 during 1948–52 as fireman, and also to the discovery of a driver's log book belonging to Bert Withers, which although it chronicles a 12-turn rostering at Swindon for a later period in the 1950s, does give a good idea of the shape and character of the link and appears to record roughly the same work that I undertook with Ted Veary in that period of recovery after the war. We are grateful to Mr. Withers' daughter, Mrs. Margaret Lowe, for access to the log.

No. 3 PASSENGER LINK

TRAIN No. 107 TO WEST EALING, week commencing 27th February 1955

This was an afternoon milk train working, for which Bert had a 'Castle' class engine, No. 4075. We'd book on at 1.45 and come off shed at 2.45 after preparing the locomotive and depart for London at 3.15 p.m. Arrival in West Ealing was about 4.40, then we went to Old Oak Sidings at 5.20. The engine was turned at Ranelagh bridge around 6.50 and we returned with the 8.30 p.m. Paddington parcels bound for Cardiff, calling at Reading at 9.21 and arriving in Swindon at 10.30 p.m. where we booked off. Eventual departure for Cardiff with a fresh crew was at 1.40 a.m. The Saturday working varied with a call at Marston Sidings at 4.5 to pick up fish traffic, and at Wantage Road, returning from London with the 9.25 Paddington parcels.

TRAIN No. 135 TO GLOUCESTER, week commencing Monday 6th March

On his week on this turn Bert had two 'Hall' class engines on the Gloucester run, a newspaper train, Nos. 5977 and 5981, with a 'County' class, No. 1012 also being employed on one day. We usually had four paper vans on this train. We booked on at 2.22 a.m. and prepared the locomotive, left shed at 3.22 and hooked onto our train at the station to leave with the 4.7 Gloucester papers, although preparing the train could result in departure as late as 4.25. Arrival at Gloucester was shortly after 5 a.m. We'd be on Gloucester shed for over an hour, then return to Gloucester Central station at 7.15 to pick up passenger coaches from a train from Cardiff, returning to Swindon with the 7.40 departure from Gloucester, which, as I recall, was a stopper calling at Stonehouse, Stroud and Kemble. Arrival at Swindon was 8.39, then we took the engine to shed where we booked off at 9.15 a.m. This week had a Sunday evening turn booked to Cardiff and back, down via the Badminton line and up via Bristol and Bath.

P.M. SPARE TURN, week commencing Monday 13th March

This was the afternoon spare turn in the link. Bert Withers' log shows that on the Monday he had no job allocated, booking on at 3 p.m. and being allowed off at 10 p.m. when it was clear no job was possible. On the Tuesday he filled in on the West Ealing milk with the return Paddington parcels, the same job he'd been on two weeks previously. The log records a signal stop at Challow on the down trip. The loco was No. 70022, a standard BR class 4–6–0 which were replacing the 'Castles' at that time. On the Wednesday again he was not required, then on the Thursday he worked Train No. 155 with a '36XX' class 0–6–0 pannier tank on the Savernake–Marlborough branch service, for which the log records 1.45 off shed, 2 p.m. at the Transfer and 2.40 at the Loco Yard, which suggests that this was a mixed train with some goods traffic. Arrival at Old Town (Swindon Town) was at 3.5, then two return trips were made between Marlborough and Savernake, leaving the former at 4.21 and 6.5. Arrival back at Swindon was at 9.20 p.m. and he booked off at shed at 10.5. On the Friday he ran the Banbury fish, which involved running box-vans from Grimsby into Marston Sidings just after midnight with BR class No. 73012. On the Saturday he ran the Cardiff milk empties. Withers' firemen during the week were Ayres, Titchener and Boase, the last-named being his regular man, as shown in the log. All jobs done were within No. 3 Link except the branch work, which, as I recall, would have been a case of the Old Town Link pinching a surplus No. 3 relief man to fill in.

TRAIN No. 170 TO BRISTOL, week commencing Monday 20th March

I suspect this was a fairly frustrating week for Withers as the train engine was No. 5068 *Beverston Castle*, which, as Mark Wilkins recalled, "wouldn't steam for nuts". We could never push it beyond 65 mph. This was a morning passenger job with seven coaches, which involved relieving the 9.5 Paddington at Swindon, departing at 10.47 for Temple Meads. This week's work reflects the policy of the roster clerk in trying to ensure that a week on p.m. duties was followed by a week on morning turns. Into Bristol near midday, the coaches were taken to Malago, the coach sidings about two miles beyond Temple Meads. After going to shed, the loco returned to Malago to pick up a fresh set of six coaches after cleaning, then ran a return trip to Swindon with a call at Bath. The crew were relieved at Swindon and booked off shed at 6.30 p.m. There was a Sunday job booked this week showing calls at Hullavington and an eventual destination of Ebbw shed. This may have been a permanent way working. No return working is shown so the crew's return to Swindon would have been 'on the cushions'.

This photo was taken at Banbury in 1944 on a '29XX' class loco when I was preparing the fire while waiting to come down with the fish train. North Eastern men had worked it from Aberdeen as far as Banbury, and we had to come off Banbury shed with our engine and take it on to Swindon. At South Marston it was shunted out – there was a section for South Wales, a section for the West of England, and a pilot engine worked a shift there each night from 8.40 p.m. shunting the fish traffic. A Cardiff crew with loco would depart with the Welsh portion at 11.50 at night, and Swindon men would work the West traffic as far as Taunton, the furthest we went from Swindon in that direction, where a Taunton crew would take over. By this time I was already in No. 3 passenger link with driver Ted Veary, working a lot of passenger trains with heavy parcels traffic.
COLLECTION GORDON SHURMER

TRAIN No. 160 TO BRISTOL, week commencing Monday 27th March

This was an evening turn with the 5.22 passenger and parcels service to Bristol with several 'Castle' class engines during a relatively easy week with local work and Good Friday off. After picking up fresh coach stock at Malago and taking water at Bath Road shed, a return trip via Badminton was made from Temple Meads at 9.25 p.m. and booking off at Swindon shed at 11.10 p.m.

A.M. SPARE TURN, week commencing Monday 3rd April

The early turn relief work undertaken again reflects the variety of work you did when you were spare. Bert's Monday involved a return working to Weston-super-Mare with a ten-coach train hauled by a 'Castle', No. 5023, possibly a Bank Holiday excursion. This was a long day, booking on at 7.25 a.m. and finally booking off at shed at 10.45 p.m. This would have been good money, with time and a half giving 22½ hours pay. On the Tuesday there was no job available, and he was allowed off two hours early. On the Wednesday, Thursday and Friday he relieved Train No. 162, the 5.5 a.m. Paddington parcels with a 14-coach stopper to Bristol hauled by 'County' class No.1012. The Saturday turn was a return passenger trip to Paddington calling at Didcot and Reading with 'County' class No. 1013. This spare week included a Sunday turn with a local job on No. 5985 to Bristol and back.

TRAIN No. 128 to BANBURY, week commencing Monday 10th April

This was a week on the 3.35 p.m. Banbury fish on which Withers had worked on a bit the previous month. We relieved a train which had come up from Cardiff, booking on either a 'Grange', 'Hall' or 'Castle', as verified by the Withers log. On his week the locos were respectively Nos. 6864, 4981 and 5023. Arrival in Banbury was just after 5 p.m. where we'd go to shed until 8 p.m., then we would return to the station to pick up the fish vans arriving from Grimsby, departing at 8.25 p.m. with about 23 box vans of fish. There would be a call to drop off traffic at Oxford and at Marston Sidings, involving a great deal of shunting, especially at the former, then arrival back at Swindon was around midnight, a fairly demanding duty with some useful overtime. The Banbury fish was not regarded as a very important job, especially by signalmen – you didn't get the road, you were not a priority and tended to get stopped at signals for everything.

TRAIN No. 105 TO PADDINGTON, week commencing Monday 17th April

This must have been one of the first diesel-hauled services out of Swindon, Withers recording Nos. 814, 816 and 825 splitting the week with No. 7035, with the 10.47 a.m. to Paddington, returning with the 2 p.m. parcels. The log suggests that the diesels were based at St. Philip's Marsh shed in Bristol at this time, to where they would have returned light after the Paddington duty. There were calls at Didcot in both directions, with the loco being turned at Ranelagh bridge. There was a booked Sunday with a return trip to Cardiff on the 9.55 a.m.. ex-Paddington and loco No. 5013, via the South Wales Direct.

Those 'Saints' were great engines and could really run at high speed. They were first introduced in 1902. This is No. 2947 Madresfield Court, *running past Twyford with a train of milk tanks c.1947.*
J. H. RUSSELL

TRAIN No. 139 to CARDIFF, week commencing Monday 24th April

We booked on at 1.35 p.m. and prepared a 'Castle' class loco to take over the Cardiff milk empties train which had originated from West Ealing. It was booked to leave Swindon at 2.50 p.m. and ran via Badminton and Severn Tunnel Junction to Newport and Cardiff where arrival was just after 5 p.m. The loco was turned on Canton shed and it would appear that for most of the week there was no booked return working for Withers, so it was back 'on the cushions', although the log does show the Wednesday with a return passenger working to Swindon, with arrival back at 9.20 p.m.

TRAIN No. 161 TO BRISTOL, week commencing Monday 1st May

This was an afternoon job on the 2.20 a.m. Bristol parcels. Withers had the new diesels, Nos. 800, 819, 842, and 847. This train called at Bathampton and Bath, with as many as 20 parcel vans on. After leaving the vans at Temple Meads and forty minutes on Bath Road shed, a set of five passenger coaches was collected from Malago with the booked return 6 p.m. to Swindon via Chippenham.

TRAIN No. 103 TO PADDINGTON, week commencing Monday 8th May

At the beginning of the week, Withers had a 'Castle', No. 5017, on this turn and the rest of the week's traction reflected the encroaching dieselisation of the railway. The service was the 8.50 a.m. to Paddington, calling at Wantage Road and Hayes. After arrival at Paddington around 10.30 there was the customary turning of the engine at Ranelagh bridge, then the return working was the 2.55 ex-Paddington with arrival back at Swindon at 4.20 p.m.

TRAIN No. 136 TO CARDIFF, week commencing Monday 15th May

This was not a popular turn as you'd be out of bed around 2 a.m. to take on the 1 a.m. ex-Paddington, a fast passenger train with ten coaches, departing Swindon at 2.55 a.m. for Cardiff via Gloucester. The engine was usually a 'Castle' and arrival in Cardiff was around 5.40 a.m. There was no return working, so at least you had a rest as you rode home passenger. This week had the fourth booked Sunday in the 12-turn cycle with a diesel job, a 1.15 a.m. to Bristol, again with no return working.

No. 2 PASSENGER LINK

I only spent a few months in No. 2 Link with driver Sid Sprules, hence my memories of it are again hazy. Sidney Sprules was born in Marlborough in 1896, and originally came from Surrey. Always interested in the working of steam ploughs and threshing machines as a child, an interest in the railway was natural for him, and he came to Swindon at the outbreak of World War I as a cleaner, lodging first with an aunt and uncle. He spent two years at Tondu in Wales during 1934–6 where he achieved promotion to driver, then he returned to Swindon where he retired in 1961. It was always one of my regrets that because of work I was not able to go to his funeral in June 1980.

Sid was a superb driver to work with, he always treated you as an equal, and was a staunch churchgoer although he never rammed religion down your throat. He was always interested in educating the next generation of drivers and when young firemen were up for promotion they used to go to Sid's house for coaching, where he would use the track and signals from his son's train set to use as a visual aid in classes. He was simply the epitomy of a clean-living man and would always do you a good turn if he could. For piecing this section together I am greatly indebted again to Mark Wilkins, who spent five years on this link during 1952–57.

7.10 p.m. TO BANBURY

We booked on at 6 p.m. and prepared a '49XX' class 4–6–0 locomotive and went to the up side of the station and collected a rake of eight coaches, pulled them out and put them back on the branch platform via the Cocklebury sidings, backing the train into the platform on the north side of the station ('on the branch') with the aid of the shunter. We left at 7.18 p.m. and arrived in Banbury about 9 p.m., calling at Oxford en route. At Banbury we used to go on shed, where we'd wait for a southbound train coming in which was part of a run from York, the 6.25 p.m., during which time we'd have our tea and sandwiches. We used to refer to this turn as the 'Aberdeen'. We'd wait for it coming into the bay at Banbury, then hook up and leave for Swindon where we'd arrive at 2.21 a.m., booking off about 2.45. We used to make about an hour's overtime on this turn.

2.10 a.m. TO WOOD LANE

This was a milk train for which we booked on at 2.05, as the engine was already prepared for us, usually a 'Castle' and often No. 5068. The train was milk tank wagons containing the West of England milk traffic which ran direct to Wood Lane depot, near Old Oak Common. We turned the engine at Ranelagh bridge and came back as the 9.15 passenger from Paddington. With fifteen coaches and leaving from platform 1, this was the heaviest train out of London. We called at Maidenhead, Twyford, Reading and Didcot.

In No. 2 Link in 1946 at Bath. This cab view gives a good close-up of the bell for the Automatic Train Control. ATC was a wonderful thing. It came in during the 1920s and was made in Swindon Works. You needed to know your signals and we Swindon men had a great reputation for safety and learning the road. ATC enabled you to run to London in thick fog without any problem. After the war, the government issued new finance to the railway companies to help them cope with problems caused by the war years, and the GWR spent their money on the ATC on its main lines. It was a safe system – you had a ramp in the middle of the track just before each distant signal and every station, set two inches above rail level. The bell in the cab rang if the signals were at clear, and a siren would buzz if the signals were at caution. If you ignored that siren, the brakes automatically came on. The driver had a handle which would cancel the siren and therefore return control to him. Each shed had an ATC man to check and clean local installations. In foggy conditions with poor visibility, the bell told you when you were passing a distant signal.
COLLECTION GORDON SHURMER

This is a typical example of what happened at Bath station. No. 4084 Aberystwyth Castle *is seen at the head of an up passenger service on the holding siding in between the up and down main lines in July 1949. On the 2.50 p.m. ex-Bristol we would pull over into this siding to allow a fast train through, then resume with a stopper to Swindon. We often took water at the column on the platform and I recall one occasion here where I was really aware of the damage to the Royal Hotel by German bombers during World War 2 – you can see the hotel behind the station to the right, and I could see clearly the scars in the plaster on the walls.*   MILLBROOK HOUSE

11.20 a.m. TO BRISTOL TEMPLE MEADS

The following week we'd book on at 11 a.m. and walk up to the station to relieve the train from Paddington which we'd worked the previous week, and take it on to Temple Meads. The train split at Swindon, the front half going to Bristol and the rear half to Gloucester. On the Bristol trip we'd always try to get up to 100 mph down Dauntsey bank, but we never quite made it. At Bristol we turned the loco at Bath Road shed, and worked a stopping train, the 2.50 p.m. back to Swindon. We called all stations to Bath, where we pulled over into the centre siding to let a fast train through, then ran all stations to Swindon, where we arrived at 5 p.m. The station took the coaches and we went to shed. That engine had done a good job, a full day's work. We booked off at 5.20 p.m.

No. 1 SPARE TURN

If, for instance, the Wood Lane milk fireman was absent, the No. 1 Spare fireman would fill in on that turn. You could relieve a train in any link as long as it was within that booked period, the early turn in this case. It wasn't very often you sat in the cabin, although Mark recalled playing 'shove ha'penny' on several occasions during the wait to be called. In this situation, No. 2 Link had priority over you, but if there was nobody off in your link you could be sent to any of the other links.

No. 2 SPARE TURN

Again, you were sitting in the messroom until allocated a job on the afternoon turn. Thinking back all those years, I can never remember being on a spare turn and not having a job. Even if it was only a factory pilot duty, you covered the depot.

7.20 a.m. to BRISTOL TEMPLE MEADS

This was a stopping train for which we would book on at 5.40 a.m. as we needed a good hour and a half to prepare a 'Castle' class loco.

This was another passenger service which was used as a running-in turn for engines just out of the Works, which had undergone their initial trial run in the Van Link. The engine could be anything – a 'Castle', 'King', a '49XX' or a '78XX'. Once the loco was ready, we would go up to the sidings by Whitehouse bridge and collect six coaches and bring them into the station 'on the branch', on the south side of the station. We ran all stations to Bristol, and at Chippenham the driver would normally get down with a feeder and put the back of his hand on the hotboxes to check that they weren't over-heating. He'd do the same at Bath. Into Temple Meads at 9 a.m. the process would be repeated with more oiling, then we'd take the coaches to Dr. Day's sidings, which was the way in which the busy platforms at Bristol were kept clear of stock. We'd be on shed at Bath Road for about an hour, then had to go back light to collect four coaches for another stopper back to Swindon, leaving at 11 a.m. and arriving back in Swindon at 1 p.m. The coaches were put back in the Water Sidings by one of the station pilots and we'd leave the loco on the engine shed rank by the coal stage ready for the attention of men in the shed & coal stage link. It was the driver's responsibility to write in the report book anything untoward concerning the running-in turn that needed bringing to the shed foreman's attention. We booked off about 1.15 p.m.

9.20 a.m. TO GLOUCESTER

This was also a running-in job, all stations to Gloucester, a passenger train with four coaches, calling at Purton, Minety & Ashton Keynes, Oaksey, Kemble (where we would take water at the column), Chalford, Brimscombe, Stroud and Stonehouse with a 10.30 arrival at Gloucester. There the shunter would uncouple and we'd go to shed, where we had a long wait before returning with the 2.20 p.m. Sometimes crews would leave the engine on shed and go over to the nearby market where you could get a good deal on

A late 1940s Swindon view in the 'narrowbacks', the back alleys between Alfred Street (to the left) and Ponting Street (right), where Sid Sprules lived at No. 67. The backs of houses in the distance were in Manchester Road. This very public-spirited shot shows Sid giving local youngsters a ride on what appears to be a GWR handcart, and was almost certainly taken after Sid brought home some scrap timber from the Works on it. Every so often there'd be allocations of wood made available to GWR employees, resulting from a coach demolition or clearance in the sawmills, which a keen DIY man might use to fashion a shelf, bookcase or other useful item at home.

CTY. SYDNEY SPRULES

These two pictures were taken in Swindon station when I was on No. 2 Link and I dimly remember that Sid brought a small camera to work and we photographed each other here, oiling the outside of the big end of an unidentified 'Castle' class locomotive, and on the driver's side of the cab next to the water column while waiting at Swindon's down platform. I can still hear him asking me "What d'y' think we should do now, matey?"

CTY. SYDNEY SPRULES

Sid sitting on the front of a 'Castle' class 4–6–0, Shrewsbury Castle, in Bath station in 1946. The single headlamp indicates that we were working a Swindon–Bristol stopper, almost certainly the 7.20 a.m. service detailed on page 149.
CTY. SYDNEY SPRULES

Again in Bath station, I am seen here in the cab of No. 5062, a 'Castle' class 4–6–0 Earl of Shaftesbury, *during my time in No. 2 Link.*
COLLECTION GORDON SHURMER

Brimscombe station on 10th October 1948, with the 10.45 ex-Paddington calling en route to Cheltenham, timetabled at 1.15 p.m. out of Brimscombe. This view looks west towards Stroud with the goods shed to the right. Brimscombe was normally served by the Chalford railcar and Swindon–Gloucester locals – the 1.15 was the only large passenger train to call there in the forties. We shunted this station on those occasions that we made it this far towards Gloucester on the pick-up goods, but if the Gloucester crew with whom we changed footplates were playing the game, we would normally swap over at Coates. On No. 2 Link our 9.20 a.m. to Gloucester that called here was a running-in job for engines just out of the L E COPELAND

No. 4995 Easton Hall *heading a four-coach stopping passenger train over the Goring troughs on the down relief on the approach to Goring & Streatley station. This presents a good view of the water troughs we used many times. This view was taken towards Pangbourne.*

plums and apples especially. We'd avoid making tea at Gloucester because of the consistency of the water there. We'd be back in Swindon at 4 p.m. and book off at 4.15. I remember doing tutoring on this run in diesel days when the Hymeks came in.

1.05 a.m. TO BRISTOL

This was a parcels train from London which we relieved. We booked on at about 12.45 a.m. and were allowed 20 minutes walking time to the station where we'd take on the train, usually an Old Oak-based '49XX' class or a 'Hall'. We would call at Chippenham and Bath to collect more vans, and parcels for those places would be removed. We'd shunt the parcel vans into the parcel bay in Temple Meads, where we would arrive at 3 a.m., then go to shed. After grabbing some sleep in the cabin at Bath Road, we'd go to Dr Day's sidings to collect four coaches, then return with an early passenger stopper to Swindon along the South Wales Direct, the 7.30 a.m. via Badminton and Little Somerford. The station pilot would deal with the coaches and we'd book off at shed about 9.15 a.m.

2 p.m. TO PADDINGTON

This was a semi-fast passenger and parcels to London, calling at Uffington, Didcot, Reading and Maidenhead. We'd book on at 1 p.m. and prepare a '49XX' class and arrival in Paddington would be at 4 p.m. We returned with a fast from London to Reading, leaving about 6 p.m., then called all stations to Swindon where arrival would be about 8 p.m.

2.55 a.m. TO NEYLAND

We booked on at 2.30 and relieved the 1 a.m. Paddington to Neyland passenger and mail train at the station which ran via Gloucester, calling at Reading, Kemble, Stroud and Stonehouse. This was usually a ten-coach passenger train which included a sleeping car. We worked this train as far as Cardiff and travelled back 'on the cushions', on a passenger train which was a return working in Swindon No. 1 link.

Another of the photos taken of me at Swindon, oiling the outside of the big end of an unidentified 'Castle' class.
COLLECTION GORDON SHURMER

Bill Hinder (1890-1979), my gaffer during 1947-55, seen at the controls of a 'Castle' 4−6−0 at Chippenham around 1949. Swindon born, he was a callboy first, then cleaner, and spent part of his early career at Cheltenham shed. Very meticulous of habit, his foodbox in which he brought his lunch to work was an Edinburgh-made tin box bearing his name on a brass plate. The wooden tip-up seats in the cabs of GWR locos were quite spartan and he always took the torn cushion with him on the footplate to try to make things a little more comfortable. It was kept in his locker for years. With his blue overalls and black tweed cap, this is just how he used to look at work − I learned a great deal from him in our seven years together.

KENNETH LEECH

CHAPTER SIX

BILL HINDER

WHEN I reached the top link as fireman in 1947, one of the most important jobs at Swindon, I remember my first meeting with Bill Hinder, with whom I was to work for seven years. He looked at me firmly and told me straight: "Promotion is rather slow at the moment, matey. It looks as though you'll be with me for some time, and I'll tell you right from the start, I like things to be right. If we get a small thing develop on the footplate we'll deal with it before it becomes a big job. Naturally, there will be times when you have to inform me of the position of signals, and when you do that, whether the signal is at caution or at clear, before you pick up that shovel and start firing the loco again, I want you to look again at that signal to check that what you told me was correct."

I never forgot those words and they still remain with me today. That was our first conversation, our first day together, on the shed at Swindon. In the seven years that we were a team we never had a single cross word. I was still single, living at home at this time. Every day Bill used to bring me in a piece of cake in his foodbox, and he used to say to me, "No steam, no bloody cake!" In other words, if I let the pressure down, then I didn't earn that treat! The type of cake varied, but it was always home-made by Bill's wife Flo. I recall there was a time when I was off work for a week or so with the flu, he came round to my house. Mum answered the door and there he was – "I haven't seen your lad for a fortnight, Mrs. Shurmer, and my missus says he has to have his cake!" He'd brought round a full cake in a round tin which his wife had baked. They lived up the top of Cricklade Road, near The Moonrakers. A Swindon man, he was very fussy – the footplate had to be kept clean, and his home was likewise.

The jobs in No. 1 Link were all pretty hard ones. One thing I really appreciated about my new boss was that he'd never let *anyone* interfere with me. If we stopped at a station and a locomotive Inspector got up on the footplate and said "Going to ride a while with you, driver", Bill would say, "OK, now you get up in my mate's corner and look out of his eyeglass, and whatever you do, don't you pester my fireman, because if he can't do it, you and I won't do it." And the Inspector would nod assent and get up there in the corner and that would be that.

Those first twelve weeks of work in No. 1 Link, if you worked it right through, included two booked Sundays. I still have paybills to prove that those twelve weeks' work all added up together came to £75 11s 6d, and in No. 1 link it was *work*, no easy jobs. It was all long-distance – London, Cardiff, Leicester. This was a very demanding link in many ways, working the fast passenger expresses, although it wasn't all non-stop services and there was a lot of arduous night work. This was the main problem for Swindon men, in that No. 1 Link had many workings which required very anti-social hours. Only with the 7.50 a.m. and 9.18 morning trains to Paddington could you work both ways within your shift and still have time to go out in the evening, so for this reason No. 1 was not considered a good link at Swindon and you really earned your money in it. But, of course, it was where the good money was, with the top passenger expresses, the 'railbenders', as we called them. Prestigious express jobs went to the drivers with seniority; if it was 'A' headlamps, and you were the senior man, you got the job.

No. 1 PASSENGER LINK *26th March 1949 (12 turns)*

4.10 a.m. TO GLOUCESTER

This was a newspaper train, six bookings for a week's work. We would book on duty at 2.50 a.m., prepare the locomotive, a 4–6–0 of the 'Hall' or '49XX' class. The train came in from London and was split at Swindon, the front half going to Bristol, the rear half to Gloucester, We would couple on to this rear half and take the train to Gloucester, with a call at Stroud at 4.51 where newspapers would be unloaded. Arrival at Gloucester was at 5.20 a.m. and after leaving the paper vans in the bay, we'd go to shed and turn the engine, then grab a couple of hours sleep before working the 9.40 stopping train back to Swindon , where we'd arrive at 10.40 a.m. This now became the 10.53 fast train to London after we'd been relieved, joining the Bristol portion of the train.

4.07 p.m. TO BRISTOL

This was five bookings to Bristol each evening, returning with a parcels train. This turn included a Sunday working in front of it, preparing a 'Castle' or '59XX' class engine and working the 12.32 p.m. fast to Paddington, calling Didcot and Reading, then working back with the 3.20 p.m. stopper which called virtually everywhere, all the wayside stations, so we were not back into Swindon until about 7 p.m.

7.50 a.m. TO PADDINGTON

This was a passenger train calling at Didcot and Reading. We booked on at 6.30 a.m. and prepared a Castle class 4–6–0. After arrival at Paddington, we would turn the engine at Ranelagh bridge, then run light to West Ealing to take on the 12.10 milk empties to Whitland. We arrived back in Swindon to book off about 4.15 p.m. and this was six bookings including the Saturday.

5.35 a.m. TO WESTBURY

We booked on at 4.10 a.m. and prepare a 'Prairie' class 2–6–2 locomotive and ran a passenger service to Westbury, calling at Chippenham at 5.52, then via Thingley Junction, calling 6.31 at Trowbridge and into Westbury at 6.48 a.m. Every other day we would work through to Frome. This was just two coaches, a Bristol Division B-set, and we returned with a similar passenger service, 8.45 out of Westbury and back into Swindon at 10.16 a.m. One occasion I recall clearly on this run was when I was working a spare

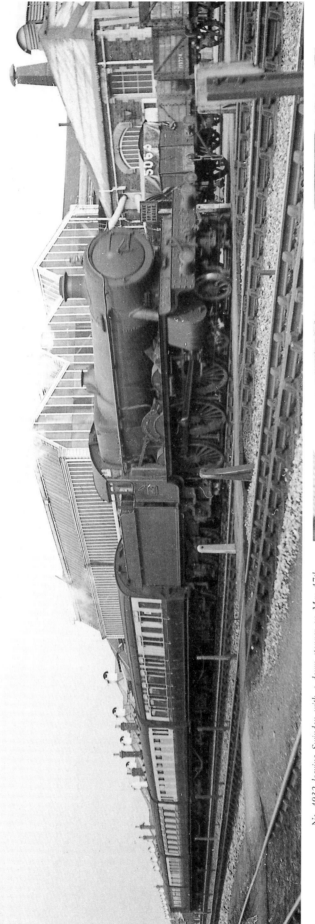

No. 4932 leaving Swindon with a down stopper on May 17th 1937.

L. HANSON

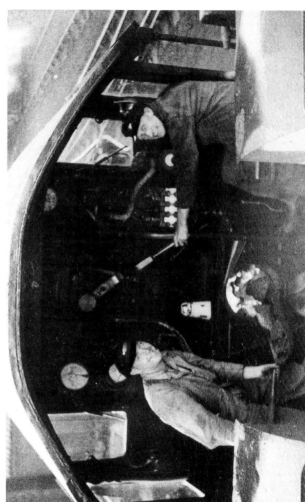

Me on the shovel and Bill on the regulator in Gloucester yard in the early 1950s. We'd already turned the engine and were waiting to come up with the 9.40 a.m. stopping train, all stations to Swindon. At Swindon our train linked up with a portion from Bristol to form the 10.53 to Paddington. The tops of two toolboxes are visible in the lower corners of the picture, the left one containing flags and detonators, the right one our foodboxes. Visible above my head is the steam pressure gauge. The four white areas above Bill's arm were the sight feeds of the lubricator, full of water. We could estimate our speed from the clickety-clack on the track and the speed at which we passed telegraph poles.

KENNETH LEECH

Gross Wages	Income Tax	Deductions	Date	Ticket No.	Net Wages		Sunday	Week Days			
7.3.7	17.0	8.3	JAN 8	351.	5.18.4	Jan 8	✓	4.10 Gloster 6 Bookings	£5	18	4
7.13.7	1.0.0	9.1	JAN 15	351	6.4.6	Jan 15	12/32 Padd	4/7 Bristol 5 Bookings	£6	4	6
6.13.7	14.0	8.13	JAN 22	351	5.11.4	Jan 22	✓	7.50 Padd 6 Bookings	£5	11	4
6.3.8	13.0	8.3	JAN 29	351.	5.2.5	Jan 29	✓	5.35 Westbury 5 Bookings	£5	2	5
11.19.4	1.19.0	8.3	FEB 5	351.	9.12.1	Feb 5	✓	9/40 Leicester 6 Bookings	£9	12	1
6.12.11	15.0	9.1	FEB 12	351.	5.8.10	Feb 12	✓	3/17 Weston-S-Mare 5 Bookings	£5	8	10
6.1.8	12.0	8.3	FEB 19	351.	5.1.5	Feb 19	✓	9.0 Padd 6 Bookings	£5	1	5
9.11.5	1.8.0	8.3	FEB 26	351.	7.15.2	Feb 26	7/6 Padd	7/6 Padd 5 Bookings	£7	15	2
6.12.11	14.0	16.1	MAR 5	351.	5.2.10	Mar 5	✓	1st Spare 6 Bookings	£5	10	8
8.13.6	1.4.0	9.1	MAR 12	351.	7.0.5	Mar 12	10.26 Padd	2nd Spare 5 Bookings	£7	0	5
7.0.11	17.0	16.1	MAR 19	351.	5.7.10	Mar 19	✓	2.35 Cardiff 6 Bookings	£5	15	8
7.18.11	1.0.0	8.3	MAR 26	351.	6.10.8	Mar 26	10.45 Padd	1/34 Oxford 5 Bookings	£6	10	8
								Total	£75	11	6

Gordon's wage slips and details of earnings.

turn with driver Bert Huntley. North of Westbury on the down trip we were stopped at the signal at Yarnbrook Signal Box – it may have been for single-line working but I can't be sure. At such a stop it was the fireman's duty to carry out rule 55 and go up into the signal cabin and sign the train register to prove he'd been up there and verify the stop. The signalman would also initial it as an indication that he was aware that there was a train stopped outside his box and that the relevant signals were at danger. I climbed up the steps, and as I opened the cabin door a raucous voice yelled "Wipe yer bloody boots!" Some of those signalmen were very fussy and houseproud in their domain, with shiny floors and well-polished levers – you'd even see some of them wearing slippers! When I got back to the loco, I commented on the miserable bugger I'd met up in the signal box. Well, as you might expect, on the return up trip, we were stopped again at Yarnbrook and it was obvious to Bert that I didn't fancy meeting my signalman chum again so soon! "Leave this to me," he grinned, and went to the oilbox and tipped out some of the contents onto the footplate. He then stepped in it several times, heels only, and proceeded on tip-toe up to the signal box, and as he opened the cabin door, even above the noise of the footplate, I heard the same stern admonition from the signalman! Except this time, Bert stumbled inside, apparently confused and surprised, traipsing a score of oily footprints all over the shiny floor! I heard further pleasantries being exchanged in the box, then Bert returned and commented "I don't think there'll be any further trouble from 'im, lad!"

9.40 p.m. TO LEICESTER

The Leicester was the best-paying job at Swindon and stands out financially very clearly on the accompanying list. It was recognised as a double week's work, and men were known to alter their holidays to ensure that they didn't miss this trip. It was part of a through service to York, and would always be a 'Hall', a '59XX' class 4-6-0 locomotive. In my day No. 5900, *Hinderton Hall,* was booked on this trip for a long time. It was nominally a passenger service although I don't recall a lot of passengers on it. We booked on duty at 9.20 p.m. and walked to the station where the locomotive was already on the train for us. We didn't prepare the engine on this run as we were going to be on it all night, a long tough trip on which I really earned my £9 12s 1d. We'd call at Oxford, Banbury, Woodford Halse, Rugby, and thence to Leicester Central, where we arrived at 1.06 a.m. if on schedule. At Leicester we'd come into contact with the LNER from Marylebone and Doncaster men from the LNER, and it was the northern men who would work the train on to York. We'd work back from Leicester at 2.14 a.m., arriving back in Swindon Junction at 5.45 a.m. and we were relieved at the station because of the long turn we'd been on, another crew taking the loco to shed. This run worked out at 88 hours' pay with the night rate and the mileage, and if we were lucky enough to work a Sunday in front of that week's work, then that was another 14 hours on top, raising it to a 102-hour week.

A wonderful photograph of No. 7037 Swindon outside the shed. This was the last of the 'Castle' class 4–6–0s to be built in the Works. The 'Not to be Moved' sign above the buffer beam was in position because work was being done on the engine. There may well have been somebody underneath. Several cleaners are seen here with oil-soaked rags and cotton waste in hand, whilst the driver is seen oiling near the cab.

AUTHOR'S COLLECTION

Bill and I at Chippenham in the late '40s, bound for Weston-super-Mare on the 1.18 ex-Paddington, having just come on to relieve a Swindon crew who'd brought the train from London with No. 6018 King Henry IV. *We'd leave for Weston at 3.05, 5.25 into Weston, then work the 8.15 stopper back to Swindon, which called at 22 stations with an 11.20 arrival.* KENNETH LEECH

3.17 p.m. TO WESTON-SUPER-MARE

We booked on at 2.45 p.m., walked up to the station and relieved the 1.18 Paddington, which was the return working of the 9 a.m. from Swindon, and we would make station stops at Chippenham, Bath, Temple Meads, and Yatton on the way. This would normally be a 'Castle' class engine, often No. 5068 *Beverston Castle*, or No. 7037 *Swindon*. After a 5.25 arrival in Weston, we'd turn the engine on the turntable there, then work the 8.17 stopper back to Swindon. This was a rough job, with the loco having been on since 9 a.m. We would pick up some milk tanks at Puxton & Worle and this run involved calls at 22 stations en route! We'd be the 9.34 p.m. out of Temple Meads, and by the time we got back to Swindon at 11.15 p.m. the tender would be empty and the clinker and ashes were rolling out of the firebox doors!

9 a.m. TO PADDINGTON

This was a crack passenger service, and we booked on at the shed at 7.30 to prepare the loco, always a 'Castle, took on the coaches from the platform where they'd been left by the Up Weston the night before, and ran to Paddington, calling at Didcot and Reading. We turned the engine at Ranelagh bridge, then reversed back into Paddington to rejoin our rake of coaches, then worked the 1.18 back to Swindon where we were relieved at 3 p.m. This was the service we ourselves had been relieving during the previous week's work.

7 p.m. TO PADDINGTON

This was a train of empty stock, a mixture of old parcel vans which had been renovated in the Works, with some new vans (as many as 12), which we took up to London with a 'Castle' class locomotive

New Year's Day, 1948, the GWR is now BR Western Region and No. 5032 Usk Castle is captured at Paddington's No. 1 departure platform, possibly with 'The Owl' referred to on page 161.

to enter service from there. Shunting engines had brought them out of the carriage shops and stood them on 'The Bank' at the east end of the station which was where we collected them. We turned the engine at Ranelagh bridge, then worked the 1 a.m. passenger to Swansea, known as 'The Owl', back to Swindon for 2.45 a.m. This was a good paying week, as there was a Sunday turn in front of it, the 7.6 p.m. Paddington.

1st SPARE AND SECOND SPARE

There were consecutive weeks of spare turns in No. 1 Link, which meant that on the first week you could be called upon to cover anything between midnight and midday on relief, and on the second you covered the midday to midnight part of the day. Spare turns could be anything – a different turn every day, or just in the messroom playing cards or, in my case, studying the rulebook, when you had no booked work, simply awaiting the foreman's orders. In front of these spare turns Bill and I always worked the 10.25 a.m. Sunday service to Paddington, returning with the 3.20 Down which stopped everywhere – Southall, Slough, Maidenhead, Twyford, Cholsey & Moulsford, Steventon, everywhere. We always had a 'Castle' 4–6–0 on this run and arrived back in Swindon at 7 p.m.

2.35 a.m. TO CARDIFF

This was our most demanding and anti-social turn of all, the Cardiff papers, the one I almost missed on one occasion through oversleeping. We would book on at 1.55 a.m., read the relevant notices about the route, then work the train which had left Paddington at 12.45 a.m., usually headed by a 'Castle' class locomotive. It was first stop Newport for us, then we'd leave the paper vans in the bay in Cardiff station around 4 a.m., and take the loco to Canton shed for re-coaling. Here we would give the coalmen armfuls of newspapers from the first paper van next to the loco, a ploy intended to ensure that we obtained the best coal, smaller pieces which didn't need a

lot of breaking up. During the War, this had been the turn on which I had fired for notorious Swindon hardman Chris Brown, who used to grab some sleep in the cab with newspapers spread over the floor of the cab before leaving with the 6.15 from Cardiff. Every other day our return train would be the boat train from Fishguard, 14 coaches, a tough job, and we would wait on the middle road in Cardiff station for the Fishguard to come in, the loco would cut off and go to shed, and we would come out and back onto the train for our run to Swindon. This was heavy work for the fireman, with calls at Newport, Severn Tunnel Junction and Badminton, with arrival at Swindon at 10.04 a.m. where we were relieved by London men. The six bookings for the week's work did not even net £1 a day in pay. Sometimes a 'County' class 4–6–0 would appear on this trip. I didn't like this class much – they were very poor at maintaining steam pressure and it seemed that no one could get them to steam freely. I was always especially annoyed when No. 1003 *County of Wilts* turned up, as this was probably the worst of the lot. I always reckoned that Old Oak put her on that run in the hope of getting rid of her.

1.34 p.m. TO OXFORD

We booked on at 1 p.m. dinner time and relieved Westbury men on a train from Weymouth. The loco would usually be a '59XX', 'Hall', but occasionally a '29XX' class 4–6–0 'Court' would appear, such as *Dorney Court* or *Madresfield Court*, and we would work non-stop to Oxford where we'd turn the engine and work an all-stations to Reading. The loco would be turned again on Reading shed, then we'd run as a stopper back to Swindon, the 4.55, which had originated as the 2.28 ex-Paddington, calling all stations to Didcot, then Steventon, Wantage Road, Challow, connecting for Faringdon at Uffington, Shrivenham and arriving back at Swindon at 6.55 p.m.

A down stopper after arrival at Swindon headed by No. 6965 Thirlestaine Hall *c.1947. Swindon's down side buildings are looking fairly dilapidated by now.*

L&GRP

A stunning view at Swindon coal stage in 1947, defining power, strength, hard graft and permanence, and yet now all gone. No. 2947 Madresfield Court was the first large passenger engine that I cleaned during my days on the shed in 1936. I often worked this locomotive on the No. 1 Link job to Oxford. Here she is seen about to receive coal for another trip. On a busy day, three men would move ninety tons of coal here, two shovelling from the wagon into tubs, the third on the tip, as seen above the cab here. At right you see an open wagon labelled 'LOCO', full of ash following the attention of the firedroppers and the ashloaders. The corrugated addition above the elevated road to the coal stage was provided so that coalmen could at least perform their arduous work under shelter.
H. C. CASSERLEY

A 1948 scene looking out from the locomotive shed across the yard, with a 'Hall' class 4–6–0 being prepared for the road at left and a pannier tank, probably the shed pilot, simmering at centre. The coal stage and the elevated road through it are seen to the right.

A. C. STERNDALE

Paddington terminus in 1951. Bill and I came through here so many times. This shows the main departure platforms, 1, 2, 3 and 4 to the left and the arrival platforms 5, 6, 7, and 8 to the right.

A. C. STERNDALE

It should be emphasised that the composition and structure of the links was constantly changing over the years, so in piecing this together it has been necessary to work as far as possible from a specific period in time as the work evolved, timetables altered and the workforce fluctuated in numbers, with roster clerks always trying to balance the work out so that road knowledge remained as constant as possible throughout the crews. Clearly, the later introduction and development of the diesels also had a great effect on the preparation and administration of the links, and it is my recollection, for instance, that at Swindon the No. 4 passenger link became mostly local passenger work undertaken by the new diesel multiple-unit sets.

My favourite job was the Leicester 9.40 p.m. out of Swindon (on the Saturday run it was 10.05 p.m.) – wonderful job that was. Every driver and fireman wanted to be in No. 1 Link because the Leicester run provided you with a double week's pay, mileage and the night rate, and on the Sunday you got time and three-quarters, so you were paid for 14 hours instead of the statutory eight. Men at Swindon shed were known to change their holidays if they discovered that they'd booked a vacation and it clashed with their week on the Leicester – it was that important. A day's work was considered to be 114 miles, and for every 15 miles over this you received an hour's pay, so with 206 miles on the round trip you can see how it doubled your money! This run was the longest worked from Swindon. Locomotive men would pay all their main bills then as that job came up every twelve weeks.

The Leicester was a passenger and parcels service, basically a mail train, although unsurprisingly there were not many passengers on it. A lot of time was spent waiting at various stations while parcels were unloaded from it, especially on the return trip, about 25 minutes per stop. Bill used to put his coat over his head and sleep in Banbury station while we were there on the way back, with a "Give us a shout when they're ready, mate!" I always brewed three cans of tea on the trip, one at Oxford going up, one at Leicester around 1.30 a.m. and another at Oxford on the way back. First call on the outward run was Oxford, where we could be stationary for half-an-hour while mail was taken off and more loaded, then on to Banbury where the wait could be up to 45 minutes. Then it was on to Woodford Halse, now on Great Central metals, Coalworth Junction, Rugby, and into Leicester at 1.06 a.m. Then we'd turn the loco on the turntable. We were grateful for this because at that time in Swindon we used to have to push our turntables round, but at Leicester the Midland Region had what was called a vacuum turntable. You would couple up your vacuum pipes on the table and the driver would create his own vacuum, with the handbrake on, and the turntable would go round on its own. We'd work back from Leicester at 2.14 a.m. back into Swindon at 5.45.

The latest engine assigned to the depot at Swindon was always put on the Leicester job. On the Monday night, Bill would spend time setting and adjusting the lubricator for maximum efficiency. By the Tuesday night she'd be a different locomotive altogether, free-running, and after he'd had her three nights she'd be as smooth as a sewing machine. It was Bill's experience that made the difference.

Another thing about the Leicester was that your loco was prepared and put on the head of the train for you, because you were on that full eight hours when you got back in! In my time only Swindon crews worked the Leicester run, but in earlier years, before the War, the work had been shared with LNER men. I think they were Leeds men, and it was a shared arrangement whereby one company would work the trip for an 18-month period, then it would pass to the other company for a similar time. The reason for this was to work off mileage that the GWR and the LNER owed to each other for working over the other company's rails, so they used the Leicester as a reciprocal arrangement to even things up. For the crews it was a double-home working – the LNER crew would work right through to Swindon from Leeds and stay in lodgings before working back next day.

I'll never forget a remarkable time in 1951 when Bill and I had a London working. It was an early-morning turn, booking on at Swindon to work the 2.08 Up postal, calling at Didcot and Reading, arriving in Paddington at 4 a.m. We only had this duty for a few weeks, and we'd walk up to the station and relieve Bristol men on a turn which had no return working. We were diagrammed to return to Swindon 'on the cushions' as passengers on the first available train, which was the 9.05 out of Paddington, so we had five early-morning hours in the capital. On this particular summer's morning it was just getting light, and I went in the messroom for a cup of tea with Bill, then decided to go out for a walk.

"Make sure you get back for the nine-five," called Bill as I left, "I'm going to get my head down for a couple hours."

I walked up the slope out of Paddington station, up Praed Street, into Edgeware Road, where I turned right to Marble Arch, then walked up Oxford Street past Selfridges, as far as Oxford Circus, then turned right down Regent Street to Picadilly, around Eros, and back, along the other side of Regent Street. As I passed Selfridges again, I was aware of the clump of my feet on the pavement and could see my nervous reflection in the window of the department store. Finally, when I got back into Paddington about 7 o'clock, it struck me that in all that distance and time I never saw a single living soul – not a milkman, not a policeman, not even a road-sweeper. The West End of London was completely deserted. It was quite eerie, and I felt I was the only person in the whole world. Back in the crews' mess room, Bill brought me down to earth with a bump! When I told him of my solitary walk, his sole comment was "What other silly bugger'd be walking about the streets of London this time o'the morning?"

The footplate was a workshop on wheels, two men and a machine working together, and if you couldn't work in harmony, then you didn't get the efficiency. Bill was a remarkable man – if we weren't doing so well and I couldn't maintain steam pressure, he'd say, "What's the matter with 'er, then, mate?" And if I could tell him I would – "Well, we've got poor coal, the fire's dirty with old clinker, I can't get sufficient heat out to boil the water, pressure is back a little bit, or the tubes are blocked and she's not drawing the air like she should." If I could tell him what was wrong, he would help me – he would ease the regulator off and coast the loco, but if I couldn't tell him, he would say, "Well, it's you, then!" And then he wouldn't help, but would just drive the loco like he always drove it. Bill was a fine engineman, who would never knock an engine about. But if we had poor coal and/or blocked tubes, there wasn't the suction on the fire which was what kept the fire bright. If the tube plate was caulked over with clinker and ashes, then the heat of fire wasn't boiling the water sufficiently, so your steam pressure would be back a little bit. If the steam pressure fell below 85% of the maximum, you had a job to keep time, because the pressure was on every square inch of the piston head, with the result that the wheels were not being turned as eagerly as they should. Clearly, to lose time would delay trains behind you.

It annoyed me when they issued poor-combustion coal to an express passenger train. You need a quick return of heat with a fierce fuel. On a long run it meant that the driver would be using more steam than a fireman could create and maintain. After the War we seldom got the fuel for which the GWR Belpaire fireboxes were designed. Although the GWR had their own coalfields in South Wales, there was still the need to economise after hostilities, so the bane of our lives was the cheap foreign coal we were given, and, worse still, the use of briquettes which were a mixture of coal dust and cement. Your face'd be like a lobster when you came home where the cement dust had burned you. This fuel came in great big squares, a foot across and six inches deep, and they had to be cracked before they'd go in the firebox. Bill once told me that Don Woodley, his fireman before me, demanded to go to Park House to see a doctor because of the problems the briquettes caused his eyes.

In all the years I worked with Bill, I never missed one turn on the 2.35 a.m. Cardiff paper train, although there was one occasion when I overslept and didn't get to the shed in time for the 4.7 Gloucester papers, and another when I almost missed the Cardiff. It's still fresh in my memory how early one morning in the early '50s, when I was still living at home, my Dad came into my bedroom and shouted:

"What time you on duty?"

"One fifty-five" I groggily replied in my half-asleep state.

"It's gone two o'clock already" Dad yelled.

I suppose I just hadn't heard my callboy. I jumped out of bed, frenziedly grabbed my clothes, shoved my boots on, never bothered to tie them up, grabbed my lunchbox which was already packed, then ran out of the house, all the way through the sleeping town. When I reached the tunnel entrance in Bristol Street, I shouted to the watchman as I clocked on "Tell the shed – Shurmer, Cardiff!"

Then I ran up the slope onto the traversing table and stood by the main line. The Cardiff was stood up at West Box and I heard Bill touch the whistle. In the bright lights around the end of the traverser I stood out on the main line, frantically waving my arms towards the train as it eased away from the signal box. I remember thinking, "Thank God he's seen me!" then I was aware that Bill was shutting the regulator, and

the train drifted towards me, allowing me to jump onto the steps of the cab with the loco in gentle motion. Bill didn't actually stop, and as I climbed onto the footplate, Jackie Lawrence, whom the Foreman had put in there to replace me, climbed down the other side, hopped down and disappeared into the night back to the shed. I was so out of breath we'd gone well past Wootton Bassett before I could fire the engine.

When I booked on next day, the timeclerk said to me "You got to see the Shift Foreman." Well, I thought he was going to compliment me for my initiative, but when I got in there, I was in for a rude surprise! George Horley, with fire in his eyes, gave me a real dressing down! "Don't you EVER do a bloody stupid trick like that again. If you or Jackie had been hurt, sprained an ankle on the ballast or, God forbid, fallen under the wheels, we should never have heard the bloody last of it!" There was I expecting praise, and got one hell of a rollicking! That was as close as I ever came to missing the Cardiff paper train!

Bill never ever made a station stop without an oil can in his hand. He'd been down on the floor going around his loco, oiling different parts. Of all the drivers I knew or worked for no one used an oil can as much as he did. He would even oil the catches on the windows! Where the whistle chain went through a chute he'd get a twig and dip it in the oilpot and push it through the chute to ensure the inside of the tube was lubricated – this used to annoy me as the oil might be dripping down on me as I was shovelling. Honestly, he would oil places on a locomotive that many drivers didn't know existed!

In November 1952 London suffered from five days of serious smog, the combined effects of fog and air pollution. So many people died that undertakers were running out of coffins, and animals were dying in Smithfield Market. Several memories stick in my mind from that time. One night we arrived in the capital in thick fog and, as usual, I liked to hang out over the side of the cab at the platform in Paddington because it was always interesting to see the detraining passengers going by. On this particular night I was surprised by Anna Neagle, the film star, who came up and said "Thank you driver (which I wasn't, of course!) for a safe journey." There were often famous personalities passing through – I once saw Alf Garnett himself (Warren Mitchell) and on another occasion Godfrey from *Dad's Army*. Fathers with young children would come up to have a look at the engine, and Bill was always very accommodating, usually asking them up to have a look around the cab.

Then there was the foggy night we arrived at Paddington a few minutes late and this pompous old boy came up to the engine. I was leaning over my side of the cab and he said to me, "You lost a couple of minutes, driver, between Paddington and here!" So I replied, "I'm not the driver."

Bill came over – "What's up?"

"I was just letting your fireman know that you lost two minutes between Reading and here."

"Tell you what, guv'nor," Bill retorted cuttingly, "I'll look for them two buggers on the way back when the mist clears!"

No. 7011 Banbury Castle ready to leave Paddington with the 1.18 to Weston-super-Mare in July 1948. This was the No. 1 Link job detailed on page 159, which Bill and I worked as a back-working from the 9.0 a.m. ex-Swindon.
R. F. ROBERTS

That's the type of man he was – very witty, didn't suffer fools gladly, and always had a rejoinder. Eight hours on the footplate with Bill was no time at all!

At night Bill was just superb. He always knew just where he was – he could tell by the smell of different factories, be it paint, chocolate, fish, or the pungent aromas around the North Somerset Junction about a mile from Temple Meads, which was known as 'Oxo' or 'Bovril' Junction, after the smells emanating from a factory where animal bones were melted down for glue production. Bill would know the rattle of different points, the presence of different foundations under the track, and the echoes under different bridges. He'd be able to estimate our speed from the ticking of the vacuum pump on the engine, as you could with the clickety-click of the wheels passing over the section of rail. This awareness was vital. For instance, there were places where bridges were rather low, and sometimes, if the engine was not doing too well, the fireman would want to get the pricker out of the back of the tender to poke the fire. On a big loco that poker was thirteen feet long. The firebox on a King class locomotive was 11ft 6 inches long and you needed eighteen inches sticking out of the firebox door for you to handle. So, of course, when I took that pricker down, it stood above the height of the cab. Bill could see a reflection of me working in the tender via his eye glass, and if danger was imminent there would be an urgent shout – "Not yet, matey!" That was because we were approaching a bridge in the dark. If that pricker had caught in the arch of the bridge, I would have been pulled out of the cab to certain death. There were instances of firemen being killed on the GWR when the pricker had caught in the ladder of a signal post or the arch of an overbridge. You couldn't let go in time and were dragged out with the speed of the train. Bill always looked after me.

We used to come thundering down from Paddington, through Slough, and there you had the branch line to Windsor. Bill'd say, "Well, matey, are we gonna go to Windsor or to Reading?" It was a very rough bit of road there and as we rattled over the points he'd say, "It's OK, we're going to

Reading, not Windsor!" When running into a station and applying the brakes, a driver didn't look at his brake gauge – he could tell exactly how the brakes were being applied by listening to the grinding. A driver would be annoyed if a fireman hadn't done his job properly and, by over-firing, was allowing the safety valves to blow steam out. This was wasteful but it took away his sense of hearing in respect of the grinding of the brake blocks. Bill hated this, and I well recall him on one occasion grumbling "If you can't keep this bugger quiet, I will!" So he'd open the regulator wider and use more steam.

One year, on the 9 a.m. Swindon to Paddington, the link in the dragbox between our tender and locomotive broke. I was firing, with one foot in the tender and the other in the cab, when I was aware of the tender starting to part from the engine. Alarmed, I screamed to Bill "Don't look now, Bill, we're running in two parts!" Bill immediately shut off the regulator so that the train came up against the tender and engine so that the gap closed. He expertly applied the brakes so we eased into Southall station and stopped without any problem, allowing the momentum of the train behind to push the loco to its final stop. Over a period of time, the tugging of the loco had sheared off the securing cotter and the main pin had worked its way out, so that the tender and the train were attached to the engine with just two safety links. At Southall, they wired the shed, and two fitters put the pin back and secured it, but we had to have a pilot engine put on the front to tow us into Paddington. When we arrived there, we were met by a concerned Locomotive Inspector who told us "When they take the coaches away from you, driver, you take this engine back to Old Oak. She's going to have a thorough examination. We've never heard of an incident like this before!" So instead of going to Ranelagh Bridge to wait for the return working, we had to go to Old Oak Common with it for checking over.

It was a normal part of a fireman's duty to make the tea and there was just one occasion in our seven years together that Bill did it. We were on a Weston-super-Mare run one winter, the 3.18 ex-Swindon (1.18 out of Paddington) which

The test run of November 1953, with 4—6—0 No. 6001 King Edward VII *heading its huge trainload through Hullavington on its way to Stoke Gifford. The point rodding leading to Hullavington Signal Box is visible in the foreground. This test was featured in a write-up by O. S. Nock in the* Railway World *magazine of January 1954. The inside of the firebox of a 'King' class loco is 11ft 6in long, so when you think that I had to reach into the tender, then turn and open the firebox doors and throw all that coal the length of the firebox to get it to the front end, that was some hard work! The 'Kings' were marvellous locomotives — there were only thirty of them, all 135 tons in working order. There are only three left now. One of the reasons why I returned home dirtier than usual was because we weren't allowed to spray water on the coal to keep the dust down, as we would have done in normal service, as that would upset the test calculations! There is a net visible on top of the tender to protect the two men who were working up there tipping down the coal. This was to prevent them from standing up tall and risk coming into collision with an overbridge. There were three men on the front of the loco behind that wooden protection screen you see on the photograph, and they were recording steam temperatures, steam pressure in the cylinders and steam chests. They were laid on asbestos blankets because it was very hot in there — the dangers of asbestos were not yet apparent. The portholes in the front were for them to look out to see where they were. The way we were working that loco was red-hot, no doubt about it. I vividly recall balls of fire bouncing off the tunnel roof going through Badminton Tunnel. Ernie Nutty from Experimental Section is seen leaning from the cab window. He was one of the recorders.* KENNETH LEECH

Another test run, a 1954 shot of No. 1000 County of Middlesex, *the first of the 'County' class, seen at Reading before a test run to Bristol. I didn't like this loco — it was not a free-steaming engine as it proved awkward to maintain maximum steam pressure. I can be seen third from the right, directly under the last '0' on the numberplate, with Bill Hinder sixth from right. Bill Andress, Locomotive Inspector at Swindon, is seen just to my right, whilst the man in the beret in the centre was Ernie Nutty, Chief of the Experimental Section, who would be in the cab recording the coal consumption. Again the tender had protective nets above to protect the two men who'd be up there tipping coal directly down from sacks.* COLLECTION GORDON SHURMER

arrived in Weston at 5.25 p.m., and we were working a stopper back from Weston, the 8.15 back to Swindon, which made 22 station stops and arrived back at Swindon at 11.15. So we had nearly three hours at Weston, where we'd turn the engine and stand on our coaches. I'd noticed some wild horse-radish over by the turntable, and decided to take the coal pick and go over and dig some. Once picked, you'd scrub it then put it through a grater, mix vinegar with it and put it on beef like they do sauce today – my goodness, that'd be hot! It was pretty dark so I took the gauge lamp with me but, unknown to me, there was a little brook flowing close to the horse-radish, and while I was digging with the coal pick I stepped back and fell in the brook! The lamp went out and in my soaked state I had to fish about in the water to find the pick. Of course, when I got back on the engine I was greeted with a frosty, "What the hell happened to you?" This was followed by an "Alright give us the tea-can!" and, muttering all the way, off Bill went to the refreshment room and made the tea while I used the warmth of the footplate to get myself dry. That was the only time that my gaffer made the tea! There was a ruling that if a crewman went into a refreshment room for hot water, he was allowed to jump the queue and be served, as of course, he had to get back on the engine – the waitress would always recognise the blue uniform and call you forward.

My most memorable experience on No.1 Link was firing with Bill on a test run from Reading to Stoke Gifford with No. 6001 *King Edward VII*. This run was an experiment because a new blast-pipe had been fitted in 6001's smokebox. This had been done because we were getting such poor quality coal, so a new design of blastpipe was needed that would force the heating ingredients out of the coal much more quickly. A sharper blast was required and, by bringing in a double blast-pipe, it was achieved. The South Wales coal that the Belpaire firebox on GWR engines was designed to burn was becoming scarce. This was just before the 'Bristolian' express was re-introduced, London to Bristol in 100 minutes. Of course, the 'Bristolian' never had the sort of load we carried on the test, never more than eight coaches at most, but it had the new blastpipe and eventually all the 'Kings' were modified with the twin version.

The steaming rate for that day was to 30,000 lbs an hour with a load of 25 coaches, a 796 ton train. We left Scours Lane Junction, a location about a mile west of Reading station, at 10.30 a.m., and when the steaming rate of 30,000 was reached, the plan was to hold it for an hour, which we did. It was a very skilled job to get the fire just right before I told Bill that we were ready to go into the steaming rate. We were two miles out of Reading on the down main before I was able to indicate readiness for the hour's test to begin, firing to keep up this particular rate. We had the dynamometer team at work in the coach just behind us, plotting coal and water consumption. One of the dynamometer team was in the cab behind us indicating with push buttons every time I finished a hundredweight of coal.

The coal consumption was approximately 4,000 lbs per hour, which is 70 lbs per train mile. It really took some doing to keep that going. I was shovelling coal at about a cwt every minute. On the return journey, the two men on top of the tender, who had been tipping the coal down, had 3½ tons to deal with ready for the next trip, and by Cholsey all of the new supply had been shovelled. With a distance of 70 miles, Stoke Gifford to Cholsey, 70 cwts of coal were shovelled, a consumption of a cwt per minute. The actual running time was 73 minutes, and we had to finish the test because there was no coal left. The highest speed we achieved on that return trip was 78 m.p.h. through Little Somerford, on a falling gradient, with a 25-coach train, a quarter of a mile long. We just cruised on back to Reading after the coal was gone. The test was chronicled in the *Railway World* magazine in January 1954 by O. S. Nock, who was on board. The notable railway historian reported;

'By any standards this was indeed an extraordinary locomotive performance. But during the turn-around time at Stoke Gifford I had an opportunity to talk with those who had been on the footplate, and I learned that the engine had steamed very freely indeed, the fireman was quite confident she was not up to her limit. The engine had been worked by Driver Hinder of Swindon; his regular fireman, Shurmer, had fired on the outward trip, with fireman Green as reserve. The enginemen had certainly entered into the spirit of this great occasion. To maintain the steaming rate accurately, watching the special u-tube manometer gauge provided, driver Hinder had hardly "fixed" his cut-off in any particular notch; very often the reverser was held midway between the two notches.'

Arriving back home at Havelock Street, my mother greeted me with "Whatever's the matter with your face? I've never seen it so black!"

"We've been on a test run. I've never worked as hard as I've done today! I've shovelled coal at a hundredweight a minute! I'm all in!"

Then I noticed there was a sprig of heather on the dining room table. The gipsy had called again. Mum would never let the gipsy pedlar go by without buying something. Mum said as the old lady had left the house, she'd turned to her and said "You have a son." Mum said, "Yes, I do." The old lady replied "You tell him from me that he'll travel far in life."

Through my mask of coal, the uniform of my day's labours, I replied "Did she say I'll have to shovel my way there and back?"

Inspector Charlie Pullen had been on the test run with us, and he saw me on the shed a couple of days later as I was turning an engine on the big turntable, and he came up enthusiastically and shouted to me "Son, they're talking about that trip the other day in Italy!"

"Mr. Pullen," I replied, "I 'spect they could hear us bloody coming!"

Bill lived to the age of 88, a grand old man who was literally worn out. He used to smoke heavily and always had his Woodbines with him at work. When we had a signal check and delay, he jotted it down on the back of his fag packet. Most drivers had a book in which to record signal checks, to

11594

Name William Henry Hinder

Aug 1911 –
(975) (Bks., 250 lvs.—O 19—7-07.)   W. & S. Ltd.

PROMOTIONS AND RATES OF WAGES.

Date.	Rate.	Position.	Date.	Rate.	Position.
				2/12/19	
			Basic Rate	24/9/24	Turns 43
2 Oct 04		Engine cleaner	12 Apl 20	17/10	
13 Mar 1911	3/-	Sht.d fireman	14 June 20	14/-	
7 May 11	3/6	3rd fireman	1 July 20	14/4	
10 June 12	3/9		1 Oct 20	14/8	
13 Mar 14	4/-		1 Jan 21	15/-	
13 Mar 16	4/3		1 April 21	14/2	
3 April 18	4/9	2nd fireman	1 July 21	13/4	
1 July 19	5/-	1st Gp. fireman	2 Dec 21	14/4	
18 Aug 19	11/-		1 Jan 22	13/8	
19 Jan 20	12/4	E man	1 April 22	13/-	
1 Mar 20	14/-		2 Dec 23	14/-	
			2 Dec 24	15/-	+8 1/1/40
			30 July 45	99/6	RSC 113.
			1 July 46	26/6	S/19448
			30 June 47	134/-	R.S.C 119.
			1 Feb 48	138/-	R.S.C 1.
			1 Jan 51	146/6	M. 416
			3 Sept 51	169/6	RS.T. 13
			3.11.52	168/6	RST.14

STATIONS AND DESCRIPTION OF WORK.

Date.	Station.	Description of work.
2 Oct 1907	Swindon	Cleaning
13 Mar 11	do	Shunting
17 Mar 14	Cheltenham	3rd Group (Junior f man)
8 Apl 17	Swindon	do (own request)
7 July 19	do	1st Group
19 Jan 20	do	E man

Retired 17.12.35

RECORD OF FINES, &c.

Date.	Locality.	Penalty, &c.	Circumstances.	Reference to Correspondence.
1 Oct 1907	Swindon		Form and colour vision normal.	J.224
18 Oct 1910	Swindon		Rejected – Teeth. Varicose vein left leg	J.61.
13 Mar 1911	Swindon		Colour vision normal. Form vision each eye acute	
			Passed satisfactorily	
22 Oct 1911	Swindon Loco. Yard.		Hinder was walking up yard, when he stepped on a clinker, slipped & fell to the ground	
			Right wrist cut. Resumed duty 6th Nov 1911.	a/34913
6 Mar 16	Swindon		Colour vision normal Form vision each eye acute	
18 June '17	Running Shed Swindon		Hinder was preparing engine 2477 when a lump of coal fell on his foot.	
			Big toe of right foot pinched & bruised. Resumed duty	A/50787
10 June 19	Swindon	Passed Inspr	Colour vision normal. Form vision each eye acute	J1
4 Sep '19	do		Form & Colour Vision normal. – W.G.a. case.	Jb.
16 Aug 19	Between Melksham + Chippenham		Hinder was working on engine 25 when a piece of hot ash from the chimney entered his eye	
			Right eye slightly burnt. Resumed 1st Sept 19	A/54567
12 Jan 20	Swindon	Passed Inspr	Form and Colour vision normal.	J1.
5 May 25	– do –		Form & Colour Vision normal	
6 Oct 30	– do –		Form and Colour vision normal.	

Extract from Bill's GWR career record.
CTY. THE NATIONAL ARCHIVES

show in their daily record and prove at which signal box the delay had occurred. When we got back to shed, he'd have to get out his fag packet and transfer the information from it when making out his ticket. He never carried a book. Bill was the boss on the footplate, make no mistake about it. No one ever told him his business there, not even the loco Inspectors. If a driver lost two minutes without reason on a regular basis, there'd be a Report, and you could expect a visit from an Inspector if you were on Report for loss of time – they'd come to check if the fireman was at fault or if the driver was not handling the locomotive properly.

It was a sad day in December 1955 when Bill retired, just after his 65th birthday. It was after I'd been made up to driver and I'd left him about a year before. I knew his last job was the 9 o'clock to Paddington on a Saturday morning, returning on the 1.18 back to Swindon at 3 o'clock. I made it my business to be around the booking office when he came off duty. When he came in, he went over to his locker and made his ticket out, threw it in the window and looked in to the booking-on clerk and dourly said "Last one!" I walked up to him, shook his hand, thanked him for the wonderful apprenticeship I'd had with him on the footplate, then he went up in the bike shed, fetched out his bike, strapped his foodbox on the back of the saddle and rode away. After 48 years' service there was nobody there except me to shake him by the hand and wish him well. No gold watch, no certificate, no glorious send-off.

Bill left the area and moved to Chester, but often returned and would look me up whenever he came to visit his son and daughter. He'd always give my son Michael half-a-crown on these occasions. Then his wife died and he ended his days in Langford House in Wroughton, just outside Swindon. I went in and saw him on Christmas Eve, just a couple of weeks before he died. I took him a couple of cigars over and he was almost blind by this time. I crept up behind him, put my hand on his shoulder and announced "I'm looking for a driver for the 2.18 Cardiff papers!" He never turned his head, just replied quietly "Matey, I can't see thee, but I shall remember thy voice forever." And I said, "I should bloody well think so, I made your tea every day for seven years!"

Less than a month later, when I stood silently at his funeral, and the reverend asked us to pause for a minute's silence for all our own personal memories, all those years came flooding back, and I knew I was paying my last respects and saying goodbye to someone who really put the greatness into the Great Western Railway. No man was more dedicated when he was at work than Bill Hinder. Most crucially, Bill was my mentor and had a great influence on the way I treated *my* firemen when I in turn became a driver. Sleep well, Bill, you deserve it.

Bill Hinder's lunch box.

I am on the right of this group in the foyer of the Regent Cinema in 1954, supervising a model railway display. The poster behind announced the arrival of Jane Russell in Double Dynamite *the following week.*

COLLECTION GORDON SHURMER

A press photograph of me pointing out something of interest to a young visitor to a model railway exhibition in the East Street Co-op Hall in 1954.

COLLECTION GORDON SHURMER

CHAPTER SEVEN

IN CHARGE AT LAST

AS a fireman you worked your way up from factory pilots to the top passenger links, then when you became a driver you repeated the whole process again. After the excitement and sheer hard graft of main-line passenger firing work, going back to work on the little pilot engines pottering around the yard at Swindon might seem like a demotion, but this was not so. Although you were now back on a shunting engine, *you* now carried the can. You were now totally responsible for that engine and for your fireman. Exchanging the shovel for an oil can was a different job altogether! I still recall my mentor Bill Hinder's words on the subject – "When you stand over here, mate, it doesn't matter who comes on board or whatever they suggest, YOU decide whether to do it or not, because if something goes wrong, the buck stops with *you*."

During my last couple of years firing with Bill, on what was now the Western Region of British Railways, a quiz competition was started between the locomotive sheds to encourage Improvement classes, and to promote excellence in knowledge of engines and their working and an awareness of safe practice. I was made captain of the team that represented Swindon shed. I suppose that with the diesel age on the horizon the idea never really caught on, but it was a good experience and the opportunity to meet and compare notes with men from other depots was beneficial. During 1952–53, we made trips to Bristol, Westbury, Exeter – the Exeter trip was the day King George VI died, I remember – and there was a trip to Newton Abbot to compete against Truro shed. We won all our contests except the one against St. Blazey, to whom we lost in the final. They were superb, especially their captain, and we reckoned that being a small depot they had lots more time than we did to do their swotting! Like I said, the idea never really caught on, but it was good while it lasted.

It is an irony, in a sense, that I spent a large part of my working life moving inexorably towards my goal of becoming an engine driver, yet when I achieved it at the age of 33, it was during those times when I could already sense the end of steam power on the railways. It would have taken me longer, of course, had it not been for those fast promotions through the links caused by World War II. Further, the older engines with which I'd grown up were now wearing out and were past their best. However, my mind was not filled with negative thoughts at all during that exciting time, with my life's ambition in sight, and I was now courting Hazel, whom I'd met for the first time in the Oxford Street Club in Swindon.

Hazel had been married before, but tragically her husband had died young at the age of only 26, so she was a very sad person when I first knew her. She gradually came round and at the time of writing we are approaching 50 years of mar-

riage. Her best friend, Joan, was married to an engine driver, so Hazel had some awareness of what life was like being married to a railwayman and what it meant in terms of hours and commitment, and through Joan she was able to check up on me a little, on my prospects and my suitability! Joan told her "He's in the top link, y'know," and of course at first Hazel hadn't a clue what that meant! We married at Christ Church in Cricklade Street, Old Town, on 3rd December 1955, and moved to a new house in Churchward Avenue, where we've

On the footplate of No. 5097 Sarum Castle *in February 1957. I was made up to driver in 1954. The loco was freshly outshopped here, facing Gloucester. The 'D' above the numberplate indicated allowed routes, in this case most main lines. The 'BT' visible on the tender indicated that the loco had to go to the 'big turntable' – this had been marked on in chalk by the shedman at the coal rank. The alternative was to chalk on the number of the road on which it was to be taken – there were nine roads, the straights. If the road had not been decided, as in this case, it was put on the big turntable so that it didn't matter whether it was down or up road on the subsequent job, as the turntable would turn it whichever way it was needed. The building visible behind is the addressograph office where the paybills were printed.*
KENNETH LEECH

A NEW LIFE. 3rd DECEMBER 1955 — MARRIAGE TO HAZEL.

Prospect Place in Old Town, Swindon, looking towards Victoria Road with the spire of Christ Church overlooking the houses. On the left was Workman's General Store.
CTY. MRS. MARY THOMPSON

I couldn't resist wearing the tiepin in the shape of a shovel on our wedding day!

Christ Church in Cricklade Street, the scene of our wedding.
CTY. MRS. CELIA FRASER

Honeymoon in London.

been ever since. I took to married life like a duck to water and used to tease Hazel about her neatness – she'd wash and iron my clothes for me and I'd say "If you keep putting my clothes away I'll never be able to find them!"

I attained the rank of driver on 29th March 1954 and on Sunday 11th April I worked my last turn as a fireman, with Bill Hinder on the 10.45 a.m. to Paddington, then back with the 3.20 p.m. Our engine was No. 7000, *Viscount Portal*, named after the GWR Chairman appointed in 1945.

I don't quite know how it happened, but for some reason I didn't work the factory link on promotion to driver, my first driving turn on the afternoon of Monday 12th April 1954 being on the Transfer link in charge of one of the station passenger pilots, a pannier tank, No. 8461. I'll never forget that feeling of pride when I booked on at the shed at 1.45 p.m. that day and walked up to the station a fully-fledged driver, to relieve the 6-2 shift. I'd finally made the move from one side of the footplate to the other, and had finished the hard slog as fireman, and now I'd proved my knowledge and the full responsibility was mine. I didn't have to wait long for the vacancy to come up to enable my promotion to take place. With the quick promotions of my firing days it didn't actually seem that long since I'd been a bright-eyed young fireman on this same link, and what a surge of power and responsibility I felt when I took hold of the regulator for the first time in charge of a locomotive!

In the early summer of 1955 there was an ASLEF strike over conditions and wages. This was difficult for me because over the previous couple of years I'd joined the Panel of Temporary Supervisors at Swindon station, and when the strike was declared on 28th May I resigned from the Panel to show solidarity with the workforce. The strike was complete – I don't think there was a single Swindon driver who came in. It lasted about 15 days, I think. The main concerns were the 48-hour week we were working and the erosion of pay differentials for drivers and firemen. The outcome was that drivers kept their differentials and the working week became five days, 40 hours, with a rest day. Membership of ASLEF in those days was 72,000, and is today down to 22,000, so there has been a loss of 50,000 over fifty years with the reduced railway network and single manning.

The exact date has long faded from my memory but late one Sunday night around 1957 on Swindon station another cherished ambition was realised for me. At that time there was a train which Old Oak men worked from Paddington to Swindon which came into Swindon at five minutes after midnight on the Monday morning. When it arrived, a Swindon crew would take over and work the loco and just the front two coaches down to Chippenham and back. On this particular night, to my delight, at the head of this train, was my favourite engine from childhood, *King George V*, and at that moment my thoughts went back more than twenty years to the night when I first saw her up on Whitehouse bridge. At last! The flagship of the Great Western and I was going to take charge of her! My whole career had been leading up to this. As I recall, this was a job in No. 4 link, but I can't be sure. Filled with excitement, my fireman Brian Stratford and I climbed aboard, and proudly steamed out of Swindon with our little train. I couldn't resist the urge to really open her up and as we sped down Dauntsey Bank I remember shouting to Brian "Look Bri, look at the speedometer!" We were doing 95 m.p.h. down the bank, and at that moment Brian caught sight of the distant signal at Dauntsey at caution and I learned a quick hard lesson there that night – at that speed you don't have a lot of braking power with just two coaches on! After delivering the Chippenham passengers to their destination, we ran around the two coaches and brought them back to Swindon tender-first, at the regulation speed of 45 m.p.h. working that way round. We left the coaches in the Water Sidings and took *King George V* to shed, where we left her on the firedroppers' rank at the coal stage for the shedman's attention. I felt so proud, so excited, and although I drove her many times thereafter, I'll never forget that first time on her footplate as a driver, and it's ironic, in a way, that when I finally took charge of her she was at the head of such a modest little local passenger run. I didn't see her the next day, of course, as she would have gone back to Old Oak Common at the head of a Paddington train.

One train I never did work but would love to have done so was the 'Cheltenham Spa Express', nicknamed the 'Cheltenham Flyer', the fastest train in the world in the 1930s. It wasn't a Swindon job, of course, being run by Old

No. 6000 King George V *outside Swindon Works on 25th April 1954.*   KENNETH LEECH

No. 4062 Malmesbury Abbey on a Swindon–Bristol service at Chippenham in 1954. This loco was often used at Swindon as relief pilot for the Cheltenham Spa Express.
KENNETH LEECH

*No. 1366 with a workmen's train
at Highworth.*

Oak men, although Pat Lawes, one of my older colleagues, who is still alive at the age of 93 at time of writing, recalled that Swindon men were involved with it in the 20s. It did affect our routine at Swindon in my time, however, because we always had a standing relief pilot ready at the shed just in case the Cheltenham's loco should fail. The service would leave Paddington in the morning and work through to Cheltenham, with a return working at 2.40. It never had more than six coaches, to allow for the maximum speed on what was a prestige speed run. She would run all stations to Swindon where, departing at 3.55, she became the 'Cheltenham Flyer' to Paddington where arrival would be dead on 5 p.m., 77¼ miles in 65 minutes. At Swindon we often had No. 4062 *Malmesbury Abbey* on the standing pilot, and the crew would have her coaled, watered and in steam ready to go to the station to hand over to the London men should the Flyer's loco need replacement. The foreman would tell the crew "If he's not needed for the 'Flyer', relieve 'Paddy's Mail' 7.6 at the station, and unless you hear any more, that's your job for the week!" They would stand on one of the straights by the shed where they'd see the Cheltenham coming off the Gloucester line, and they could see she was fine and would wait until the train had cleared Didcot, by which time the driver would say to his mate "Well, she's gone now, mate, back to the cabin." So if the standing pilot was not needed, the crew would now walk up to the station and relieve the crew of 'Paddy's Mail', a stopper from Didcot. The Swindon crew on that job had been on a long turn, having gone up with the 12.5, so the pilot crew would relieve the crew of the Didcot and allow them to book off promptly while they took the stopper's loco to shed.

I think Management used to worry about the speeds on the Cheltenham after one driver did the run between Swindon and London in 57 minutes 46 seconds, maybe concerned that the 'Flyer' might end up in Praed Street in trying to beat the speed record. So they issued an edict that all running times, 65 minutes for the 'Flyer', were to be strictly observed. Mind you although we provided that cover at Swindon for the 'Flyer', I don't recall it ever failing there, so it was always the Didcot duty for the pilot crew.

One job I always enjoyed in the Van link was the local branch service to Highworth, where the GWR had run workmen's trains to bring employees to the Works since 1890. These trains were provided free to the workforce. During the days when there was a full passenger service to Highworth, I worked over there many times as a fireman, although by the time I was a driver, only freight and workmen's trains remained. We'd take in foodstuffs and farm machinery, and a great deal of rugs, carpets and coconut matting came from a factory there. The most difficult section to work was from Hannington up into the terminus at Highworth, and I've known it when the sand wasn't being discharged from the sandboxes adequately and the wheels would slip badly on that section. There are tales of waiting workmen at Highworth enjoying the crew's embarrassment as they struggled to get the train into the station and the cheer that went up when they finally made it into the platform! I can recall a time when I had my fireman down on the ground scooping sand out of the sandboxes with his teacan lid and chucking it down under the wheels!

At Stanton there was a little level crossing and a watchman's hut. I think the gates are still there today. These gates were knocked down many times by branch trains. There was one particular driver, who, upon promotion to the Van link, was so worried by the tales of the vulnerable gates at Stanton that he cycled over there on the day before his first turn on that service, and affixed a bicycle reflector on one of the gateposts on the driver's side of the curve. Not only did the line curve there, but it was also a falling gradient at that point, and he was so preoccupied with keeping a lookout for the

Herbie Scarratt, one of the best-liked railwaymen at Swindon, seen here in driving days before he became shed foreman.

little red disc that he missed it and without sufficient restraint his train took out the gates as it slid around the bend with locked wheels!

Another old colleague of mine once told an interesting story of how he succeeded in shutting the Highworth branch down for a day in 1959! He was in the Relief link, and he'd relieved a goods train from Severn Tunnel Junction which he was running up the main line early one July morning. When they came to Highworth Junction, the signalman informed them that he couldn't get the signal off for them to go into the loop so he gave them permission to pass the signal at danger. This straightaway threw the responsibility onto the driver. He could see that the points were set correctly for access to the loop, but forgot to check the other pair inside the siding itself, which is where the problem was. They were, in fact, open a little, and as the engine, a '28XX' class 2–8–0, hit them, it came off the road, all wheels. Fortunately, they were not going very fast, and when they got down to have a look the loco had actually regained the road but the tender and the first three wagons had derailed. There was the cause of the problem – there was a wooden key, one of the wood-blocks from the track, wedged in the tongue of the point, possibly put there by locals as a prank. Well, now the Highworth branch was blocked until the freight could be put back on the road, and, to cap it all, it was a Trip day! There was a train full of Works men waiting to come out main line so they could get into Swindon to connect with their holiday specials. So buses had to be put on to get the Highworth contingent into Swindon Junction. Moreover, those three wagons off the road contained urgent shipment traffic, so a Transfer pilot had to come with fresh wagons for tranship-ment of the loads via the goods shed at the Transfer.

We had some great characters at Swindon shed, and none more so than my old friend Herbie Scarratt. Herbie had started at Swindon in the mid-30s not long before I did and was one of those who cycled to Shrivenham to offer assistance on the night of the accident there when an Old Oak driver was killed when his locomotive struck the back of a freight train that had become divided. Herbie was a keen sportsman and a well-known funny man who was an expert in the art of gurning, not in any way the typical picture of a formidable shedmaster! He left Swindon briefly for promotion to shed foreman but soon returned to us in that capacity. Once when I was talking to a chap from Westbury shed, naturally Herbie's name came up in conversation.

"You know Herbie Scarratt?" he laughed. "I'll tell you about Herbie Scarratt! That man should have been a come-dian! I'll tell you a story about Herbie. I was on duty at the shed one night and he came in the messroom and told me and my mate 'Here, there's 5980 on the shed. Go and get him ready for spare pilot.' So we walked around the shed and couldn't find it. In the end we found it was up against the stop block with a sack over its chimney and a label tied to the handrail on the side of the cab which read 'to be forwarded to Swindon Loco Works for repair'. So we went back to find Herbie and told him 'That loco's got to go to shop for

repairs!' And you know what Herbie said? 'Well, just go do the best you can with 'im!'" Yes, as the Westbury man said, Herbie should have been a comedian and was almost too likeable a bloke to be in such a position. Foremen dished out a lot of flak and also took a lot from drivers. At the shed you could give the foreman a real bollocking, receive one back, and still keep your job! It wasn't like that in the Works, though, where it would be instant dismissal if anyone spoke abusively to the foreman.

Another character with whom I got on very well and for whom I fired several times on relief was Chris Brown. Born at Baunton in Gloucestershire, he had left Swindon shed to go to Tondu in South Wales for promotion and returned later to work through to retirement in 1955. Chris was one of the toughest of the Swindon men, a real hard case. I've seen him turn up for work in the depths of a cold winter with his shirt open to the waist, and on the Cardiff paper train he'd spread newspapers on the floor of the footplate and grab a couple of hours' sleep in Canton shed before working back up to Swindon. He'd always re-assemble those newspapers and give them to the coalmen, a ploy which earned him supplies of the best coal for his loco! Chris invented a device known as the 'jimmy', a damper that fitted over the blast pipe and helped you get better results from your boiler. A lot of drivers were very grateful for the 'jimmy'.

Of the jobs we worked from Swindon, quite the most challenging was freight work through the Severn Tunnel. At Swindon, we referred to it as 'The Arcade'. The tunnel was opened on 1st December 1886, and prior to that traffic from South Wales to London was worked via Gloucester. It was 4 miles 624 yards long and 2¼ miles of it was below the Severn itself. Some 3,628 men were employed in its construction over thirteen years and over 76 million bricks were used. It is still pumped continuously to keep the tunnel dry, to counter the 30 million gallons of water that percolate daily. From a driver's point of view, the difficulty was that it slopes at both ends with a flat section in the bottom, and is also on a curve, and the secret was to keep the coupling chains tight on your freight train all the time. The guard would keep his brake on slightly all the time to keep them taut. There was a danger that when you went along the flat middle section, then opened up the regulator to go up the other side, you could get a snatch which would risk breaking a coupling and divid-ing the train. We had banking engines there to assist, always kept at Severn Tunnel Junction on the Welsh side. With an express you were in the tunnel only about six minutes, but with a freight it would be as much as 16 minutes. You were always very wary in the tunnel, but, as I said, the secret was keeping that tight chain, relying on your guard. The other problem in there was slipping and losing the momentum of your train when you needed it on the gradients coming out on each side. I experienced this once with a Britannia class 4–6–0 on the front. We were in a 15 m.p.h. speed restriction and, when Bill opened her up, she started slipping and went to a standstill. We'd taken the train on at Swindon and, unbe-known to me, there was wet sand in the sandboxes. I had to

Inside the 1908 section of Swindon shed on 30th September 1956, with 3846, 75023, 7815 and 6848 on the large electrified turntable.

KENNETH LEECH

4−6−0 No. 4096 Highclere Castle *standing on one of the straight roads into the 1871 shed on 30th September 1956.*　　　　KENNETH LEECH

No. 6124, a 61XX class 2−6−2 locomotive, seen in 1955 on one of the nine 'straights' outside Swindon shed. This loco would typically be seen on passenger suburban trains such as Paddington−Southall. When allocated to Swindon, its main duty was on the 8.50 pick-up goods to Westbury, a hard night's work which involved shunting every yard on the way. Empties would be picked up and brought back to Swindon Transfer around 5.0 next morning. The two windows to the right of the loco were the shedmaster's office − a Mr. Morgan was shedmaster at this time.

　　　　LENS OF SUTTON

go out to the signal box with a wrong line order so an engine could come into the tunnel and pull us out.

Diesel locomotives were first introduced onto the railway in 1955 and it took a period of 13 years to fully integrate them into the network. The year 1968 was when the last diagrammed steam train ran and, of course, during those thirteen years all drivers had to go back to school.

During the early part of this period, I was an instructor at Swindon Improvement Class, which was held in a building in Emlyn Square. I had been involved from about 1945 and I realised that I would be called upon to tutor on the new locomotives. The Improvement Class took place every Sunday morning from 11 a.m. to 1 p.m., during which time drivers would teach firemen. Drivers would pose questions to the younger men on such subjects as how you would realise you were losing power, rules and regulations, and the correct procedure to adopt when the communication cord was pulled. Occasionally, visual aids would be used, such as models of Stephenson's link motion and the Walschaerts valve gear. I can still recall Alfie Guyatt, a fine old Great Western veteran, with his piece of waste in one hand and a bit of chalk in the other. Alfie was a legendary Swindon character who many times on the road, if stopped at a signal, would be heard to say 'Never mind the signals, where's the nearest pub?" But, of course, behind this mischievous exterior was a very professional and expert railwayman.

The class had existed since well before I first joined the GWR as a young cleaner, and I began attending while still on my cleaning duties. I gradually worked my way up until I was eventually invited to be an instructor myself, well before I was asked to become a tutor driver on the diesels. Getting to understand the diesels on the Western Region of British Railways was more complex than elsewhere because we were what was known as the Experiment Section. We had several classes of diesel locomotives – the multiple units, the '47XX' diesel-electrics, the Cromptons, the Parkinsons, the Class 3s, the '68XX' class, and of course, we also had the hydraulic locomotives, which were the '800s', the Western '52s' or 'Maybacks', and the 'Hymeks', so there was a great deal for drivers to learn. The other BR Regions had just one class of locomotive – the Midland, for example, with the English Electric.

In those days, on the Western, before the introduction of the diesels, there were no tutors at all for drivers. Firemen became drivers through the tradition of older men teaching them on the footplate during the course of normal rostered work. Unbelievably, we never even had any books on steam locomotives provided by the railway until they were on the way out and being replaced by the diesels. All we ever had was a rulebook. The only steam-related books that we did have were what dedicated men wrote themselves and sold for a couple of shillings to their colleagues. With dieselisation, however, we had literature on every single class of locomotive.

In steam days there were two examinations we had to pass – the first was the passenger fireman's, for which we went to Park House where we had to prove to the Locomotive Inspector, who had previously been a driver himself, that we were familiar with the rules and regulations so that in the case of an emergency, such as a driver failing to turn up for work, as a passed fireman, providing you had knowledge of road, you could now take on the driver's duties. You would be asked about the working parts of the locomotive and what symptoms would result if certain parts broke. For instance, if you were running along the road getting four puffs to the turn of a wheel, and you suddenly lost a puff, and therefore a beat of the loco's rhythm, what had gone wrong? When a vacancy for a driver arose you were returned for your last examination, which was a little more difficult as the questions involved faults on the large four-cylinder engines which required more intense exams, and if you passed this you were appointed as engine driver permanently. If you failed the first time you were given two more chances, but if you failed the third time then you would be offered a job as a labourer at the shed and therefore would have no chance of ever taking charge of a locomotive. Some men failed miserably and those were the chaps who ended up firedropping, coaling the engine, tube-cleaning, ash-loading – all the tough jobs at the shed. We had a local agreement at Swindon whereby if you reached the age of 40 and still hadn't been made up to driver you could apply to come off main-line work and do shunting in the marshalling yard in the 'Over-40 Link'. It was up to the men, if they wanted this.

Of course, steam tuition had all been voluntary. It was only when they wanted diesels brought in quickly in 1955 that it became a paid duty, because they wanted men tutored with all speed. The railway simply *had* to provide professional training. There were two tutor drivers at Swindon at first, although this number was soon doubled as dieselisation increased. For some of the older men approaching 60, the GWR old guard, it was a tremendous task, to have only two weeks' tuition on the new diesels, and there were many who took the golden handshake rather than adapt so late in their careers. Such rapid tuition had not been been needed previously because if you were firing for 15 years you simply learned the job as you went along. I'd been several years on tutoring when the diesels first came in, and teaching elderly men on the verge of retirement was a very difficult thing to do. All their lives they had been in charge of a locomotive where they made the decisions – if the steam pressure was down, the driver would tell his fireman that they would stop at the next signal box and have time to put things right. With the diesels you had no idea of imminent problems until lights started to flash warnings. Blue indicated everything was fine, amber meant a problem, and red indicated that the engine had stopped. Men sixty years of age and over had to forget all their steam training and take on this new idea and being on their own in a strange situation with these lights really did force a lot of the old stalwarts out. Those that stuck it would be keeping their fingers crossed that nothing would happen out on the road, and their legs crossed too, as there was nowhere on the new locos where they could relieve themselves! There was a move to build the driver's seat as a commode, but the Unions understandably objected to it.

One key new thing that had to be learned on the diesels was how to steam-heat the train. In steam days you'd just put your steam pipes together between the locomotive and the coaches, and opened a valve on the loco which let steam from the boiler back through the train and you could steam-heat fourteen coaches. When it came to the diesel, there was no massive boiler where steam was created, so you had to have a miniature boiler in the middle of the diesel for the sole purpose of creating steam to heat the train. There were many different types – the Stone generators, the Claytons and the Spanners, and the drivers had to learn them all and pass a different examination for each one. You were given three days to learn how to create steam for the diesel loco and get it back through the train, and blow the boiler down after you'd completed the heating. So a big difference now was that whereas in the steam age you had to pass two examinations, you now had to pass an examination on every single class of diesel locomotive, and there were many, added to the several different exams on the steam-heating boilers.

People often have remarked to me what a great shame it was that steam went, and it was, but of course the main reason that steam was replaced by diesel was economics. A steam locomotive could only work up to 16 hours a day with two sets of men, eight hours each, and when it came to shed after those 16 hours out on the road, the tender would be empty of coal, the fire would have to be cleaned, the tender re-coaled, the engine re-lit and re-oiled, so out of 24 hours the steam loco would require eight hours in the shed. Its new diesel counterpart could come into shed and if there was nothing wrong with her either electrically or mechanically, and there were no repairs booked, then she'd take on 800 gallons of fuel, 1200 gallons of water, spend no more than an hour on shed and be back out on the road in revenue-earning service, so you now had a machine that could work 23 hours out of 24, on passenger trains by day and freight at night, with only one man aboard. That was the difference. So economics *did* change the face of the railway, whatever way you look at it. A steam locomotive was a wasteful machine because every puff of steam up the chimney was wasted energy, gone forever.

On the diesels there wasn't a lot for the second man to do, beyond dealing with the steam heating. Promotions and retirements eventually did away with the second man – they were ex-firemen, of course, and you couldn't sack them because they were the generation of future drivers. The number of diagrammed single-manned services was gradually increased until all firemen had been made drivers. I still believe that two heads are better than one. I was having a discussion with an Inspector about this around the time the second man was being phased out. His view was that you could be talking to each other and lose concentration. I told him I couldn't agree with that and, when he asked me why, I recalled a time when I was on a train from Swindon heading east, and as we were going through Ashbury an amber light came on, indicating a fault. I asked my second man to go back and check and he reported high water temperature. I asked him to re-set the relay, which he did, my amber light

went back to blue and there were no more problems. Approaching Didcot, having already passed Foxhall Junction at about 80 m.p.h., my colleague suddenly blurted out "Don't we stop here?" Indeed we were supposed to call at Didcot, we could see the passengers on the platform, and we were about to go straight through! I put on the emergency brakes and made the best stop ever in the platform, the only time in my career that I was close to running through a station by mistake! No, the second man didn't do much – he made the tea, he learned the road, but he couldn't be sacked, and thinking back to that experience when my focus on the journey was disturbed by the water temperature problem, I still say two heads are better than one!

Throughout the late 50s I was tutoring steam to the men but regularly working diagrammed diesel services. The first diesel loco I ever saw at Swindon was a diesel-electric shunting engine outside the 'A' shop in the Works, which they called the 'Class 8'. Even with these little shunters, and just being in a marshalling yard pottering about with wagons, there was a lot to learn. The diesels were assimilated gradually – we didn't have all the different new classes at one time as that would have been far too much new knowledge to take on board. For a considerable time we had only the diesel-mechanical type, the multiple units, known as the 'dmu's' which dealt with the suburban work in three-coach sets. They were Swindon Works-built and they were my first experience of driving diesels during 1957, my first rostered turn being a 9.40 a.m. working to Gloucester, calling at Kemble and Stroud. The bigger locomotives were built by English Electric. The diesel locomotive that I liked the most was the 47 Class, with 2750 horse-power, a marvellous engine for power and very quick on acceleration.

Being made up to driver in 1954, I hadn't actually been driving that long when I took on the tutoring. From 29th August to 30th September 1955 I attended Faverdale College, near Darlington, sent there by the Western Region, with a view to honing my ability to impart knowledge to colleagues, very much with an eye to the future. I shall never forget arriving there and going to see the principal of the college and he said to me "Mr. Shurmer, if you've come here to learn about your job, you may as well go back home, because we know nothing about your job whatsoever. You are here for us to teach you *how to put it over*, but of course the knowledge of the job is up to you." So I learned the art of transferring knowledge, the use of your eyes when you watched your pupils, the way you dressed and, when you were illustrating a particular point with an object as a visual aid, we were taught not just to leave it out where the class could gaze at it and be distracted, but to put it away in a drawer out of sight, so the group could focus on you properly.

During the month at Faverdale, I had to present five 40-minute lectures to the other students, all of whom were railwaymen of different grades – signalmen, guards, porters, plate-layers, fitters, Ambulance people – from all over the country. Of course, today I still use many of the things I learned during that time when I talk to the visitors on the engines at the *STEAM* museum. One of the lessons you gave

On the course at Faverdale College, Darlington, in 1955, with myself second left on the back row, and the Head Prefect of the college, Lt. Col. Anderson, at centre of the front row. I was there to learn to put over my railway knowledge to colleagues. COLLECTION GORDON SHURMER

Evening meal at Faverdale with the Head Prefect at the head of the far table and myself on the same table, nearest the camera on the left. We'd stand to attention behind our chairs until Lt. Col. Anderson came in, at which point he'd command us to sit with an imperious "Be seated, gentlemen." Note the superior upbringing of the three gentlemen at right on the near table, with their soup dishes tilted the correct way!

COLLECTION GORDON SHURMER

Faverdale College, Darlington, scene of my month's 'in-service' course in September 1955.
COLLECTION
GORDON SHURMER

was taped and then they took you aside afterwards and you listened to the tape and they would point out where things needed to be improved. The Head Prefect of the college, Lt. Colonel Anderson, was a military man with a very formal bearing and no one messed around with him. When we went into dinner each night we stood behind our chairs until he entered and instructed everyone to sit down. The group photograph we had taken just before we left is a reminder of the strict, autocratic approach of the Colonel – the photographer was a couple of minutes late, and in front of everyone the Prefect gave him a severe dressing down and swept aside his excuse about a late taxi with a stern "If this happens again, you will lose the business of this college."

We were able to get home for weekends but if you had a lecture to give early the following week you spent most of the weekend studying. When I had completed the course, I had to go and see the Superintendent of the Bristol Division and he informed me that I had been the only GWR driver there. He further told me that I had represented the Western Region with distinction and had received a very good report, which stood me in good stead for when I was eventually invited by Management to become a diesel tutor driver in 1962.

Of course, during the mid-50s, I was very aware that times were changing irrevocably, and it had always been my dream to be in charge of a steam locomotive. I was always totally fascinated by steam and I know in my heart that had there been a diesel locomotive at the front end of a train when I was a boy I don't think I would have wanted to become an engine driver. But now, the point was that I'd reached the moment where management were saying "This is the new type of traction, this is the future. The choice is yours – either you learn it, or you have to leave." There was no choice. So I made the best of it and adapted. Being a realist, there's great com-

fort with a diesel locomotive, and when I think back to the days of steam, being exposed to all weathers, conditions on the footplate could be terrible. The fireman could always keep warm, working as he was close to the firebox, but drivers crouched up in the corner always wore a great thick overcoat in winter time to protect them from the icy blasts swirling around the cab. But in the steam age we knew nothing different. We accepted it as a way of life. But to book on at 2.00 a.m., walk up to the station and relieve the paper train, first stop Newport, climb up the sides of the cab with icicles hanging on the steps and handrails, and the coal so tightly-packed with the frost that you had to really attack it with the coal pick before you could shovel it into the firebox, was a tough existence not for delicate souls. On that locomotive, the concentration and effort of the crew was just as great at 2.00 a.m. as it was at 2.00 in the afternoon.

Many of the newer breed of firemen of that period were quite happy on a shunting engine in the marshalling yard, content on a slow freight, but when it came to the railbenders, what we called the hard-hitters, where you'd be running long-distance, non-stop, with high water and coal consumption, many packed the job in, in an era when times were changing and people were becoming more aware of alternatives. In Swindon, many left the railway to take on jobs with more attractive hours at firms such as Pressed Steel. Of all the hard-hitting jobs on the railway, the example I always like to give is running the 'Cornish Riviera' with a 'King' class locomotive on the front, running non-stop for four hours between Paddington and Plymouth. The 'King' class could not work beyond Plymouth because its 135 tons was too heavy for Saltash Bridge, the weight on the driving axles being the deciding factor, so a 126-ton 'Castle' would take over for the line west of Plymouth. The fireman would boil nine to ten thousand gallons of water into steam on that

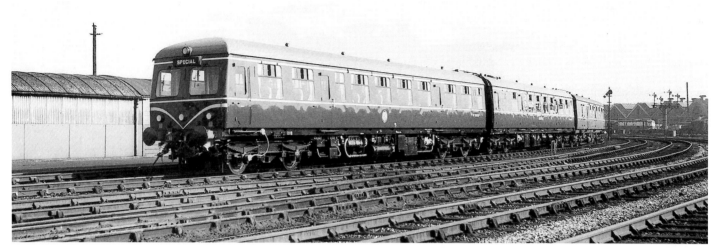

The Swindon-built diesel multiple units were the first of the new motive power to work out of Swindon shed in the '50s, with cars numbers W50658, W59261 and W50697 seen here at Swindon on 16th February 1958. In the far distance can be glimpsed an old GWR diesel railcar.
W. POTTER
CTY. KIDDERMINSTER RAILWAY
MUSEUM

This photo at Swindon Town station is a happy reminder of days on the diesel tutoring, and shows my friend and colleague George Watts (3rd left) on a teaching duty with three new driver candidates. There were four of us on the tutoring team at Swindon — George, myself, Jack Nurse and Noel Butcher.
CTY. GEORGE WATTS

BR's diesel railbus No. W79978 seen at Swindon shed in 1961. This was allocated to work on the Tetbury branch as part of the railbus experiment on the Tetbury and Cirencester branches.
W. POTTER
CTY. KIDDERMINSTER RAILWAY
MUSEUM

London-Plymouth trip, thirty to forty gallons per mile. He would shovel on that same journey six to seven tons of coal and as the tender held only four thousand gallons of water, they would have to pick up water on the run, by lowering the scoop as they went over water troughs at Aldermaston, Fairwood Junction, Cogload Junction and Exminster, picking up 3,000 gallons in 15 seconds each time. When these troughs were full, they held up to 6,250 gallons. Beside the track there would be a pumping station with a tank which held up to 40,000 gallons of water and those troughs would be full again within three minutes. Of course, the troughs had to be placed where the ground was flat and near to a good supply of water. That's how it was, the glory of steam, just brute force and boiled water!

The furthest we worked from Swindon was Taunton, with fish and parcels traffic, not passenger. In the other directions our limits were Paddington, Leicester and Cardiff, although, with the onset of dieselisation, the Welsh outpost became Swansea with the ability of the diesels to go further with less attention. The toil and sheer physical effort of my younger years was now replaced and rewarded with a job with no physical effort. Both my promotion to driver and the gradual changing of motive power seemed to emphasise this physically easier existence, and I had more time to enjoy the runs, which seemed different each time as the seasons changed. My favourite run was always the trip to Paddington, the excitement of the high-speed journey along Brunel's great construction in sharp contrast to the leisurely pace of my local much-loved favourite, the Midland & South Western Junction line down through [Swindon] Town to Andover.

In the summer of 1958 I was involved in a difficulty that almost blemished my clean driving record on the railway. I was in charge of a diesel freightliner which had originated at Parkeston Quay. I had taken it on at Stratford and its destination was Cardiff. During daylight hours these trains had to reduce their speed to 60 miles per hour between the hours of 12 noon and 9.00 p.m during summer. I brought the train down from Acton Wells onto the main line at Acton and I knew I was running in front of the 11.45 ex-Paddington and was hoping to keep out of the way of that particular train. I managed to get as far as Steventon when I was switched into the loop for the 11.45 to go by. As was normal practice in this situation, I stopped at the end of the loop and went to the signalman to let him know I was the driver on the Acton Wells freightliner. My loco was a Class 47 diesel electric and, of course, by this time we were on single manning.

The signalman said "That's all right, driver, but there's an Inspector up here on the phone in the box who wants to talk to you." So now I was communicating with Reading Panel Box, and this fellow came on the phone and asked me "Driver, are you aware of the speed of your train?"

"Yes, sixty miles an hour."

"Well I clocked you at sixty-five between Pangbourne and Cholsey!"

'Not according to my speedometer," I replied firmly.

"Well, I'm taking you off. You'll be relieved at Swindon."

"Of course I will. That's my home depot! It's the end of my shift. I'm coming off anyway!"

When I got back to Swindon, the Supervisor, came out and told me I'd been suspended. "It's alleged that you've been speeding with a freightliner."

The next day I was in the driver's cabin, not allowed to drive, and Len Smith, our ASLEF Union rep came in to see me.

"What's the problem, Gordon?"

When I told him the situation he said "Come on. We're going up the station to see the Area Manager."

Well, the Area Manager didn't know anything about it! Len was indignant. "You mean to tell me that one of your top drivers has been taken off and you don't know a thing about it! Well, I'll tell you something right now – get this man reinstated, back on his job, because if you don't, I'll have this entire depot out on the streets! And they'll support this man one hundred per cent!"

So it was arranged for Larry Whitney, the Chief Locomotive Inspector, to come and see me, and he informed me "Gordon, I've looked through your records and you've got nothing to worry about."

"Of course I haven't! But I want an interview with Mr. Bartlett (who was Superintendent of the Bristol Division). The fact is I have been accused of overspeeding with a train when I *know* I was doing my job correctly."

So they arranged the interview for me. I told the Super I was driving correctly and he told me the loco had been examined and the speedometer in it was found to be recording 5 miles per hour low! So, in other words, when you thought you were doing sixty you were actually running at sixty-five! Mr. Bartlett told me it wasn't my fault.

But I wasn't entirely satisfied. "So Mr. Bartlett, the next time I'm on an express at 90 miles an hour, and I'm behind time, do I run 85 or 90?"

"What!" he thundered. "Man with your experience! Maximum speed!"

"And if I've got a faulty speedometer next time and I'm running at 95 are you going to take me off?"

Whitney, the CLI, looked at Bartlett and said, nodding, "He's right, guv'nor."

And that's how it ended. That Inspector in Reading, how did we know his watch was reliable? To me, it just wasn't good enough, not a correct way of doing things, to take me off driving without the necessary checks being undertaken.

Life changed again forever with the birth of our son, Michael, on 2nd January 1960. He became very interested in the railway and eventually went into the Works as a machinist until it closed in 1986. One memorable short conversation with my son sticks forever in my mind, and he wasn't more than about eight years old at the time. It was an unpleasant, cold and wet morning as I looked in to say goodbye to him before heading for work on my bicycle, and I commented to him upon the unfairness of it all as I prepared to brave the

No. 48589 on a parcels train on 23rd January 1963.

The winter of 1963 was a testing time for us on the railway, but looking back it amazes me to remember that I don't think we ever had to cancel a service. Cancelling a train was a serious matter, but the weather never beat us. On the main picture here we see the 9.05 Paddington–Cheltenham service, 10.10 out of Swindon, taking the curve for the Gloucester line on 29th January 1963. Swindon station and West box are visible in the background. Our main concern at the shed was to make sure your injectors didn't freeze because they put water back into the boiler. You had two, an exhaust injector and a live injector, and you worked them alternately. My colleague Dave Jones, who used to cycle in from Brinkworth in all weathers, recalled being on the Leicester overnight run and being delayed at Oxford and Banbury by points clogged up with snow, and a blizzard making them four hours late back into Swindon. There were icicles in Charwelton Tunnel which rang like bells when you struck them. COLLECTION PETER TIMMS

Swindon station on 1st January 1963 after a heavy snowfall the previous day.
COLIN MOUNTFORD

A quiet scene in the 1960s on the down branch platform at Swindon, with a DMU set in the platform and luggage trolleys outside the shunters' cabin, which was behind the right-hand window.
LENS OF SUTTON

Diesels on Swindon shed with an '800' class 'Mayback' outside on one of the straights with a Drewry 0–6–0 shunting engine. We often referred to these 'Maybacks' as the Bo-Bo class on account of their four-wheel bogies.
W. POTTER, CTY. KIDDERMINSTER RAILWAY MUSEUM

elements in order that the railway might keep running. Back came the muffled reply from beneath the sheets – "*Your choice of jobs, Dad!*"

My route onto tutoring on the diesels was quite simple. I had learned both driving on the diesels and tutoring on them at more or less the same time, had passed on three classes of diesels, the diesel-multiple units, the 'Hymek' (hydraulics) and the diesel-electric '47' class, and on 14th January 1962, Sam Morgan, our shedmaster at Swindon, approached me to invite me to become a tutor driver, as one of the team was retiring and he considered me the ideal chap to fill the vacancy. Well, of course, I'd been a tutor all along for years in the Sunday morning Improvement classes, and realised that steam would be eventually fully replaced by the new traction, and I wanted to be as well up on it as possible. So I immediately agreed, and went on a course with the Inspectors to prepare me for it, starting on 16th January 1962. My attitude, as I have already indicated, was that I needed to adapt to stay in work, that diesels were the coming thing and there was no going back. Further, I had discovered through the Improvement classes and my Faverdale experience that I really enjoyed the teaching side of railway work, and derived great personal satisfaction from imparting skills to others, so it was an easy decision to make. The rules and regulations would be the same, but the type of traction was to change completely. My training runs on the dmu's were usually Swindon to Gloucester, and there was a turn to Bristol. When the hydraulics and diesel-electrics came in, it could be anywhere, including Paddington. The dmu's were gear-driven, so you changed gears like on a car, whereas with the bigger diesels the gears changed automatically with your speed. That was something I had to get used to.

The voluntary Improvement class had now more or less come to an end, because you were now tutored privately by the Railway on each locomotive that you were going to drive. On the first diesel that you ever learnt you were given three weeks, but after that sometimes you were allowed as little as three days. I was given a brief outline of the job and then more or less taught myself by reading books. I'd study the manuals, then put it into my words that I knew the men I would be teaching would understand, using railway language. There were four of us tutoring at Swindon and I never had a pupil of mine fail his examinations, a record of which I was very proud. It was a job where you had two men on one locomotive and never ever did you have two men of the same ability, so you had to be very careful to ensure that the man who picked up things very quickly did not do so in a way that caused the slower man to lose confidence. I'd always try to give the difficult questions to the man that was more advanced so that the fellow lagging behind could learn off his back, so to speak, with easier questions for him to answer and develop his confidence.

I was issued with a little blue card by the superintendent, which allowed me to take two men out on the road for tutoring and I could show it to any driver, on any service, anywhere, and take over that train. That relieved him of his command and I was now solely responsible for the running of the train while I was teaching the two men. I would inform the booked driver "I am taking this train from here to Westbury for tutoring." The driver would travel 'on the cushions' while I worked with the men, and for that job I would receive 2/6d a day extra over my normal driver's pay. When we reached a destination on those teaching runs, I would tell the men to clear their heads, forget all about it, as I reckoned that 40 minutes was the maximum time they could take things in properly. I'd learned that at Darlington. I'd tell them to have a walk into town, visit the shops, get some fresh air, then we'd come back to the station and ride home as passengers, during which time we would have questions and answers on the journey.

On one of these training runs we went to Trowbridge, and walked up into the town and passed a shop that was selling garden ornaments. In the window was a little painted stone rabbit, priced at 1/9d. I had the two trainees with me, on this day Bernard Smith and Arthur Gover. Arthur was a bit of a character and with a grin he said to me "I suppose you're going to buy that rabbit with that half-a-crown they paid you today?"

"Yes," I replied, "and I'm going to name that rabbit after you two buggers! How about Bernhardt? No, hang on a minute, I've changed my mind. Having you two with me for a fortnight has given me heartburn, how's that!? That'll be his name. Heartbern! Named after you two!" And that same ornamental rabbit, minus its paint, still stands in my back garden in Churchward Avenue today!

Preparation of a diesel locomotive was only about a twenty-minute duty. There was nothing to look at bar your fuel. There was no motion to oil, but you'd check your fire bottles to see that the dates were correct – all diesel locos had

'Artburn, my souvenir rabbit from the tutoring trip to Trowbridge, still sits in my back garden today.
COLLECTION GORDON SHURMER

Both steam and diesel traction are in evidence in the distance in this dingy interior view of the running shed on 9th May 1964. This was the 1871 section of the shed, with a 40ft turntable with 21 short roads, and five through roads leading onto the table and two straight dead-end roads. Pannier tanks were usually seen around this turntable, which remained manually operated to the end. The larger locos used the adjacent 1908 building with the 65ft table. This view looks south towards the coal stage.

V. R. WEBSTER CTY. KIDDERMINSTER RAILWAY MUSEUM

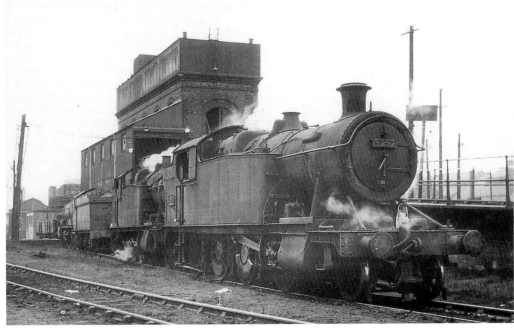

Ex-GWR 42XX class 2–8–0s 5252 and 5246 by the coaling stage at Swindon shed on 28th January 1964. 'Castle' class 4–6–0 No. 7004 Eastnor Castle is visible beyond. This was the western side of the coal stage, showing the sheltering built for protection of the coal men during coaling operations.
W. POTTER
CTY. KIDDERMINSTER
RAILWAY MUSEUM

fire bottles that we could detonate by pressing a button. Diesels did occasionally catch fire. The only time I recall this happening to me was at Haresfield one day, coming up with a train from Gloucester, when I saw flames coming from the underside of a coach. The fire alarm bell sounded and I stopped the train and we herded all the passengers into the back power car. With the fire dealt with, an assisting engine, a Hymek, came from Gloucester and our train was taken up to Stroud where the Area Manager met me on the platform. "All right, driver, we'll put you in the siding and we'll stop the next up fast and put you all on there!" I'll never forget it, the fireman on the assisting loco firmly told the local official "Here, this bloke's been on 'is own, had enough to contend with – Oi'm making 'im a cup o'tea before we do anything!" Of course, we'd run all our working lives with fire aboard and thought nothing of it, but fire aboard a diesel was a great hazard.

I never found the diesels difficult – in fact it was a far easier job, cleaner, quieter, but the love had gone. I was never so proud climbing out of the cab of a diesel as I had been out of steam. You simply had a different relationship with a diesel to the one you you had with a steam loco. As long as there was fire in her belly and water in her boiler, with steam and smoke rising, she was always a sleeping giant but always also alive. With the diesels, the driver just came in, pressed a button, and that was it. They could stand in the shed quiet for a month, just another vehicle, until activated by the press of a button. With steam you had a total physical and mental experience. With diesels it was more in the mind, a dead experience. At night on the diesels I often had to put the side window down to allow the night air to flood the cab in an effort to stay alert. Drivers often used to refer to that time after midnight, if you were coming out of Paddington with a

late train, as 'The Dead Patch'. There were times on those turns when I would look across to that empty seat and feel sure that the old man, my old gaffer Bill Hinder, was there watching over me.

The main difference in driving a diesel locomotive was that the power was always there, always ready on tap, whereas with the steam loco there was the essential and lengthy preparation and, out on the road, if you knew that a few miles ahead of you you had a steep gradient to climb, the fireman would be working for that, ensuring that he had a full head of steam ready. With the diesel you had no such concern, as you just waited until you reached the foot of the gradient and then opened the controller just a little wider. It was all there, the engine revved a bit harder, the dynamo generated more electricity, and the power was there simultaneously. There was no build-up, and with the modern high-power 125 mph diesels there's 2500 horse power *at each end*, so you have a 5000 horse power train. Of course, with change came hardship, whereby men of a certain age found it hard to accept the changes – in the steam era the driver was always the boss – he would look at the steam pressure, check the amount of water in the boiler, and if it wasn't working as it should and he considered it needed to be stopped to have attention, he'd pull up at the first signal box and when the signalman came to the window, the driver would say "Gone off the boil a bit, mate, we need a few minutes to put ourselves right." But with the diesel, you didn't know that until your lights started flashing. You knew that an amber light indicated a fault, but now the question became, is the fault where you've lost power, or is the fault where you haven't lost power? Is it just high water temperature, and what's causing this? Is it the oil? When you were on your own in the middle of the night, this was a daunting prospect, and many of the men who had been the

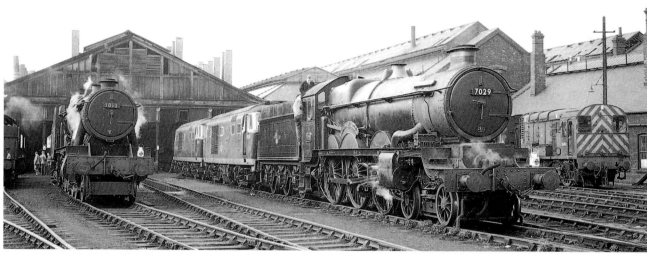

On 26th April 1964, GWR-designed 'Castle' class 4–6–0 No. 7029 Clun Castle *and 'County' class 4–6–0 No. 1013* County of Dorset *outside Swindon shed, in the company of two Hymek diesel hydraulic locos and a diesel shunter.*

BRIAN MOORE, CTY. KIDDERMINSTER RAILWAY MUSEUM

An undated view of Hymek diesel D7021 facing London in Swindon station, with colleagues Con Mason and Brian Kervin aboard. I fired for Con during World War 2. He was an interesting character who knew no fear. He lived just two doors down from us in Churchward Avenue. Still recalled in our road is the time he wanted to remove a troublesome tree stump from his back garden and decided to do the job with gunpowder! Having prepared it, he lit the fuse and retired indoors to await the explosion. Unfortunately, the lady next door came out to hang her washing just as the explosion rocked the neighbourhood. The tree stump was successfully removed and the poor lady fainted!

KENNETH LEECH

This is how Swindon station looked in the early 1960s with DMUs on local trains.

boss in the steam age found that they were now working with a machine that was effectively in charge of them.

With the growth of the diesel era in the 50s and 60s, it meant that Swindon locomotive shed had to be equipped to offer dual facilities to both steam and diesel. They were both together for a period, and a part of the shed was ruled off for diesel locomotives only. Initially, of the nine straight roads into the shed, numbers 8 and 9 were apportioned for the new traction. With dieselisation, many of the smaller sheds eventually went altogether – Chippenham, for example, was never a diesel shed, and by the time steam was finally phased out, the allocations were concentrated in the remaining large depots – Old Oak Common, Slough, Reading, Swindon, Tyseley – with big gaps in between. By October 1968, when the last diagrammed steam service ran from Paddington, the diesel fleet had increased sufficiently to enable the date to be fixed for the final withdrawal of steam. The atmosphere in Swindon shed had changed completely, with the main jobs now being electricians, refuellers and fitters replacing the tubers, smokeboxers and coalmen. In most cases the men took early redundancy. The shed still required to be kept clean in its final years, but diesels didn't require the constant clearing up after them that their predecessors demanded. A new building, all asbestos and girders, known locally as the 'Elephant House', was erected close to Swindon station for use by fitters and refuellers, housing just one loco at a time, to replace the ailing shed, which was retained for a time, until demolition, as merely a signing-on point.

Early on Boxing Day in 1969, my Dad passed away. I had spoken to him earlier on Christmas Day when he'd been admiring one of my models, a Tudor-style Christmas street with stage-coach, telling me it was the best I'd ever done. He'd got his wish, to go quickly, and was never a burden to anyone. Mum passed away just over a year later, in January

1971, on my 50th birthday. In Autumn of that year I was settling up business on our old home in Havelock Street and went to the house to lock up for the last time. Upon an impulse, I went up to my old bedroom and, it was flooded with sunlight. The evening sun was shining through that back bedroom and with the door open to the stairs, the whole house was illuminated by it. I'd never seen that old house lit up like that in all the years we lived there and the memory will live with me forever. Both Mum and Dad had left Havelock Street not knowing they'd never return to it. It was a happy home full of memories.

I completed my tutoring years on the diesels in 1969 and went back to driving on the now all-diesel network. The tutor-drivers were disbanded and it was decided that the Locomotive Inspectors who did the examining would do the tutoring themselves. By 1980, I was having trouble with my hips which caused me problems in moving around, and I was considering early retirement when the Management asked me if I would consider going round the schools to talk to the children about the dangers of playing near railway lines. I took this on and really enjoyed my stint in the world of education, going to schools as far away as Reading, Box, Calne and Stroud. The biggest problem for me was finding the schools, as I had to travel by train and bus as I was physically unable to drive any more, although I once cycled to Purton in the rain and, as I swung into a near-flooded playground, the headmaster greeted me with "You look more like the commander of a submarine than an engine driver!" I think the thing that really struck me about my school visits was how much times had changed in education since my own schooldays. I even once heard a pupil address a headmaster by his Christian name!

However, I fell down at work in 1981 and couldn't stand up properly, and that's when I had the first of many hip oper-

This picture of me in charge of a Class 46 Crompton & Parkinson diesel locomotive, No. 46015, was taken at Didcot on 24th June 1976. We had taken over a train of coal from South Wales at Swindon and took it on to Didcot Power Station, then ran empty back to Swindon. John Sherman was my second man, I remember.
COLLECTION GORDON SHURMER

ations and had to leave the railway for good. It was a very sad day for me in 1981 when the Medical Officer had me down to Bristol, following the October operation on both hips. The Area Manager came to see me at home on 31st July 1982 to inform me that my status would only allow BR to pay me for another twelve months. I was philosophical – "Well, Mr. Brown, you don't ever back a horse that's not going to run any more." In Bristol, I knocked on Dr. Anderson's door, and as soon as I stepped inside the M.O. told me "Don't sit down, laddie. Get back to Swindon on the next train. Put in your resignation because you'll never drive a train again. You can throw that old peaked cap away!"

He must have seen the shocked look on my face because he continued "I'm not saying you *couldn't* drive a train, but you could never deal with an emergency if you had to leave the cab. You're disappointed?"

"Yes, guv'nor. If I could have gone to 65 I'd have done half a century."

"Don't come down here and boast to me! Get off home and put in your resignation and get your railway pension."

So that was it. They told me "You'll have to resign. We can't even offer you a job in the car park." But I'd completed 46½ years on the railway, which wasn't at all bad, was it? The problem with my hips wasn't the result of a specific incident, it was just general wear and tear. Mr Young, the surgeon, told me "I've seen worse hips than yours, but not very often!" So I resigned there and then in the booking office at the station where I'd been based all my working life. The railways never gave a great deal away – we had to fight for our overalls, conditions of service, classification of drivers, sick pay, although our ASLEF Union did a lot of good work in securing these rights over the years. I always remember Sir Winston

Churchill saying "Watch ASLEF!" They did indeed become very powerful.

So that was my career on the railway. I'm so proud that I was associated with the days of steam, but, like many of the senior generations locally, I mourn the loss of the railway in the life of my hometown. With the closure of the Works just five years after I was forced to retire, Swindon ceased to be a true railway community. The ability of the diesel locomotives to go farther with less preparation eradicated the need for many of the running sheds of the era in which I first learned my trade, so today there is not a single locomotive shed remaining between London and Bristol. Lost also has been the gradual build-up that I enjoyed as a child to the passage of a train through Swindon – the anticipation I remember from those days as the signalman pulled the lever, the sound of the bell code, the hum of the wires, the movement of a signal arm, then in the distance the approaching rumble, which increased in intensity until the steam giant and its train roared through the station, and the whole process repeated itself in reverse.

I think you'll find that a top driver these days earns around £37,000 a year salary, sat on their cushions and with their footwarmers in a cosy cab, not shovelling their guts out as I was. But I don't want to sound as if I begrudge them their better conditions. It's what ASLEF fought for, after all, but I remain grateful for my involvement in both eras, for the inspiration and personal satisfaction I derived from being part of the pre-war generation who carried on the great GWR tradition, and the pride I had in being able to adapt and practise my belief in education in passing on skills to the railwaymen of post-steam days.

Swindon is today a museum of industrial archaeology, with a host of new industries which have enabled the town to thrive in another age which has seen the population almost double in the last forty years. The railway past is preserved in the local archives, in books such as this, and in the new museum at STEAM, where I and several old work colleagues are able to present that history to visitors on the preserved steam locomotives there, and also re-live our careers together over a cup of tea. We also meet in sadness and respect every so often at the Crematorium to pay tribute to another old workmate from the iron road who has passed away.

Today the building which housed the main offices of the GWR and the drawing office, where I first entered my GWR employment nearly 70 years ago, is now occupied by the National Monuments Record Office. The stone reliefs of a broad-gauge locomotive still remain on the south-facing wall overlooking the site of Swindon's first locomotive shed of the 19th century, proudly drawing the attention of 21st-century passengers on the main line to an era of skilled and dedicated industry at Swindon and a railway livelihood of which I was proud to be a part.

Looking back through my life as most people do at my age, I often find myself reminiscing about the steam age and

I am grateful fate allowed me to achieve my great ambition in life, which was to be an engine driver. The work that was accomplished with a steam locomotive by a driver and fireman with skill, brute force and boiled water was truly remarkable.

Tribute should also be paid to the women, those who worked for the GWR, and to the wives of the men who served as I did, especially my wife Hazel, who had to tolerate the unsociable hours inflicted on their menfolk and run the home with dedication and uncomplaining fortitude. I would

also like to say how grateful I am to author Mike Fenton, with whom I've worked on this book for what seems an age now, who skilfully transferred my memories into readable material for this work.

Finally, as much as I missed the job when I was required to retire after 46½ years through ill health, what I missed even more was the camaraderie with the men with whom I worked. They were and always will be to me 'the Salt of the Earth'.

Right from the start of the research for this book, these two bas-relief depictions of a Broad Gauge locomotive on the wall of the Main Office block, now the National Monuments Record, have constantly come up in conversation betwen Gordon and Mike Fenton. Their presence here is a link with and a recognitition of Swindon's Broad Gauge history, because these stone panels were located originally on the masonry ends of the original Broad Gauge shed of 1841, and today appropriately overlook the site of the old shed in full view of main-line passengers between London and Bristol. They are thought to depict the locomotive Centaur *of the 'Firefly' class, built by Nasmyth, Gaskell & Co. of Manchester in the days before the GWR began to produce its own engines at Swindon Works.* Centaur *was one of 62 locos of its class, a 2–2–2 with 15in by 18in cylinders and 7ft diameter wheels, first produced in March 1840. It was delivered to the GWR in December 1841 and ceased work in November 1867. With the threatened demolition of the old shed about 1890 to accommodate a proposed extension to the Works, with the abolition of the Broad Gauge imminent, the reliefs were removed into safe custody, which is why later photos of the building do not show them. As it happened, the shed was not actually demolished for another 40 years! When the further storey was added to the Main Offices to provide a new drawing office during the early years of the 20th century, the reliefs were brought out and incorporated into their now familiar position.*   M. FENTON

Chris Brown (1894-1968), one of the toughest characters at Swindon. He attained the rank of driver very young, at the age of 27, and was a well-known instructor in Improvement classes.

CTY. MRS. IRIS HACKER

Charlie Pullen (1896-1968) was the Inspector featured in the Midland & South Western Christmas Day chapter. He always took a great interest in my career.

Cleaners Dowdeswell, Conlon, Tarrant and Rumbelow (front) at the back of Swindon running shed about 1938. Cleaning was a way of getting youngsters familiar with the engine, learning the names of the parts and how they worked but at the same time doing an essential job. It helped you overcome fears and develop confidence.

CTY. CYRIL TARRANT

Shunters in the Cocklebury yard c.1950, with driver Jefferies (centre).
DAVE 'BRINKWORTH' JONES

Mark Wilkins, Fireman. Mark had two years as cleaner on Malmesbury loco shed before coming to Swindon. His recollections of work in No. 2 Link were invaluable to this book.

A typical sight all over Swindon for many years — cleaner Colin Trembling cycling to the shed from Stratton St. Margaret in 1951.
CTY. COLIN TREMBLING

24914

(975)
6 bks., 250 lvs.—1/37—Est. 231 [26]

Name **Gordon Albert George Shurmer**

PROMOTIONS AND RATES OF WAGES

Basic Seniority Date :— 1.2.37

Basic Date for Advances : 9.6.39 Turns 129   Basic Date for Advances 22.3.56 Turns 6

Date	Rate	Position	Date	Rate	Position
2.3.36		Office Boy	2.11.52	143/-	RSNT. 14
1.2.37		Engine cleaner	6.12.53	147/-	RSNT. 15.
3.7.39		Acting Fireman	24.1.54	151/6	RSC.13
25.9.39		(Temp. S.S.) Engine cleaner	29.3.54	159/6	Driver
6.11.39	9/6	Fireman	4.10.54	172/6	RSNT16
9.6.41	10/6		24.1.55	175/-	
9.6.43	66/-		22.3.55	180/-	
30.7.45	74/6	RSC113	15.6.55	187/-	RSC20
1.7.46	102/6	S/9448.	23.1.56	200/-	" 22
30.6.47	110/-	RSC 119.	22.3.56	212/-	
1.2.48	117/-	RSC 1.			
1.1.51	126/-	M.1221			
3.8.51	136/-	RSNT 13			

STATIONS AND DESCRIPTION OF WORK

Date	Station	Date	Station
2.3.36	Swindon		
1.2.37	do		
3.7.39	do.		
25.9.39	do.		
6.11.39	do.		
29.3.54	-do-		

Date	Locality	Penalty, &c.	Circumstances	Reference to Correspondence

24914

Date of Birth **31st January 1921**

EYESIGHT							EYESIGHT							MEDICAL			INSPECTOR	
Date	Form			Colour			Date	Form			Colour			Date	By whom Examined	Result	Date	Result
	R.	L.	B.	W.	B.	E.G.		R.	L.	B.	W.	B.	E.G.					
29.1.37	6/6	6/6	6/6	✓	✓	✓								29.1.37	Dr Bennett	Passed	3.2.47	Passed
31.10.39	6/6	6/6	6/6	✓	✓	✓								31.10.39	-do-	-do-	24.8.50	Passed
4.11.40	6/6	6/6	6/6	—	—	✓								4.11.40	-do- (Boils on arms)	-do-		
9.6.41	6/6	6/6	6/6	—	—	—								9.6.41	Dr Bennett (Scarlet Fever)	-do-		
9.6.41 S'don	6/6	6/6	6/6	✓	—	—												
1.11.46 Swindon																		
24.8.50	6/6	6/6	6/6															

Date	Locality	Penalty, &c.	Circumstances	Reference to Correspondence

ASSEMBLING THE LINKS
Reminiscences of Roster Clerk Danny Williams

I was roster clerk at Swindon shed from December 1956 and found that my experience on the footplate was very useful when it came to working out the turns in the links, as I always took the view that I should work out the rostering in a manner that I would have appreciated myself if I'd still been a fireman, and I seemed to get on well with all the crews. I had a pretty good idea of how the links should look, what was practical, and would always put myself in the position of the crews. I'd started as a cleaner at Burry Port on 1st December 1947, then came to Swindon as a fireman on 1st November 1948. I progressed through the Swindon links as far as No. 6, the lower goods link, but had to come off the footplate because of ill health. I went into the Swindon office on 24th January 1955 and nearly two years later took on the rostering work upon which I worked until 1985. I was trained in the job by Tom Crowley, who used to relate stories of an earlier roster clerk, Harry Ann, who used to put up the roster sheets every Saturday morning, then scarper on his bike before anyone could make a fuss with him over their turns. Harry was a big Swindon Town follower and didn't want to get caught on match day!

I lived in Stratton in those days and used to come into work on the Highworth workmen's train in the morning, boarding at Stratton on the branch. My working day was 8.0 a.m. to 5.0 p.m. with an hour's meal break. When there were big changes in the links we would have to work many extra hours, including Saturdays and Sundays. There were two of us and we used to roster all the drivers, firemen, engine cleaners and all the shed staff — the firedroppers, boilerwashers, coal stage men, and also the Works shunters who came under the control of the shunters' foreman at that time. Our office was on the corner of the running shed, right opposite the addressograph office, along with the Chief Clerk's office. It also served as a pay office on Thursdays. The line into the shed big turntable separated the addressograph office and our office.

You have to understand that the links were constantly changing, with amendments being made each month and jobs being switched from one link to another. If a certain train service or turn was discontinued, then you had to try to balance the link and you had to maintain a balance of work in the links and equalisation of earnings, which would be quite a thing with the men. The diagramming people at Paddington used to send the diagrams to the depots every May and October and you really had to make the best of it, arranging the turns to suit the work allocated to the depot. We had a diagram from which the roster clerk worked, and he would keep a master copy of this. He also kept a copy which was posted in the notice cases at the running shed, and also had a copy for each driver to take with him in a plastic folder. These were left with the timekeeper and when the driver booked on he'd ask for his turn by number and the timekeeper would hand him the diagram which he was expected to return at the end of his turn. He didn't always remember, of course, and if he was on a turn for a week in the normal way and was sick for a day, this would cause problems, and the timekeeper would have to go round to the noticeboard and scribble out a quick replacement for the covering driver.

An important consideration for the roster clerk was to ensure that each driver maintained good road knowledge. It is an oversimplification to say that No. 1 link was all the fast passenger trains and that the bottom passenger, No. 4, was all the local stoppers as is sometimes assumed. There would be London jobs, for instance, in all the passenger links, in order to ensure that continuation of route knowledge, as this kept train crew costs down. If you had a Paddington turn in No. 4 Link and the driver was promoted to No. 3 and there was no Paddington job in that link, you then had the cost of teaching him the road again when he reached No. 2 Link by the need to cover his turn of duty in No. 2 while he was learning. Eventually that might lead to upgrading a passed fireman to a driver and paying him a higher rate of pay as a driver, or replacing him further down as a fireman with a senior fireman and then having to upgrade a cleaner to a fireman. The continuity of road knowledge avoided this and made things easier all round.

On the rosters there was a daily slip of paper with all the drivers in all links on it, and that slip would be put on the chart for Monday's turns, then we would produce another slip for Tuesday, and so on throughout the week, a separate one for each day. Now when the clerk looked at the sheet, he might notice, for instance, that there was a man on a rest day, so I had to cover the 6.50 Paddington on a Monday and he'd make a note to do this on a scrap sheet. On the Leicester overnight turn, they had a local agreement that if the Spare 2 man wasn't available, he would take the man off the 6.50 Paddington to work the Leicester to ensure it had a driver who knew the road through already being in the link, as road knowledge to Leicester was only in No. 1 Link and you would then cover the Paddington job by whatever means you had.

Our day in the office was basically spent on the paperwork, and going out into the noticeboard area if alterations needed making. There were seven boards here held in glass cases, where the turns would be posted every day, numbered 1-7. No. 1 board contained all the passenger links, Nos. 1-4, and No. 2 board had the Goods Links, Nos. 5 and 6. No. 3 board contained the huge Control Link on its own, over 70 turns to cover through freight work. I always thought this was an odd name for a link, but basically there were freight control offices all over the system, ours being at Swindon Transfer. The main office was at Bristol, and this link provided good experience for men going into the Swindon goods links. No. 4 board had the Van and Old Town links on it, and No. 5 was for daily alterations through sickness and leave. No. 6 board listed the Transfer and Shed/Coal Stage links and No. 7 was the factory pilots. We had to send out an office messenger to inform drivers of altered turns after rest days. If a driver was off on a rest day on a Monday, a call note would be sent to him informing him of his Tuesday duty if it was altered. It was very rare for drivers to have a telephone back then. It was also common practice with the shift foreman that if he had a truck of sand arriving for the sandhouse and he wanted it unloaded quickly, if no shed staff were available, he would get two or three engine cleaners to do it and they would be

COMMENCING 13/6/55.

SWINDON TURN 151

MEN   On Duty 10.52 M-S

Relieve Turn No. 150 men on
No. 73 engine at Station.

Swindon Jcn.		11. 7	P	SX
Swindon Town	11.15			
Swindon Jcn.		11.13	P	SO.
Swindon Town	11.21			
Change footplates with Turn 153 men				
(72 engine)				
Swindon Town	11.30	5/45	Shunt	
Change footplates with 5/50 ex				SX
Swindon Jcn.				SX
Swindon Town		6/ 4	P	M-S
Chiseldon	6/12	6/20		
Swindon Town	6/27	6/35	LE	
Shed	6/50			

Off Duty 7/ 5 8Hrs.13Mins.

SWINDON TURN 152

MEN   On Duty 8. 0 M-S

Prepare engine for 10.15 Swindon Town. -
Cheltenham.

Shed		9. 0	LE	
Swindon Town	9.20			
Change footplates with 6.40 Cheltenham men				
Swindon Town		9.48	Fgt.	
Andover	11.37	11.45	LE	
Shed	11.50	2/10	LE	
Andover		2/35	P	
Swindon Town	3/55			
Relieved.				

Off Duty 4/50 8Hrs. 0Mins.

SWINDON TURN 153

MEN   On Duty 5.20 SX

Prepare No. 73 engine.

Shed		6. 5	LE	SX
Swindon Jcn.		6.20	ES	
Shrivenham	6.32	7. 0	P	
Swindon Jcn.	7.11	7.20	LE	
Swindon Town	7.28			

On Duty 6.25 SO.

Prepare engine No. 73

Shed		7.10	LE	SO
Swindon Town	7.30			
Swindon Town		8. 9	P	M-S
Chiseldon	8.17	8.25		
Swindon Town	8.33	9.30	Shunt	
Change footplates with Turn 150 men,				
Turn 72 engine.				
Swindon Town	9.30	11.25	Shunt	
Change footplates with Turn 151 men				
Turn 73 engine.				
Swindon Town		12/38	P	
Swindon Jcn.	12/47			
Relieved at 1/ 0				

Off Duty 1/20   8hrs SX
               6¼ 55m SO

Taken from official papers for June 1955.

paid as a firing turn for the day. If I ever ran into difficulty over the rostering, I would go and discuss it with the LDC staff before putting it down on paper and, of course, it always helped that I'd been a fireman myself.

The question of balancing the links was really a matter of common sense. You couldn't put all the early morning turns in one link because the men in that link would then be on early starts all the time. You had to split it all up so that everyone had a variety of work, so it was always a week on early turns followed by a week on nights, afternoons or late turns. Jobs were put in to suit the work in the link and although No. 1 Link had the top jobs, sometimes a turn had to be moved to another link to balance things up. As one of our colleagues once stated, 'The top link was for seniority, the best work, but they had to have some of the rubbish as well.'

When assembling the goods links, Nos. 5 and 6, it depended on how much freight work there was. During my early years on rostering in the mid-50s, I remember there being as many as 16 turns in each goods link, but if there wasn't enough freight work allocated to the depot, they would add a couple of relief turns to make it up. If there weren't enough turns in these links, some Control Relief turns from No. 7 would be substituted to prevent men being dropped back through the links. There was more loose-coupled work in the lower link, No. 6, with more vacuum-fitted trains in No. 5, a better class of work with freights that could go faster. However, it really depended on how the LDC wanted to share the work out. If there was a lot of vacuum-fitted, they would have to allocate some of those jobs to No. 6 link. The main thing was to do it economically and without loss of road knowledge. The Gloucester pick-up goods would typically be in No. 6, the lower link, jobs which normally started at Swindon, whereas No. 5 contained more of relieving booked through trains such as the Barry bananas and the Rogerstone loco coal trains. It is my recollection that pick-up trains to Bristol ran on the Badminton line to Stoke Gifford whereas the goods trains to Bristol in the Bath direction were worked from Chippenham with Chippenham and Bristol men. The Westbury pick-up from Swindon covered the Swindon–Chippenham section, although there was, I remember, a Chippenham–Swindon run late in the evening which ran into the Cocklebury yard, bringing out goods from the Calne branch, and it took a fresh engine back after bringing up one for boiler washing. I also do recall a time when No. 5 Link had so much work that it was renumbered 5a and 5b, but this did not last for long.

1955 extracts from Bert Withers'
driver's logbook from No. 3 Passenger Link.

When George Measom published his Illustrated Guide to the Great Western Railway in 1852, borrowing from Bourne's earlier work but presenting it in a more blandly poetic way ('... but hark! The bell rings!'), he included this 'view from the gallery of Swindon station'. It gives an early drawn impression of the junction in 1852, which, allowing for artistic licence, does contain some interesting features. The word 'gallery' refers to the footbridge between the up and down sides of the station. The running shed features in the distance, arrowed, to the left of the early disc-and-crossbar signal. A single pilot engine, possibly a station pilot, is depicted on the Up line, whilst there appears to be a passenger train with some of the earliest most spartan carriages coming into the station from Gloucester. A single crossover road from the Down side at left gave access to the Gloucester branch, with another station pilot simmering on the Down branch platform road. The buildings of New Swindon in the left distance can be dismissed as being fairly inaccurate, although St. Mark's Church is a fairly easily recognised landmark. In the right distance are the workshops and chimneys of the embryonic Swindon Works, with the engine house, standing at right-angles to the running shed, indicated by the small arrow. Easily the most interesting feature here is the track running at right-angles to the main lines with the small turntable to moving new wagons from the factory onto the running lines, and one can be seen in close proximity to the turntable ready to go into traffic.

APPENDIX
A HISTORY OF SWINDON'S LOCOMOTIVE SHEDS

'That the Principal Locomotive Station and Repairing Shops be established at or near the Junction with the Cheltenham and Great Western Union Railway at Swindon'. With these words, in a resolution of 6th October 1840, did the Directors of the Great Western Railway, acting upon advice from Isambard Brunel and Daniel Gooch, confer upon Swindon a date to instigate a century and a half of association with the railway and a tradition of honest, skilled industry with which the town will be forever associated. Swindon at that time was a sleepy hilltop town overlooking the flat plain of north Wiltshire, but the inspections of Brunel and Gooch during the Autumn of 1840 had determined that the area which was to become New Swindon was the ideal place for locomotive operations for a number of reasons.

Swindon was the point at which there was a significant change in gradient on the main Paddington–Bristol line, in those days requiring a change in motive power; so with a different class of engine needed for each section, it was an obvious choice for a locomotive shed. It was also, of course, the junction with the line through the Golden Valley to Gloucester and Cheltenham, and a convenient spot at which to house banking and pilot engines, bearing in mind the close proximity to inclines at Wootton Bassett and Sapperton. Further, the junction was close to the North Wilts Canal, which Gooch considered advantageous for the cheap delivery of coal and coke, although one wonders if he had not fully considered the new railway's potential for freight carriage at this point in time? The only apparent problem was thought to be the lack of an obvious water supply, but construction of reservoirs north of the line and the eventual link with Kemble soon remedied this difficulty.

Locomotive sheds at Swindon span a total of 123 years, from the opening of the first broad-gauge shed in 1841 to final closure of its standard-gauge successor in November 1964. Broadly the history can be looked at in three phases – the broad gauge shed which stood on the north side of and parallel to the main GWR line to Bristol, the new 9-road shed which was opened in 1871 out on the east side of the Gloucester branch, and thirdly, the 1908 extensions to the 1871 building which provided a new 65ft turntable under cover.

Gooch originally envisaged an engine establishment of the roundhouse form in the triangle formed by the GWR main line and Cheltenham & Great Western Union Railway, with a western loop joining them, a loop which never materialised, but ultimately the sensible decision was taken to construct a straight-road rectangular shed just a short distance west of that first envisaged. It was considered that Swindon was an ideal stopping place for passengers to take a break from the journey, and both the Engineer and Gooch were of like mind in recommending to the Board of Directors as to the suitability of the location for a locomotive shed and Works. Hence, in 1841 the Directors authorised the construction of the new depot at Swindon so that a change of engine 'may be advantageously made and the trains stopped for the purpose of passengers taking refreshment'.

There was an early awareness that the lengthy preparation of an engine for the road required to be done under cover, and it is also worth considering that at that time it almost certainly took longer than it did for the engineman's counterparts of fifty and a hundred years later with their accumulated experience. In the 1840s, engine cleaners, firemen and drivers were a new breed of men working with a new technology as yet not fully developed, added to the fact that the GWR at first ordered its locomotives from factories elsewhere in the country. The railway records of the period are rife with reports of exploding boilers and the perils of running at speed in close proximity to several hundred gallons of boiling water. Gordon Shurmer's generation learned from their predecessors – the stalwart enginemen of the 1840s had no predecessors. Moreover, the vagaries of the British weather and the privations in those days of a cold winter and early darkness made it vital that adequate preparation of a steam locomotive was a job that needed to be done under shelter and close to adequate tooling, water and coaling facilities.

The original broad-gauge shed was built of timber which was the obvious choice for the main construction material as it was abundant, economical, and easy to erect. Posts were sunk in the ground at convenient centres and boarding placed horizontally between them to form the walls. Roof trusses were then fixed onto the posts and purlins, and timber rails running longitudinally were fixed onto the rafters of the trusses. The roof was of timber boards covered with slates, although there was an early exchange between Brunel and the Directors about the comparative costs of roofing in either canvas, zinc or slate. At the meeting of the Directors in Reading on 6th May 1841, the following figures were presented by Brunel:

Statement on Comparative Roof Expenses

	Open Engine Shed	Engine House	Fitters' Shops
In canvas	£2929	£3680	£911
In zinc	£3131	£3915	£911
In slate	£3306	£3915	£964

The reference to the 'open' engine shed is clearly an indication that the engine shed as first built had no doors at either end. Upon the recommendation of the Engineer that zinc be used instead of canvas on the centre roof of the engine house, and slate on the roofs of the open engine shed, the fitters' shops and the tender shop, the Directors approved Brunel's ideas on condition that the whole additional expense did not exceed £1,000.

It is important at this point to make a distinction between the use of the terms *engine shed* and *engine house*, as confusion is easily compounded by Bourne's famous lithograph of the 'house' with its impressive timber and wrought-iron roof and traverser platform which could move engines intended for repairs from the shed to the repair bays in the engine house and back again. This building was *not* the shed. There was a clear emphasis on the 'shed' being close to the operating lines and used for the running and stabling of engines and minor repairs carried out by the crews themselves. The 'house' was the building where the locomotives could be temporarily withdrawn from service to undergo more serious attention, with more skilled staff. Fortunately, Bourne's *History of the Great Western Railway* is quite clear on the subject, with two separate descriptions of the two buildings:

'At some distance west of the passenger station, on the north side of the line, is the Engine Depot; its arrangements are upon a large scale, and capable of accommodating about 100 engines; these consist of the engines in actual use, of the stock of spare engines and of those undergoing repair. At this station every train changes its engine, so that from this circumstance alone, at least twice as many engines are kept here as at any other part of the line. The Engine Shed is a rectangular building, 490ft long by 72 broad, and capable of holding upon its four lines of rails 48 engines and tenders; the two ends are open, the roof is of wood, slated, with louvres at intervals for the escape of steam. The engines standing here are all in serviceable condition, and a sufficient number of them are ready with their steam up to carry on the business of the Railway.'

1846

This early plan of the GWR at Swindon shows clearly the position of the original broad-gauge engine shed on the southern edge of a somewhat (at this stage) very embryonic Works. The building running at right-angles from the shed, labelled as the 'repairing shop', was in fact Bourne's 'Engine House', where running repairs could be mostly carried out by the drivers themselves. A traversing table, which could be moved into the running shed to enable locos to be moved on it into the engine house and into repairs stock, ran the length of the building and the diagram inset shows how this traverser's rails were extended into the loco shed to provide connection with the running lines there. Turntables and coking stage are shown to the east of the engine shed, and the early railway village provided by the Company for its workforce is already in place with several streets of New Swindon already established and named after locations to be served by the Great Western. St. Mark's Church and its neighbouring school to serve this community are also visible. Works facilities already exist for boilermakers, carpenters, smiths, turners and steam hammers, with erecting shop, wagon shops, offices and stores, and a small gasworks. Swindon's first GWR station is shown to the east of the junction with the Gloucester branch. An early signal box is located out on the up side of the main line to Bristol.

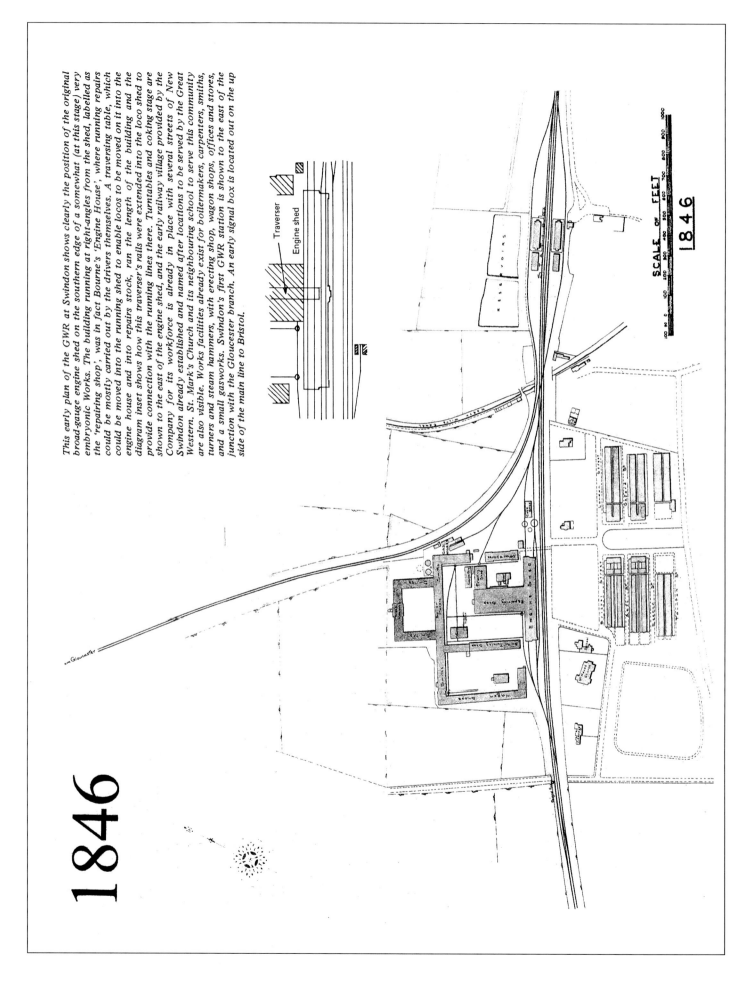

SCALE of FEET

1846

It was this building thus described which was Swindon's original running shed, and Bourne confirms the doorless ends previously mentioned. A report from the GWR Board meeting at Paddington of October 1841, which refers to the 'contemplated Engine Establishment at Swindon Junction', would confirm that the full provision there was not at that time available. Indeed, the new Locomotive Works became fully operational on 2nd January 1843, but it is thought that the running shed must have been operational by early or mid-1841, with surviving plans for it dating from 1840. There were four roads through the shed which had an internal width of 67ft 8in and the stabling tracks were in pairs at 13ft 2in centres. The south wall of the building was wooden with timber columns at 12ft centres and about 17ft from rail level to the underside of the timber roof trusses. There was also a row of similar timber posts along the centre of the building, giving intermediate support to these trusses. Between the support posts of the south wall were timber panels of windows or louvres. These posts were joined and bolted at ground level to tapered hardwood piles 12ft deep driven firmly into the clay subsoil. The internal tracks were mounted on longitudinal brick foundations with an inverted arch cross support, giving a shallow pit of maximum depth of 2ft below rail level. Large square pagoda-style smoke vents were provided over the tracks every 24ft. Indeed, this building was so well-constructed that it

lasted for the better part of a century, until long after it ceased to be in use as an engine shed.

As shown clearly on the accompanying plans and from glimpses on the few photographs that exist, the corners at each end of the shed were built in stone and the roof formed a gable over the open entrances at each end. Doors were added at a later date. On a masonry pediment above the return walls at each end of the shed facing the main line were carved stone bas-reliefs depicting a 2-2-2 'Firefly' class locomotive, thought to be *Centaur*. About 6ft by 3ft, these impressive panels were recovered from the building after its closure with the end of the Broad Gauge in May 1892, and in 1906 were re-erected on the outer wall above the entrance to the main office block when its upper storey was added, appropriately overlooking the site of the original shed. They remain there today in full view of passengers on main-line trains.

At the centre of the south wall of the running shed was a matching stone pediment of the same classic design as the ends, although there was no actual access there, being purely an embellishment. Inside the building on the opposite side, was a large arched opening of 40ft clearance, which opened into the main repair shop of the depot, Bourne's so-called 'Engine House'. The north wall of the shed was of stone construction but with similar timber panels between the stone pillars. Outside the east end of the shed was the

This view at Swindon in broad-gauge days of Electra *of the 'Firefly' class, with Driver Copplestone on the footplate, also affords us a tantalising glimpse of the stone gable on the end of Swindon's original broad-gauge engine shed. This locomotive was one of 62 engines in this class and was built by Nasmyth, Gaskell & Co. of Manchester, being delivered in March 1842 and working until withdrawal in January 1867. It was one of four 6-coupled 2-2-2 goods engines of 1842, a group which resulted from an instruction by Daniel Gooch to the builders to construct them, not as passenger engines, but as trial goods engines by altering the frames and wheels. Hence* Electra, *as shown here, was one of only four 6-coupled locomotives on the Broad Gauge to have the frames outside the wheels. No more locos were built for the GWR after 1842, the Company starting to construct its own in Swindon Works. This view gives some idea of the rough conditions endured on the road by enginemen during those pioneer days — the open unprotected footplate where the crew would take the full force of wind and winter conditions, working a 12-hour shift as they thundered along the track, continually blinded by dust, and feeding fires with coke from small tenders. A curious feature of this photograph is the complete absence of any background beyond the engine and the shed, which leads one to believe that this was taken close to the coking stage at the east end of the shed, before the Works began to develop on the south side of the main line.* COLLECTION PETER SHELDON

Bourne's famous 1846 lithograph from his History of the Great Western Railway depicts Swindon's 'engine house' with its impressive roof, showing the traverser, and the moving platform which brought engines from the running shed into the maintenance bays for repairs. A 'Firefly' class locomotive can be seen being moved between the platform and the repair bay.

J. C. BOURNE

coke plant, where the engines were fuelled, measuring 100ft by 25ft, and two turntables of 30ft and 40ft in diameter. It is believed that by 1871, when the new narrow-gauge shed became available, only the outer gable bay was given over to stabling broad-gauge engines, the inner bay being used for engines awaiting factory attention. By 1887 all the roads through the shed were mixed gauge to conform with the main line and with the demise of the Broad Gauge in 1892 the whole shed became incorporated in the Works, and was known as 'A' shed, until its eventual demolition in 1930. The opinion has been expressed that just the two outer roads inside the south wall of the shed were utilised as the actual engine 'shed', and 1870 plans, which show how the traverser road from the engine house extended into the shed to give access to the engine house from the two inner roads of the running shed, tend to lend weight to this belief.

The engine house which ran northwards from the shed was a quite impressive structure of stone walls and timber roof captured so classically in Bourne's 1846 lithograph. His description is correspondingly graphic:

'In the centre of and at right angles to this shed and abutting against its northern side is the Engine House. This is an oblong room 290ft by 140ft, divided by two rows of columns into three compartments; the engines stand in the side compartments transversely, as horses in the stalls of a stable, and the central part, 50ft broad, is occupied by a large platform, travelling on wheels from one end of the house to the other, by means of an engine which can be readily transferred between the central part and any one of the stalls. Here the engines receive their lighter repairs, those which the enginemen themselves are for the most part capable of executing. The roof of this shed is of timber and wrought iron, covered in with slating; the stalls will contain 36 engines and tenders. At the northern end of the Engine House are placed the buildings employed in the repairs of locomotive engines. The Erecting House, in which the parts of the engine machinery when repaired are put together, is a building communicating with the Engine House, and capable of holding 18 engines.'

There must have been a good feeling of spaciousness in this building, enhanced by the double-rise roof forming the central span, 51ft out of a total of 140ft between the walls, contrasting with the more claustrophobic smoky feel of the running shed. One can only guess at the atmosphere in these early sheds – the hiss of steam, the echo and clatter of tools being used on metal surfaces or being dropped on the traverser, the curse words of the men as they learned their trade in the new technology, the rumble of the moving double-tracked traverser platform and the continual movement of locos in and out of the engine shed as New Swindon assumed its role as a major railway centre and the GWR a major provider of employment locally.

In October 1849, according to a GWR Minute of 22nd October 1849, there were 11 drivers and 11 firemen based at the fledgling shed at Swindon. There were 5 men listed as being 'in shed' which one assumes to be engine cleaners, with 3 engine turners, 2 fitters and a carpenter. Other employees listed included in the staffing were cleaners by contract (14), cokemen by contract (3), traffic labourers (9), water (1), foremen (6), draftsmen (3), clerks (21), housekeeper (1), erectors (104) and stationary enginemen (5). The allocation of Broad Gauge locomotives at the shed during the two weeks ending 27th July 1850 totalled nine, comprising:

Actaeon – 'Firefly' class 2–2–2 – built by Nasmyth, Gaskell & Co. Manchester, delivered December 1841. This locomotive exploded at Gloucester in February 1855. It ceased work in March 1868.

Bright Star – 'Star' class 2–2–2 – built by R. Stephenson & Co., Newcastle, delivered April 1841. It was withdrawn from service in April 1864.

Mazeppa – 'Firefly' class 2–2–2 – built by G. & J. Rennie, Blackfriars, London and delivered to the GWR March 1841. It was withdrawn in March 1868.

Milo – 'Firefly' class 2–2–2 – built by Nasmyth, Gaskell & Co. Delivered June 1841, ceased work in February 1866.

Orion – 'Firefly' class 2–2–2 – built by Nasmyth, Gaskell & Co. It was delivered in March 1842 and was withdrawn by July 1870. It was converted to an 8-wheel saddle tank engine, similar to some of the 'Star' class.

Peri – 'Prince' class 2–2–2 – one of the GWR's own early Swindon-built locomotives, built as a passenger engine in November 1846 and withdrawn in July 1870.

Pollux – 'Firefly' class 2–2–2 – also originating in the Manchester factory, delivered in July 1842, ceased work February 1866.

Priam – 'Firefly' class 2–2–2 – building and delivery details as for *Orion*. Withdrawn June 1864.

Sylph – 'Prince' class passenger engine 2–2–2 – another of the early Swindon-built locomotives, its career running from March 1847 to April 1870.

Gordon Shurmer recalls that the GWR was a very strict employer, but the men knew that as long as they toed the line and worked to the best of their ability, they had a job for life. Company discipline, according to staff records, appears to have been strict in Victorian times, as the archives are full of reprimands and fines for such misdemeanours as 'taking bank engine unnecessarily', 'taking oil from lamp room', 'moving an engine that was under repair', 'not signing for coal at the time it was delivered to the engine' and, more seriously, 'passing signals at danger'. The first recorded Swindon-based employee at the shed was one James Stokoe, a fireman during 1852–54. A certain Henry Derbyshire (not his real surname), born in 1833, was also an early employee at the running shed, where he became a fireman on 1st December 1858. In 1866 he passed for engineman on a rate of 5/6d a day. Unfortunately, Derbyshire was an individual of a somewhat spiky disposition who seems to have learned his trade at Company expense, and the records are full of cautions and fines involving damage to locos through his injudicious handling of the stock. In May 1878 he was fined 2/- at Swindon for 'using abusive language to the Coalman at the goods engine shed'. This last is an interesting reference – what exactly was this, so described? Is this an indication that perhaps when the 1871 shed was

Actaeon

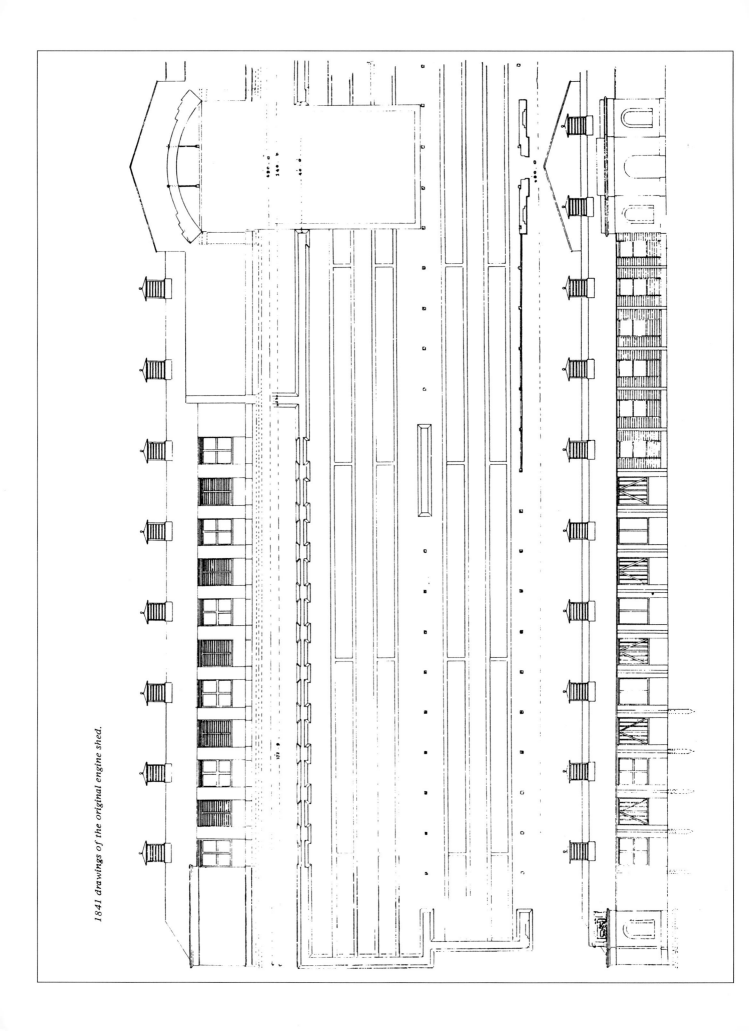

1841 drawings of the original engine shed.

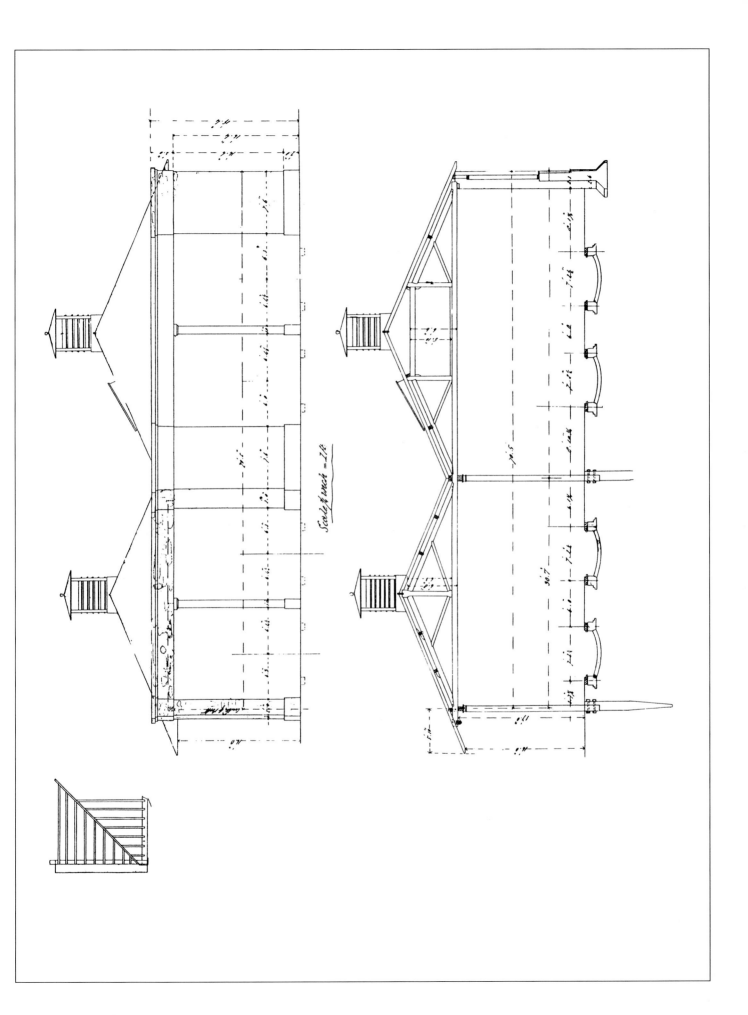

Scale ¾ inch = 1 ft.

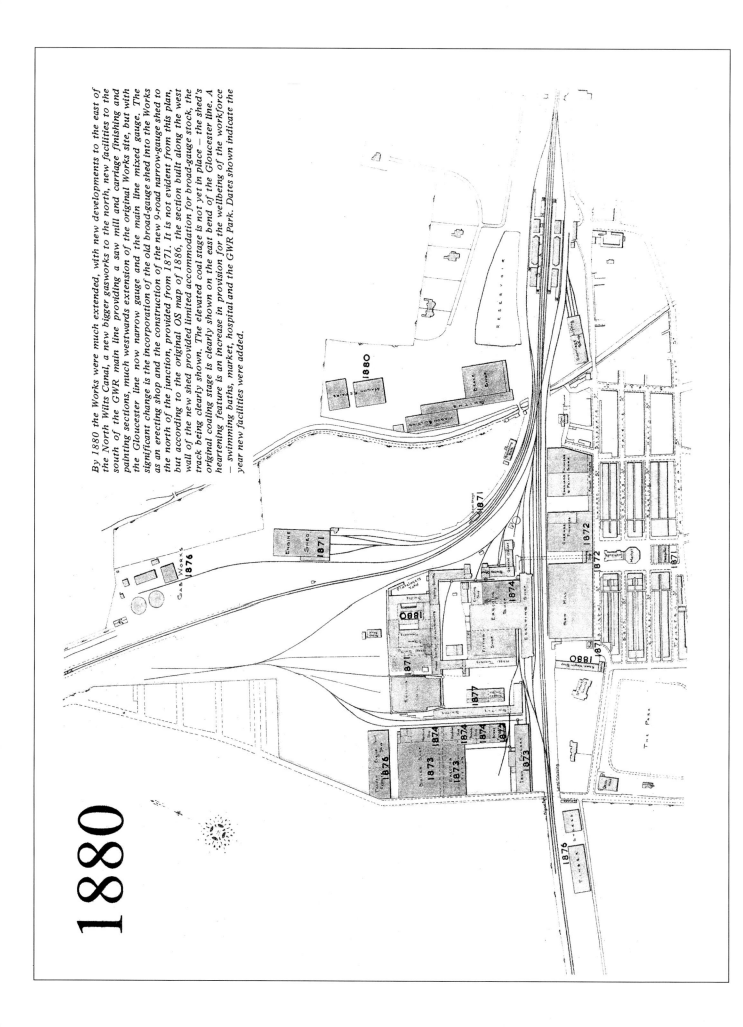

1880

By 1880 the Works were much extended, with new developments to the east of the North Wilts Canal, a new bigger gasworks to the north, new facilities to the south of the GWR main line providing a saw mill and carriage finishing and painting sections, much westwards extension of the original Works site, but with the Gloucester line now narrow gauge and the main line mixed gauge. The significant change is the incorporation of the old broad-gauge shed into the Works as an erecting shop and the construction of the new 9-road narrow-gauge shed to the north of the junction, provided from 1871. It is not evident from this plan, but according to the original OS map of 1886, the section built along the west wall of the new shed provided limited accommodation for broad-gauge stock, the track being clearly shown. The elevated coal stage is clearly shown on the east bend of the Gloucester line. A heartening feature is an increase in provision for the wellbeing of the workforce — swimming baths, market, hospital and the GWR Park. Dates shown indicate the year new facilities were added.

built the old Broad Gauge shed was in use for goods engines and the new for narrow gauge passenger stock? By this time, passenger trains on the Broad Gauge through Swindon were rare. It's a possibility. Driver Derbyshire was eventually discharged from the GWR in 1896.

We know the Broad Gauge shed at Swindon was still in use as a running shed in August 1891 as there is a reference to Joseph Jones, then an engineman on the pilots, who, whilst oiling engine 3022 in the 'Broad Gauge shed, Swindon', slipped off the feedpipe and bruised his side and knee. Jones's luck ran out the following year – on 17th June 1892, whilst oiling his engine in the up siding near 'E' signal cabin, he was knocked down and fatally injured by an Up mail train.

By contrast, Luke Higgs, born in 1834, who was a cleaner and lighter-up at Oxford shed in 1852, moved to Paddington for promotion to fireman, then came to Swindon first as an engine turner in 1861. He progressed to engineman and appears to have been a popular figure who enjoyed good health and was allowed to remain on the payroll as a shunting engineman at 5/6d a day until he was 70, when deterioration of his eyesight hastened his retirement.

With the development of the narrow gauge on the GWR, there was a need to replace the original shed and a new nine-road straight shed measuring 370ft x 155ft was built on land on the east side of the Gloucester branch, with a 45ft turntable built at the rear with 23 'lengths' off it. Up to the 1870s, most GWR turntables conformed to this size, in under-girder style and boarded over. Similar to that at Reading, the shed was built with brick walls with piers carrying the timber roof trusses and slates. Light throughout was important and there were raised glazed vents and glazing along the roof slopes and gable ends. Timber smoke troughs were in use by this time to provide better ventilation, and between each roof truss a stack led through the roof to allow escape of the smoke from the trough. As originally built, this shed had a section along its western wall which provided limited Broad Gauge accommodation, confirmed by pho-

During 1846 to 1851, the GWR produced 23 'Iron Duke' class locomotives at Swindon Works, 4–2–2 passenger engines with huge 8ft driving wheels. Tartar, seen here in about 1885, presents a great contrast to the earlier 'Firefly' class with its cab which gave the crew more protection from the elements. Tartar was built in July 1848 and ran 731,817 miles in service in its original condition. This class of engine greatly exceeded in size and power all locos previously built for any railway, and they became the GWR's standard express passenger engines until the abolition of the broad gauge in 1892. Tartar weighed 35.5 tons in working order, had a water capacity of 1,800 gallons and a fuel capacity of about 1½ tons of coke. This photograph has several other features of interest. The track was mixed gauge here, and had been so since the third rail was added to the Swindon–Thingley Junction section in the summer of 1874. At left we can see the stone abutments of the eastern end of the engine shed, clearly showing the relief stone casting of a broad-gauge locomotive in its original position. A similar bas-relief design adorned the shed at its western end. Above the tender appears the GWR's main office block extension which dates to the 1860s, here in its original two-storey form before the addition of an extra floor in 1906. It was in this building that Gordon Shurmer began his GWR career, as an office boy, in 1936. The stone castings of the broad-gauge 2–2–2 locomotive were later re-erected on the south wall of this building after closure of the original engine shed, where they remain today.
R. L. BLEASDALE, CTY. REV. CANON BRIAN ARMAN

This mid-1880s view, looking west from Swindon Junction station, illustrates perfectly the nightmare the GWR had on its hands with its early adherence to the broad gauge while the other major railway companies were working with the narrow, later standard, gauge of 4ft 8½in. MT6 plans of the east end Transfer yard show clearly the complexities resulting from Brunel's persistence with the broad gauge — Swindon was a chaotic mixture of broad, narrow and mixed gauge, with a sole mixed-gauge siding with narrow-gauge loop leading west for connection with the loco yard and the Gloucester line. Mixed-gauge tracks and crossovers of the main line to Bristol are prominent on the left whilst the narrow-gauge lines disappear round the bend at right in the direction of Gloucester. The original broad gauge shed can be seen in the distance, arrowed, but all the prevailing activity here was on the narrowed track, with factory pilot engines at work around the yard. The GWR General Manager's Report to the Board of May 1871 stated that the cost of mixing the gauge between Didcot and Swindon was expected to be about £80,000, and it was estimated that about 800 trucks, broad and narrow gauge, per month, were detained at Swindon on an average two days waiting for transfer at Swindon, and 'a lot of extra work could be got out of those trucks in two days'. The third rail for mixed gauge between Didcot and Swindon was laid between the summer of 1872 and February 1873, with provision of extensive transfer sidings at Swindon for the narrow-gauge Gloucester/Cheltenham line. Not surprisingly, Inspector Tyler, in a Board of Trade report of May 1872, commented: 'The most important place on this length and in some respects the Great Western system is the Swindon Junction and yard. The very extensive works in connection with that yard and the lines and sidings in it and about it, have grown from time to time during a series of years into a condition of complication. They require general re-arrangement and improvement with the introduction of modern appliances for working points and signals with locking apparatus . . .'

Armstrong stated that during 1871-2, a 12 month period, he would send out of the Swindon shops 72 narrow-gauge engines, 60 tenders, 150 carriages and 1,200 wagons, many of which, if the line was not mixed gauge, would have to be loaded up on broad gauge trucks at Swindon and unloaded again at Didcot as was then the case. He was further of the opinion that North Country coal would be more extensively used at Swindon if the expense of the transfer could be avoided — 'It is probable that a considerable quantity of goods now sent to Swindon via Gloucester and transferred at Gloucester would go direct to Didcot thus having a big saving on transfer expenses at Gloucester.'

West of Swindon, the third rail was added to the Swindon–Thingley Junction section during summer 1874, and by August 1875 there was narrow-gauge provision on all GWR tracks. The nearby Faringdon branch was not converted until 1878, but was not actually absorbed by the GWR until 1886, so that branch was the last piece of broad gauge east of Bristol. By the 1880s, broad gauge trains east of Bristol were rare. The main line at Swindon remained as mixed gauge until 1892, when the broad was finally abolished during May, the work emanating from Swindon as many narrow-gauge engines were sent from Swindon that month on broad gauge crocodile trucks to Newton Abbot, Plymouth and other West Country depots so they were in place ready for operations on the new tracks. A broad gauge train from Swindon conveyed 457 men and their tools to the West for the conversion, putting them up during the work in goods sheds, loco sheds, station buildings and tents all over the system, and thus did the remaining 182 miles of broad gauge and 252 miles of mixed pass into history.

So the Swindon Junction, as depicted here, was in need of an overhaul. Conversion of the line to Gloucester began on 23rd May 1872. The Up line was in the possession of the engineers at daybreak on that date, with the Down line worked as a single line with a modified service of trains, by pilot engines and pilotmen in three sections, Stroud and Kemble being the crossing stations. Then the single-line working was transferred to the Up line, now in narrow gauge. The Up line was ready on 26th May and the last broad-gauge train of empty stock left Cheltenham and Gloucester after the midnight mail early that morning. A special engine ran announcing the closure of the broad gauge and opening of the narrow gauge line. Ordinary Down line working resumed as usual on 29th May.

Swindon was equipped with numerous signal boxes at this time, all denoted by letters of the alphabet. The one visible at the junction of the main line and the Gloucester branch was Box 'E', a 40-lever cabin with 25 spares.

The buildings on the left were the down side carriage shops, with the spire of St. Mark's Church appearing over the top of them. The building seen to the left of the tall signal post at right was the original Medical Fund swimming baths – you can make out the title on the nameboard running just below the guttering.

CTY. SWINDON LIBRARIES

A view of the Swindon running shed of 1871, which must have been taken about 1887. In the left distance is the new Stock shed which was built in 1886 to house engines fresh from Works repair while awaiting allocation to a depot, but as yet there was no sign of the elevated coal stage road on the right of the photograph, which was erected in 1888, hence the conclusion that it is roughly 1887. At that time, the GWR denoted its signal boxes with letters, and in the Swindon area they ranged from 'A' (Highworth Junction of 1883) to 'K' (Rushey Platt). The one shown here by the Up line from Gloucester is Box 'G', built in 1877, and renamed Swindon Locomotive Yard Signal Box on 22nd January 1909. It was replaced under the same name in January 1924. According to 1898 plans, Box 'G' was an 18-lever box with no spares. The building behind the telegraph pole is a total mystery, as it does not even appear on the 1886 original edition OS map. The most striking aspect of the loco shed is the forest of smoke chutes and this view shows several tank engines standing on the straight roads into the shed, with a tender engine steaming away behind the snowplough — one wonders how many times this was used? The building partially visible behind the mystery shed was presumably part of the Gasworks, which came into use in 1874.

By far the most exciting aspects of this view are the broad-gauge features still in situ only five years from the final abolition of the 7ft gauge. The shed at the centre of the photo along the western wall of the 1871 structure was a broad-gauge shed, and it is strikingly different in appearance to the rest of the new building. Its doors give it away as a broad-gauge building, but one wonders when it was built? It certainly could have been provided earlier, during the days

before the Gloucester line was narrowed, but no maps have been found to substantiate this. Gordon Shurmer clearly recalled seeing broad-gauge track embedded in cobblestones in there when he was a young fireman, and this is confirmed by the 1886 OS map which shows a mixed-gauge track in the yard which becomes 7ft gauge in the approach to this shed. Clearly the GWR believed that some limited broad-gauge provision was still desirable at this end of the station in the 1870s, with a link to the Transfer Yard at the east end of the station. In Gordon's day, this old shed was used as stores, he also recalling tinsmiths at work in it and some repairing of headlamps being done. The northern end of it was used as a sandhouse, its chimney visible, as are sandtrucks outside the building here. Cleaners would empty these trucks of sand and throw it on top of the sand furnace in there to dry it out. One Joe Waters was in charge of the sandhouse in the 1930s, a Company man kept on the payroll after being hurt on main-line work. There is a mixed-gauge crossover visible on the Up line of the Gloucester branch, leading into the shed yard, again tying in exactly with the OS, and we can see old broad-gauge wagons standing on what was clearly mixed-gauge track on the inclined road beyond the telegraph pole. This view looks towards Gloucester, with the narrowed track of 1872 sitting on transverse sleepers, and, bearing in mind the isolation of the shed from the station and the much-photographed Works, and its distance from areas frequented by the public, this is a quite valuable railway view.　　　　CTY. SWINDON LIBRARIES

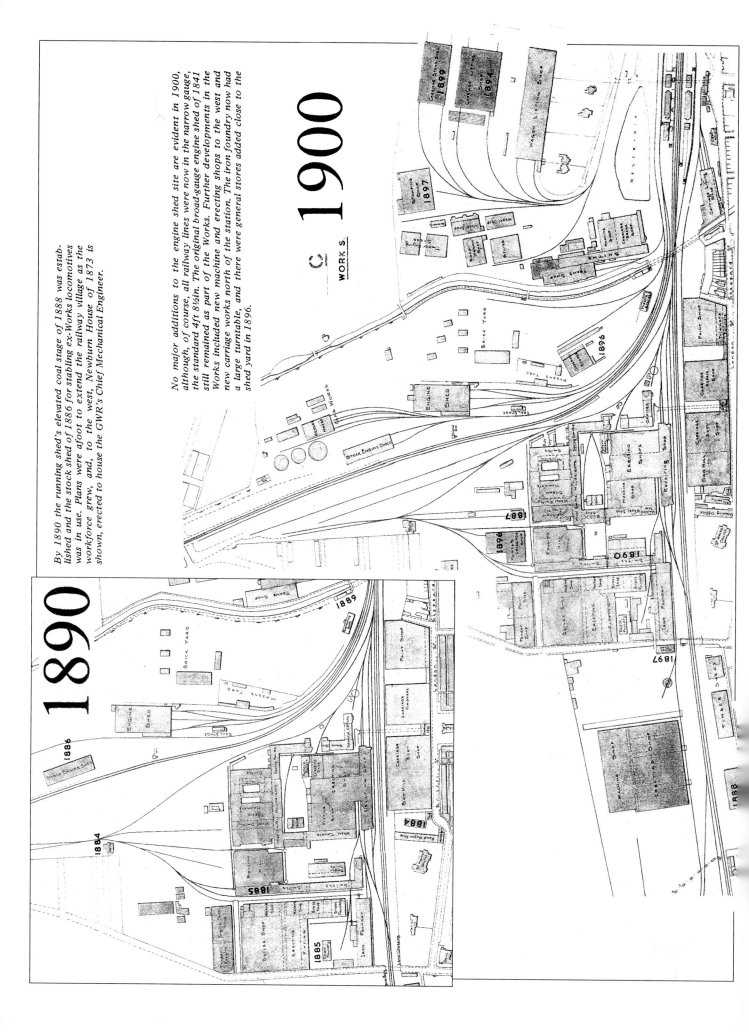

By 1890 the running shed's elevated coal stage of 1888 was established and the stock shed of 1886 for stabling ex-Works locomotives was in use. Plans were afoot to extend the railway village as the workforce grew, and, to the west, Newburn House of 1873 is shown, erected to house the GWR's Chief Mechanical Engineer.

No major additions to the engine shed site are evident in 1900, although, of course, all railway lines were now in the narrow gauge, the standard 4ft 8½in. The original broad-gauge engine shed of 1841 still remained as part of the Works. Further developments in the Works included new machine and erecting shops to the west and new carriage works north of the station. The iron foundry now had a large turntable, and there were general stores added close to the shed yard in 1896.

c 1900
WORKS

1890

1910

By 1910 the locomotive shed extensions of 1908 were complete, with the new 'big shed' providing a 65ft turntable added to the east wall of the 1871 shed. There were new offices and stores also added. The reference on the plan to the extra floor added to the Company offices in 1905 was the part of the Works where Gordon Shurmer started his GWR career in 1936 as an office boy. It is worth remembering that these plans were intended to show the growth of the Works and should not be regarded as comprehensive as regards track and signalling — only one signal box is shown here, the Box 'G' which served the loco yard and was eventually replaced by Swindon Locomotive Yard Signal Box. Before modernisation of the signalling provision in the first decade of the 20th century, there were numerous signal cabins in the Swindon area, all named with a capital letter.

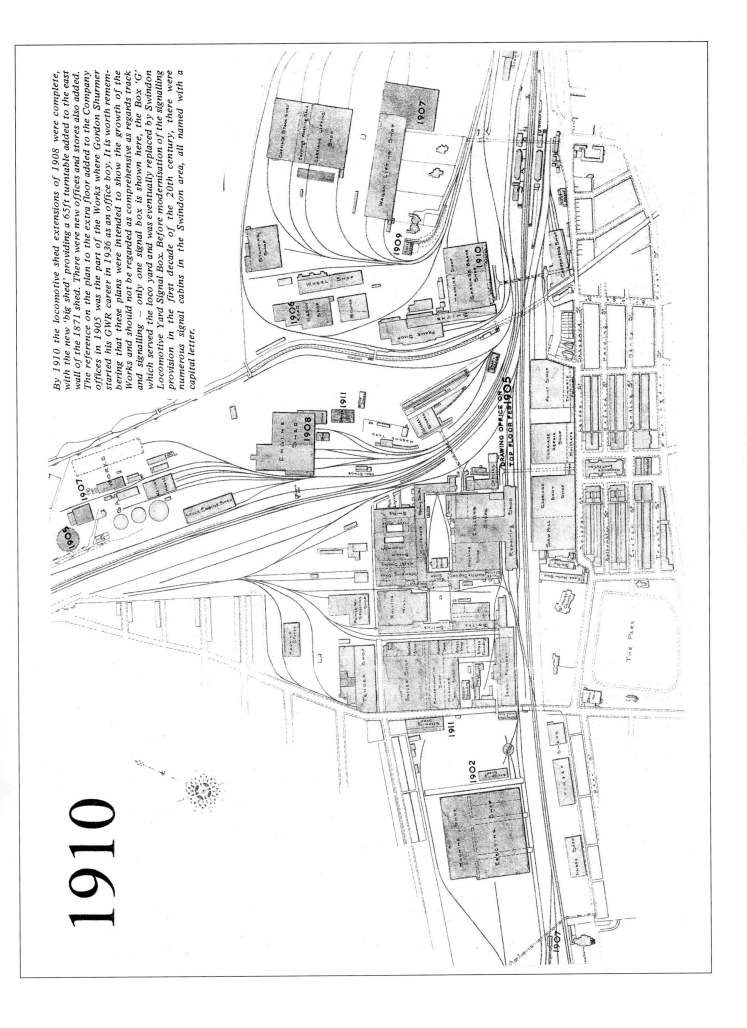

The big shed addition of 1908 in clean, new condition, showing the new 65ft turntable.

NATIONAL RAILWAY MUSEUM

tographs, Ordnance Survey evidence and Gordon Shurmer's memory. With the disappearance of the wider gauge, this building eventually became a store and sandhouse. In 1871 the coal stage for the shed was located further south, closer to the main-line junction, but in 1888 an improved and larger replacement was built with an elevated coal delivering siding closer to the shed, 91ft x 20ft and covered by a huge 80,000 gallon water tank.

Water supply had always been a problem at Swindon and it was decided to tap the water source at Kemble, close to the source of the River Thames, and pipe this supply to the Works. During 1903, gangs of Swindon Works men, supported by a special train with steam crane, excavated trenches along the west side of the line between Kemble and Swindon and laid in a new water main connecting the pumping station and boiler house at Kemble with Swindon locomotive yard. The work was completed on 28th July 1903. Water was fed into the high-level coal-stage water tank at the running shed, and thence linked to the pattern stores tank in the Works.

In its February 1906 edition, the *Great Western Railway Magazine* reported on a paper presented by Mr. H. Arkell on the subject of 'Locomotive Engine Sheds' at the meeting of the Swindon Junior Engineering Society held on 12th December 1905:

'Engine sheds vary in type according to the conditions of site, etc. There are "straight" sheds, "turntable" sheds, and American "roundhouses". The first is the simplest form and is always adopted for small sheds, but there is a limit to its utility, as, if several engines are placed on a straight road with a dead-end, obviously the inner ones cannot get out without shunting the others. This defect is overcome by adopting "through" sheds, in which engines work in at one end and out at the other, and can be fairly well-arranged in their proper turns. This arrangement, however, requires twice as much yard room, and on that account cannot be adopted everywhere. Examples of this type on a large scale may be seen at Crewe and Eastleigh.

'The "turntable" sheds are favoured in this country. The Great Western lately adopted them as the standard for large sheds, and the Midland Company uses them almost exclusively. Convenience and adaptability to awkward sites are their chief advantages, but they are extravagant in covered space, requiring about 50% more room per engine than a "straight" shed.

'The "roundhouse" type is adopted almost without exception in America. The chief objection to its use in this country is the large amount of ground required.

'The details of construction of the various types were explained by the aid of diagrams and drawings, and tables given showing the comparative capacity of each type. In concluding, Mr. Arkell advanced the suggestion that a "straight-through" shed might be adopted, with traverser at one end, upon the opposite side of which might be placed the lifting shed, which would combine the best features of the "straight" and "through" types without their disadvantages.'

By the early years of the 20th Century, with a great increase in the size of the locomotives coming out of the Works, notably the larger 4–6–0s being built under the auspices of Churchward, the 1871 shed was proving inadequate, as reflected in a report of the Locomotive Superintendent of 12th April 1905:

'For some time past the number of engines stabled at Swindon shed has been 76 whereas the existing shed will only accommodate 34, and consequently some of the engines have had to be put in the Stock Shed which was built for the purpose of storing engines after repair, in consequence of which the work is carried on at great inconvenience and unnecessary expense, so it is recommended that the engine shed be extended to accommodate about 32 mixed engines at an estimated cost of £20,000.'

On 11th October 1905, the Board approved the expenditure of the £20,000 for the extension of the shed. The Locomotive Superintendent reported that the scheme was to include the provision of new offices for the staff of the divisional Superintendent and that, as a preliminary to the work being commenced, it was necessary to remove the buildings then in use as offices.

Thus in 1908, an extension, with improved water supply, the standard single turntable 'roundhouse' shed, similar in design to Old Oak Common, was added with new offices and stores. The new turntable shed measured 216ft x 182ft with messrooms provided for crews, cleaners and labourers along the eastern wall measuring 110ft x 15ft. The new stores were in two buildings of 72 x 84ft and 165 x 60ft. The latter of the two buildings eventually became the bike

1. Store (former broad gauge shed)
2. Sandhouse
3. Smithy
4. Fitters' workshop
5. 1871 building
6. Big turntable
7. 1908 building
8. Messrooms
9. Stores
10. Mr. Morgan's office and addressograph office
11. Bicycle shed
12. Site of boiler house
13. Coal stage
14. Locomotive Yard Signal Box

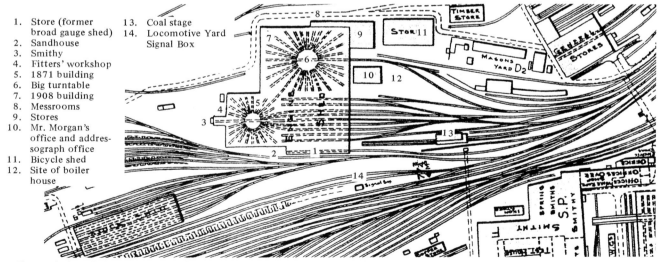

The roads into Swindon shed's original 1871 building were numbered from 1 to 9 from the Gloucester line end and known as the 'straights'. No. 1 was always regarded as a dangerous road — drivers would not prepare a loco there because engines were coming down from the coal stage, over the points just outside the shed and there was always a worry that an engine could run away and collide with stock on No. 1 road. The dangers to engines and crews there were obvious — apparently such a thing had happened there. No. 3 road was where the factory pilots were stabled overnight and with the turntable they could be moved out at either end. No. 5 road which ran through the turntable, was always kept clear, as distinct from the stabling roads, and was an outgoing and ingoing road worked in either direction. At the coal stage, the only tip ever used was the one nearest the shed, the other being a spare which was hardly ever used. Locomotive Yard Signal Box controlled movements in and out of the vast sidings across the Gloucester line, and opened on 1st January 1924.

Swindon Locomotive Shed Staff Allocation 1925

Foremen					
Locomotive Shed	1	Chargemen, Engine Cleaners	3	Shed Labourers (General)	10
Running	4	Engine Cleaners	59	Stores Issuers	4
Locomotive Shop	1	Shed Chargeman 'C'	1	Toolmen	4
Locomotive Yard	1	Ashfillers	2	Tube cleaners	6
		Boilerwashers	10	Yard Foreman	1
Foremen's Clerks	2	Callers Up	3	Locomotive Shunters	52
Clerks	5	Coalmen	8	Shop grades	54
		Firedroppers	9		
Engine Drivers	147	Firelighters	6	Total	549
Firemen	147	Lamp trimmers	3		
Shed Enginemen	3	Messroom Attendant	1		
Shed Enginemen's Mate	1	Sandman	1		

A 1921 view of the running shed, with the buildings of the 1871 shed in the centre of the picture. The 1908 additions housing the big turntable are partially obscured by the shedmaster's office, where Mr. Morgan was in charge when Gordon was a fireman. This building also housed the addressograph office where the wage paybills were printed. An addressograph was purchased for use here at a cost of £92 10s 9d in October 1908 when the office was built. On the extreme right a former store was used in Gordon's day as a bike shed. The building to the left of the bike shed housed the offices where the roster clerks worked on preparing the turns in the links. You could leave anything in those days — "The only crime we knew was riding a bike after dark without lights, or keeping a dog without a licence! The only glue-sniffing we knew was running alongside a council steam-roller getting a whiff of the tar!" NATIONAL RAILWAY MUSEUM

For Drainage of WC's see
Drawing Nᵒ 30081.

56'8¾"

MECHANICS MESS ROOM

65 ᶠᵀ Turntable

17 16 15 14
18   13
19   12
20   11
21   10
22   9
23   8
                   7
24   6
25   5
26   4
27 28   3
     1 2

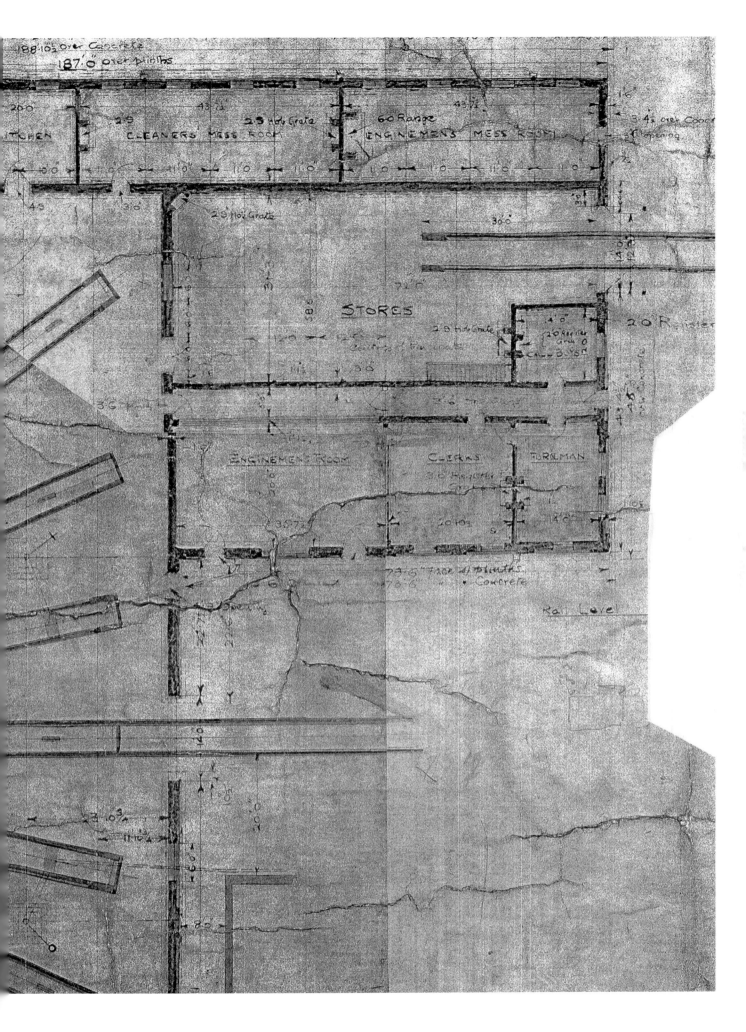

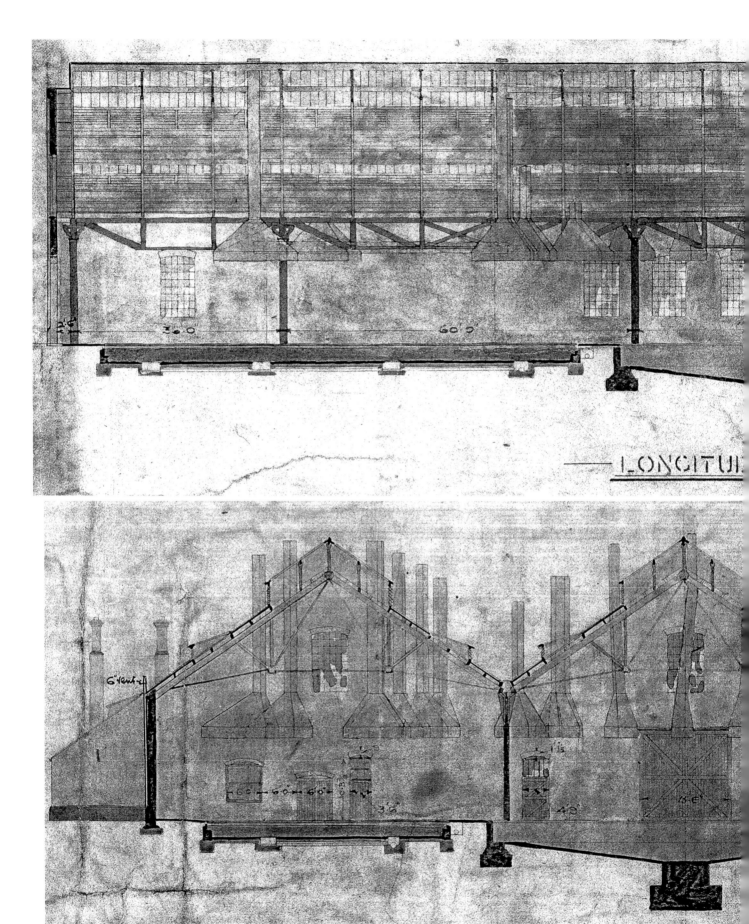

LONGITUI

CROSS SEC

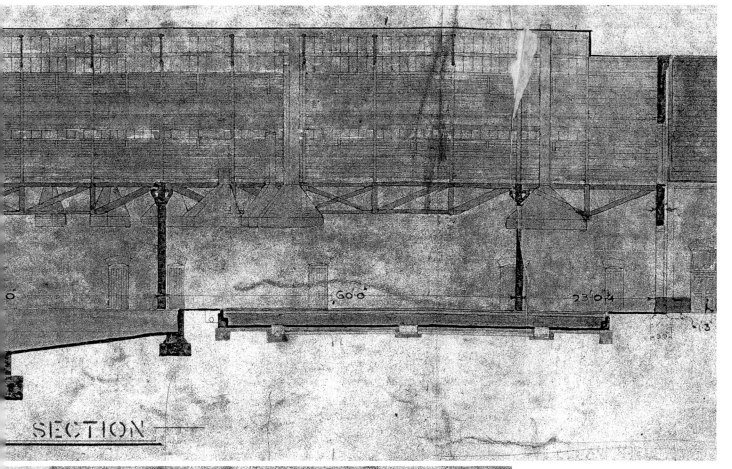

SECTION

NORTH ELEVATION

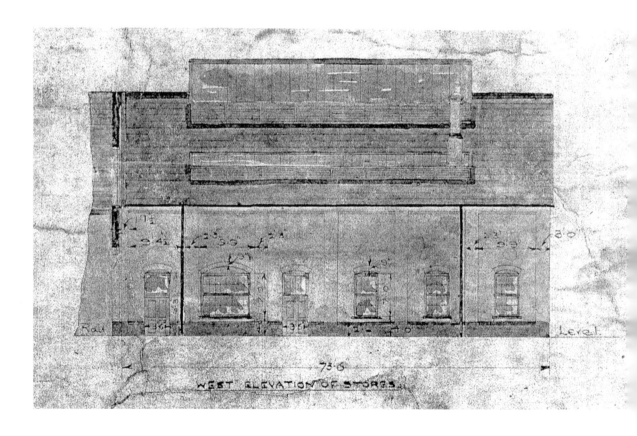

WEST ELEVATION OF STORES

Decay and disuse in the mid-1960s, Swindon running shed passing into history.

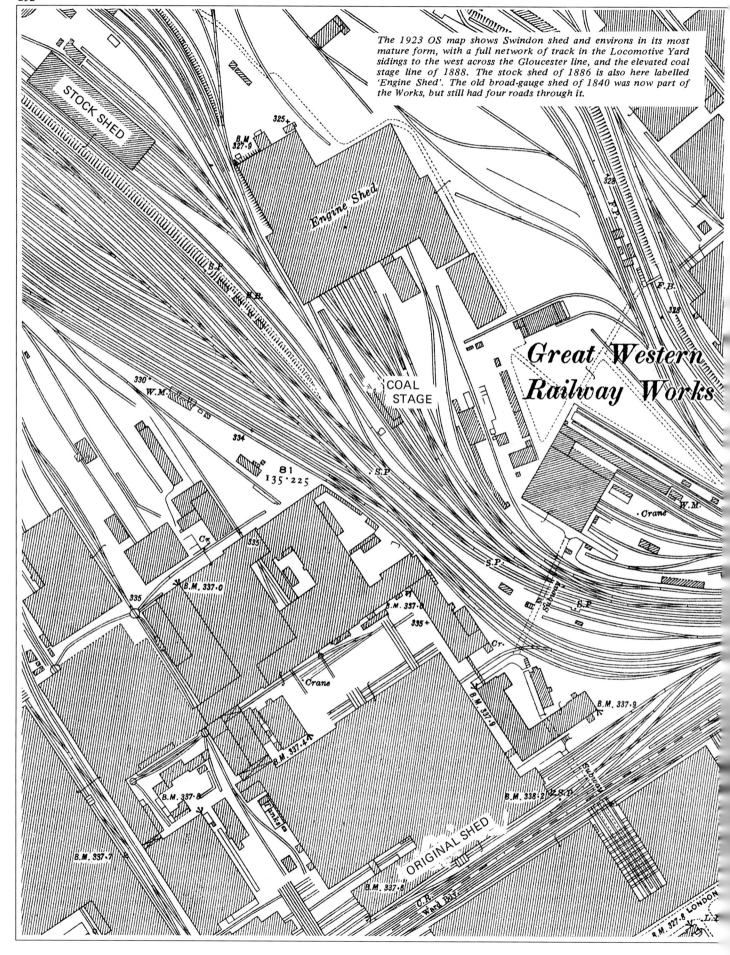

The 1923 OS map shows Swindon shed and environs in its most mature form, with a full network of track in the Locomotive Yard sidings to the west across the Gloucester line, and the elevated coal stage line of 1888. The stock shed of 1886 is also here labelled 'Engine Shed'. The old broad-gauge shed of 1840 was now part of the Works, but still had four roads through it.

STOCK SHED

Engine Shed

COAL STAGE

Great Western Railway Works

ORIGINAL SHED

shed, and a single-storey building eventually provided outside the southern wall of the 1908 shed housed the shedmaster's office and the addressograph office. During the '30s, in Mr. Duck's reign as shed foreman, the stores adjoining the messrooms provided the fore-man's office, a store upstairs for uniforms and other clothing, and also the stores where crews collected their supplies such as tools and oil, and cleaners their waste. The normal practice was for the large tender engines to be stabled in the roundhouse whilst shunting and smaller locos were stabled in the old straight shed. The new turntable was of the 65ft diameter brought in for roundhouse sheds by Churchward, with 26 lines radiating from it for stabling locos. The old Broad Gauge shed on the west wall of the main shed eventually became the sand furnace.

Eric Mountford, well-known ex-GWR Works employee and historian, recalled that the siting of Swindon shed had its disadavantages for enthusiasts:

'Swindon shed was sited in a most inaccessible place for the railway enthu-siast, not visible from any public place apart from a train on the Gloucester line. It could only be reached by continuing through a second long tunnel directly following the the main tunnel entrance to the Works. From the end of this second tunnel the shed was still some distance northwards, reached across numerous sidings. Thus it was never included in normal Works visits, and visitors were only taken there by special arrangements beforehand.'

In the earlier years of the GWR, the network was divided into two main areas, North and South Divisions, with Swindon the divisional

Swindon's original broad gauge shed after being incorporated into the Works, seen looking east in 1929, a year before its demolition. The timbered walls had survived nearly 90 years. The stone casting of the broad-gauge locomotive had been removed from the end stone section to its permanent home on the south wall of the Main Offices block. NATIONAL RAILWAY MUSEUM

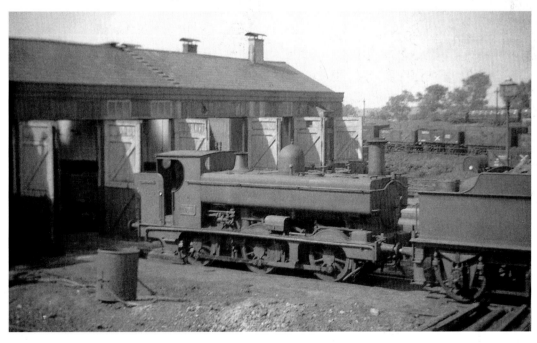

The stock shed was built in 1886 specific-ally for storing engines waiting to be allocated to a depot after coming out of the factory until such time as another shed required an engine of that particular class. The stock shed did not come under the juris-diction of Swindon running shed – it was owned and maintained by the Works.
BRIAN MOORE
CTY. KIDDER-
MINSTER RAILWAY
MUSEUM

A wonderful 1930 line-up of 'Kings' and 'Castles' on the straight roads outside Swindon shed. Pat Lawes, born 1913, was a cleaner on this gang and remembered this cleaning session, also the presence of the 'Cheltenham Flyer' headboard (extreme right) which is a reminder that in those days the 'Flyer' was a Swindon job — "The cleaners on here were all older chaps, mid-30s, married with two children. The chargehand who was in charge of these blokes was quite frightening — you can see him in front of the third loco from the left. There was one chargehand, Joe Austin, a little short Irish bloke with a bowler 'at, very strict. You couldn't go in the cabin and have a bit of lunch — you had to sneak in, get your lunchbox and come out and eat by your engine. I've seen grown men see him coming and be so scared of getting caught they'd throw their sandwiches in the bloody pit! In those days we'd clean a loco for the 'Cheltenham Flyer', come off shed about 3.30 p.m. and the loco would be changed at Swindon. I remember there was a fireman called Bill Platt and I heard the rest of the cleaners remarking that bloody Platty's on the 'Cheltenham Flyer' again! Of course, it became an Old Oak Common job, like it was originally. I think the first engine on it was Launceston Castle. That's about half the men on the day shift on that cleaning gang, and I'm sure I'm on there somewhere! You could go home for lunch on the day shift. Promotion was very slow back then. When I started there in the '20s, there were 59 cleaners at Swindon shed, I was number 60. I stayed on the bottom of the list for four years and no one started after me."

CTY. GREAT WESTERN SOCIETY

236

headquarters of the south and Wolverhampton the north. As the network expanded in the latter half of the 19th Century, with an increase in the number of running sheds, the strains imposed on two divisional centres necessitated a reorganisation so that by the time the Broad Gauge was finally removed, there were seven divisions, London, Bristol, Newton Abbot, Wolverhampton, Worcester, Newport and Neath, with Swindon being a part of the Bristol Division.

Following G. J. Churchward's reorganisation of the Locomotive and Traffic Departments in 1916, the effects of World War I required fresh thinking. With large numbers of available engines being commandeered for war use, locos ended up all over the network, and shedmasters needed to know when their engines would be returned. In 1918 a new coding system was introduced to identify sheds, and by the 1920s locos were bearing both the divisional code and the code of the depot where they were allocated. After several experiments, the preferred marking on engines became the abbre-

viated letters of the shed name being painted beneath the running plates just behind the buffer beam, Swindon becoming 'SDN'.

In the 1930s, as small sheds were reduced to sub-sheds and their locos allocated from a major shed, e.g. Malmesbury from Swindon, Yatton from Bristol Bath Road, and as these sheds were still operative and stabled engines, it became necessary to recode all sheds for clerical purposes using numbers. Hence Swindon became 132, the '2' representing the number of the Division, in this case the second division (Bristol) out of nine, and the '13' being Swindon's alphabetical position within the Division. By the same system, Chippenham was 62, Frome 72 and Westbury 172. Brimscombe's banking engines were housed at shed 15, reflecting its first position alphabetically in Division 5, Worcester, with Chalford 35, Tetbury 205 and so on. With nationalisation, British Railways changed the codings, with an 8 to represent the Region (Western), followed by another figure to show the division, this figure being the same divisional number used by the GWR, and after this double number was

During 1929-30 the original broad-gauge shed at Swindon was finally demolished and the site incorporated into Swindon Works. Using the tall signal post as a marker, it is easy to see how the location here changed during that year. Known as 'A' shed, it is seen above in November 1930. GREAT WESTERN RAILWAY MAGAZINE

Swindon running shed on 3rd March 1935.

H. F. WHEELLER

This picture of ROD 2—8—0 No. 3022 at the shed in June 1932 provides a closer view of the coal tip at the south end of the stage.

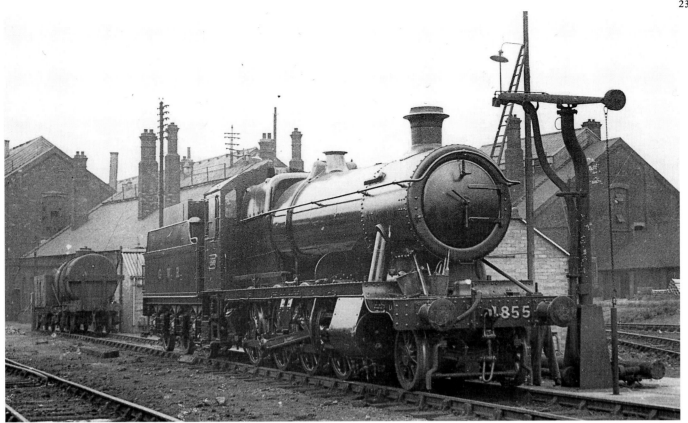

Between 1945 and 1947 the GWR carried out a programme of oil-firing in an effort to combat the shortage and rising price of coal following World War 2. Twenty 2–8–0 locomotives were converted to use oil at Swindon and a refuelling depot, seen here, was established along a siding located close to the divide between the 1871 shed and its 1908 extensions. The Anglo-Iranian Oil Company assisted Swindon Works with the conversions, which used a special burner at the front of the firebox. Steam was used for atomising purposes as well as keeping the heavy fuel mobile enough to flow by gravity to the burner from the 1800-gallon rectangular fuel tank occupying the bunker area on the tender. Gordon Shurmer's friend and colleague, Freddie Simpson, had some experience of working oil-fired locomotives and he recalls it as being a very much easier job for the fireman, as all you had to do was light up with a long rod with lighted waste, check the temperature on a thermometer on the tank, and turn a wheel, which regulated the steam pressure and the flow of oil from the tank to the burner. On one occasion in London Freddie turned the wheel the wrong way, which resulted in thick clouds of black smoke around Westbourne Park! According to Freddie, the training was very much on the job. There was an Inspector, Tom Stephenson, who came in to do the teaching, but it appears to have been on an individual basis, with no classes as such because the job was fairly uncomplicated.

In June 1946 one of the 'Hall' class 4–6–0s, No. 5955 Garth Hall was converted to oil, and in the following year another ten passenger engines were so altered. They were given new numbers in the 39XX series. Five of the 'Castle' class were adapted in 1946/7. Freddie Simpson worked 'Castles' and 'Halls' out of Swindon under oil power and thinks that the 9.00 London job in No. 1 Link was run with an oil-burning loco, as was the 1.18 Paddington to Weston-super-Mare. There was enough oil in one filling of the tank to run from Swindon to Paddington, then to Weston-super-Mare and back to Swindon. There was one occasion when he worked on No. 1 Link with driver Dai Davies and they had problems with an interfering Inspector on the 1.18 ex-Paddington, and there was an altercation in Reading station on the footplate, which concluded with Davies telling Freddie, "Fred, shut it all down and do it like you normally do!"

Top left: The Swindon depot with No. 5083 being refuelled, the large fuel tank on top of the tender being clearly visible. Below left: Travelling rail tanks replenishing the 36,000-gallon capacity oil storage tanks at Swindon, by means of steam pumps. The building with the window was part of an old boiler house. Top right: '28XX' class 2–8–0 No. 4855, formerly No. 3813, in the Swindon depot. This loco was renumbered in June 1947 and was eventually shedded

at Laira. Above: A general view of the depot, showing the pump house. In October 1948 the converted locos went into storage because of a national oil shortage, and the GWR abandoned the experiment and reconverted all the locos back to coal burning by the end of 1948. Oil-powered engines also had difficulty in achieving and maintaining high speeds, and with oil proving expensive and its supply difficult to guarantee, it was a shortlived period in GWR history.

A 1950 view in the shed yard, showing the northern end of the elevated coal road with pannier tanks in steam nearby. The white 'X' on the wagon indicated that the vehicle was limited to no more than 3 miles on the main line. It is likely that this wagon stored equipment that was needed around the factory.
DAVE 'BRINKWORTH' JONES

Approved expenditure at Swindon running shed, from Locomotive, Carriage & Stores Committee Minutes

January 1903 – repairs to centre portion of roof of running shed, provision of a larger area of skylight and renewal of smoke bonnets and chimneys £950

October 1907 – whitewashing and painting of running shed £400

December 1907 – new engine shed, Swindon, £20,000 authorised, expenditure to date £19,007 3s

December 1907 – provision of incandescent gas fittings, Swindon running shed £200

October 1909 – renewal of water mains at running shed £300

October 1910 – repairs to pits at old engine shed £950

October 1911 – painting and whitewashing of engine shed, and renewing smoke trough £1,450

March 1912 – widening of doorways of engine shed £800

October 1929 – repairs to 65ft turntable No. 15 at running shed, including making good running on and off and surrounding roads £2,450

June 1931 – repairs to engine shed £2,700

July 1932 – renewal and extension of boiler washing plant at running shed £630

January 1934 – major engine shed repair £3,800

January 1935 – shed roof repairs £350

Other Wartime expenditure on Swindon shed

January 1944 – repairs to the road in the running shed £440. "They were always messing about with the roads. The roof too – always leaking."

March 1944 – works ordered by Ministry of War Transport, cost to be borne by the Government, £539 for provision of accommodation for enginemen.

April 1944 – renewal of pit rails in engine shed £105
Repairs to incoming road to turntable £200

May 1945 – running shed yard, renewal and repair of crossings, drains and manholes £365

a letter for each parent shed in the Division. Hence, Swindon became shed 82C, and this lasted until closure.

The straight roads into the shed were numbered from one to nine from the western end. No. 1 road was never used for preparing engines, as it was felt there was always a danger from locomotives coming off the coaling road. There were instances of engines running away here and smashing into locos on this road. No. 3 road was used for stabling the factory pilots overnight, and No. 5 road, the central turntable road, was always kept free for access.

Built along the east wall of the engine shed was a building containing messrooms for crews, cleaners and shed labourers. The crews' section had wooden forms around the outside fixed to the wall, with tables in the centre and a large iron circular brass urn which was always on the boil, 365 days a year, to keep the men supplied with

tea. The pipe from the stove went up through the roof, and around the top was a circular iron band from which hung metal coat-hangers. Less popular inhabitants of the messroom were the crickets, which you could hear but never find!

As the diesel age progressed during the 1960s, servicing was concentrated on Reading and Bristol, so Swindon shed was closed from 2nd November 1964. Most of the yard sidings to the gasworks and stock shed were lifted during 1965, with final removal of shed sidings and roads taking place during 1970. East and West boxes and Highworth Junction Signal Box closed on 3rd March 1968, and Locomotive Yard Signal Box was taken out of use on 28th July 1968. The whole area was incorporated into the multi-aspect signalling (MAS) controlled from Reading.

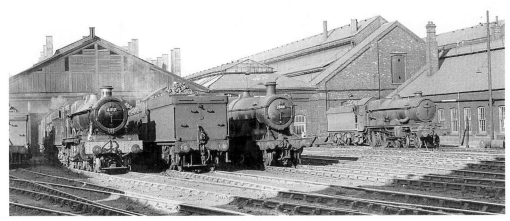

Swindon shed in February 1960.

Gordon's favourite No. 6000 King George V, *on shed at Swindon on 17th October 1962.*

COLIN SPIRES

PIECEWORK COALING AT SWINDON, 1935

Days	Dates	Turn of Duty	Coalman	Hours Worked H.M	Coal Put On T Cwt	Piecework Total H.M	Balance %
Week Ending 26th October							
Sun	20th Oct	6.0-2/0	Bush, F.	7.30	17.10	11.40	55-4
		2/0-10/0	Poulton, F.	8.0	19.10	13.0	62.5
Mon	21st Oct	2/0-10/0	Bush, F.	48.0			
to	to	2/0-10/0	Savoury, A.S.	48.0	448.0	298.40	55-5
Sat	26th Oct	2/0-10/0	Payne, W.	48.0			
		2/0-10/0	Poulton, F.	48.0			
Mon	21st Oct	10/0-6.0	Stratton, F.	48.0			
to	to	10/0-6.0	Hole, W.	48.0	423.0	282.0	46-9
Sat	26th Oct	10/0-6.0	Reynolds, H	48.0			
		10/0-6.0	Edmonds, W	48.0			
Mon	21st Oct	12.0-6.0	Mackman, J	6.0	15.10	10.20	72-2
		6.0-2/0	Ludlow, W.	8.0	14.0	9.20	-
Tues	22nd Oct	6.0-2/0	Mackman, J	40.0	168.10	112.20	-
to	to	6.0-2/0	Ludlow, W.	40.0			
Sat	26th Oct						
Week Ending 2nd November							
Sun	27th Oct	6.0-2/0	Mackman, J.	7.30	18.0	12.0	60-0
		2/0-10/0	Ludlow, W.	8.0	12.10	8.20	4-2
Mon	28th Oct	2/0-10/0	Ludlow, W.	48.0			
to	to	2/0-10/0	Stratton, F.	48.0	432.10	288.20	50-17
Sat	2nd Nov	2/0-10/0	Savoury, A.S.	48.0			
		2/0-10/0	Mackman, J.	48.0			
Mon	28th Oct	10/0-6.0	Bush, F.	48.0			
to	to	10/0-6.0	Payne, W.C.	48.0	403.0	268.40	39-9
Sat	2nd Nov	10/0-6.0	Webb, L.C.	48.0			
		10/0-6.0	Poulton, F.	48.0			
Mon	28th Oct	12.0-6.0	Hole, W.	6.0	22.0	14.40	144-4
		6.0-2/0	Edmonds. J.	8.0	21.0	14.0	75-0
Tues	29th Oct	6.0-2/0	Hole, W.	40.0	186.10	124.20	55-4
to	to	6.0-2/0	Edmonds, J	40.0			
Sat	2nd Nov						

Days	Dates	Turn of Duty	Coalman	Hours Worked H.M	Coal Put On T Cwt	Piecework Total H.M	Balance %
Week Ending 9th November							
Sun	3rd Nov	6.0-2/0	Ludlow, W.	8.0	9.0	6.0	-
Mon	4th Nov	2/0-10/0	Hole, W.H.	6.30	20.10	13.40	110-2
&	&	2/0-10/0	Bush, F.	16.0	144.10	96.20	50-51
Tue	5th Nov	2/0-10/0	Hole, W.H.	16.0			
		2/0-10/0	Reynolds, H.H.	16.0			
		2/0-10/0	Edmonds, W.J.	16.0			
Wed	6th Nov	2/0-10/0	Stratton, F.G.	24.0			
to	to	2/0-10/0	Hole, W.H.	24.0	235.10	157.0	63-54
Fri	8th Nov	2/0-10/0	Bush, F.	24.0			
		2/0-10/0	Edmonds, W.J.	24.0			
Sat	9th Nov	2/0-10/0	Bush, F	8.0			
		2/0-10/0	Stratton, F.	8.0	71.0	47.20	47-8
		2/0-10/0	Edmonds, W.J.	8.0			
		2/0-10/0	Reynolds, H.H.	8.0			
Mon	4th Nov	10/0-6.0	Savoury, A.C.	48.0			
to	to	10/0-6.0	Ludlow, W.C.	48.0	372.15	248.30	29-4
Sat	9th Nov	10/0-6.0	Mackman, J	48.0			
		10/0-6.0	Wilson, A.C.	48.0			
Mon	4th Nov	12.0-6.0	Payne, W.C.	6.0	18.0	12.0	100
		6.0-2/0	Poulton, F	8.0	17.0	11.20	41-7
Tues	5th Nov	6.0-2/0	Payne, W.C.	40.0	175.10	117.0	46-25
to	to	6.0-2/0	Poulton, F	40.0			
Sat	9th Nov						
Week Ending 16th November							
Sun	10th Nov	6.0-2/0	Poulton, F.	8.0	15.10	10.20	29-2
		2/0-10/0	Payne, W.C.	8.0	19.0	12.40	58-3
Mon	11th Nov	2/0-10/0	Bush, F.	48.0			
to	to	2/0-10/0	Payne, W.C.	48.0	433.0	288.40	50-34
Sat	16th Nov	2/0-10/0	Mackman, J	48.0			
		2/0-10/0	Poulton, F.	48.0			
Mon	11th Nov	10/0-6.0	Stratton, F.	48.0			
to	to	10/0-6.0	Hole, W.	48.0	366.0	244.0	27-08
Sat	16th Nov	10/0-6.0	Edmonds, W.	48.0			
		10/0-6.0	Reynolds, H	48.0			
Mon	11th Nov	12.0-6.0	Ludlow, W.	6.0	6.10	5.40	-
		6.0-2/0	Savoury, A.C.	8.0	22.0	14.40	83-33
Tues	12th Nov	6.0-2/0	Ludlow, W.	40.0	189.10	126.20	57-9
to	to	6.0-2/0	Savoury, A.C.	40.0			
Sat	16th Nov						

SWINDON RATES, October 1926

Ash Loading
Per Engine Lighted Up	15 mins
Per Truck of Fine Ashes	4 hours

Cleaning Fires, Ashpans & Smokeboxes
Per Engine - Smokebox only	15 mins
(6.0 a.m. to 2.0 p.m. Turn)	

Fire Dropping
28XX, 4-6-0s and RODs	60 mins
Intermediate Classes	54 mins
Metro Tanks & small shunting engines	30 mins

Coaling Engines from Stage
Direct from Stack by Steam Crane	40 mins/ton
Direct from Stack by Hand:	
up to 10ft from rail	50 mins/ton
10 to 20ft from rail	65 mins/ton

NOTE: Swindon at this point had an
old pattern tip stage

PIECEWORK RATES FOR FIREDROPPING AT SWINDON - November 1936

Grate Area (Sq. Ft.)	Classes of Engines	Per Engine (Mins)
26 - 34	{ 28XX, 29XX, 40XX, 47XX, 49XX, 59XX, 60XX, 68XX, 78XX and ROD	60
20 - 21	{ 26XX, 31XX, 33XX, 34XX, 41XX, 42XX, 43XX, 51XX, 52XX, 53XX, 56XX, 61XX, 63XX, 66XX, 72XX, 73XX, 83XX and 93XX	54
15 - 17	{ All other classes except 4-coupled tanks and small shunting engines	48
Up to 14	{ 4-coupled tanks, small shunting engines and stock engines on receipt from Factory	30

SWINDON RUNNING SHED
STAFF - 2nd November 1932

Name	Address
Advisory & Clerical	
Mr. A.M. Duck	170 County Road
Mr. W.C. Dowse	12 Gambia Street
Mr. C.J. Sheppard	159 Kingshill Road
Mr. A.A. Holder	144 County Road
Mr. G. Gregory	87 Rosebery Street
Mr. A. Kent	9 Whitworth Road
Mr. G.F. Joyce	11 Beatrice Street
Mr. H.A. Ann	32 Ponting Street
Mr. G.W. van de Perk	76 Drove Road
Mr. W.G. Griffiths	68 York Road
Mr. W.T. Reeves	43 Pembroke Street
Mr. F. Allen	88 Avenue Road
Mr. H.C. Taphouse	'Berwyn', Pleydell Road
Telephone Attendents	
W.F. Russell	28 Cheltenham Street
A.J. Durbridge	47 Exeter Street
A.H. Bailey	23 Beckhampton Street
Adult Callers	
E. Rogers	7 Pinehurst Road
G. Whitehead	'Walton Villa', The Street, Stratton
J. Clifford	28 Poulton Street

SWINDON RUNNING SHED
Telephone Directory - July 1952

Title	Extension No.
Shedmaster	2422
Foreman (Running)	2426
Foreman (Workshop)	2427
Foreman's Clerk	2423
Locomotive Supervisor (Passenger Station)	2428
Stores	2425
Time Office	2424

SWINDON ALLOCATIONS

DECEMBER 1850 - Broad Gauge

Class	Type	Name
Fire Fly	2-2-2	Damon, Ixion, Mentor, Milo, Orion
Prince	2-2-2	Peri, Sylph
Star	2-2-2	Red Star, Rising Star,
Sun	2-2-2	Zebra

JANUARY 1901

Class	Type	No.
Atbara	4-4-0	3390
Badminton	4-4-0	3307
Bulldog	4-4-0	3364, 3366
Duke	4-4-0	3312
Armstrong	4-4-0	7
Achilles	4-2-2	3013, 3074
26XX	2-6-0	33
Barnum	2-4-0	3206, 3208, 3211, 3212, 3213, 3214, 3215, 3219, 3222, 3224, 3225
481	2-4-0	28
3232	2-4-0	3234
1883	2-4-0	1883
Standard Goods	0-6-0	432, 495, 604, 607, 609, 612, 668, 670, 679, 783, 1113, 1115
2301	0-6-0	2302, 2320, 2327, 2353, 2356, 2359, 2382, 2404, 2409, 2415, 2418, 2423, 2438, 2464, 2465, 2531, 2563
2361	0-6-0	2364, 2373
850	0-6-0	858, 864, 871, 873, 997, 1908, 1957, 1981, 2011
1016	0-6-0T	1039
1076	0-6-0T	950, 1150, 1272, 1294, 1295, 1567, 1606,
1661	0-6-0T	1667, 1692
1854	0-6-0T	1757, 1792, 1879
2721	0-6-0T	2722, 2723, 2769, 2770, 2780
Nth. Pembroke	0-6-0T	1378
Severn & Wye	0-6-0T	1353, 1354
Cornwall Min.	0-6-0T	1393, 1399, 1400
517	0-4-2T	554, 574, 576
W. Cornwall	0-4-0T	1391

JANUARY 1914

Class	Type	No.
Saint	4-6-0	2904, 2907, 2915, 2980, 2998
Bulldog	4-4-0	3323, 3337, 3400, 3413, 3438, 3440, 3441, 3442
County	4-4-0	3821
3521	4-4-0	3543, 3546
28XX	2-8-0	2806, 2812, 2818
43XX	2-6-0	4337
26XX	2-6-0	2645, 2665, 2672, 2673, 2676, 2679
Barnum	2-4-0	3211
Stella	2-4-0	3511
Standard Goods	0-6-0	434, 882, 1190
2301	0-6-0	2315, 2348, 2355, 2386, 2399, 2408, 2426, 2430, 2434, 2438, 2457, 2480, 2511, 2522
850	0-6-0T	853, 858, 859, 860, 988, 994, 996, 1948, 1983
1076	0-6-0T	1169, 1613, 1619, 1660
1661	0-6-0T	1672, 1678
1813	0-6-0T	1851
2021	0-6-0T	2069
2721	0-6-0T	2760, 2769
Cornwall Min.	0-6-0T	1394, 1398
517	0-4-2T	549, 1154, 1476, 1484
3571	0-4-2T	3576

JANUARY 1927

Class	Type	No.
Saint	4-6-0	2913, 2923, 2942, 2947
Atbara	4-4-0	4128
County	4-4-0	3803, 3810, 3817, 3838
Bulldog	4-4-0	3300, 3319, 3326, 3430, 3431, 3443, 3444, 3451
Duke	4-4-0	3260, 3263
M & SWJ	4-4-0	1120, 1121
28XX	2-8-0	2815, 2853
30XX	2-8-0	3054, 3056, 3085
43XX	2-6-0	4311, 4314, 4330, 4349, 4367, 5333, 6320, 6347, 6375, 6390, 7307
M & SWJ	2-6-0	24
2301	0-6-0	2518, 2524, 2570
M & SWJ	0-6-0	1007, 1009, 1013,
M & SWJ	4-4-4T	25
Metro	2-4-0T	1447, 3588
M & SWJ	0-4-4T	23
850	0-6-0T	94, 858, 869, 994, 1928, 1933, 1934, 1964, 2012, 2015, 2017
1076	0-6-0T	1139, 1576
1813	0-6-0T	1852
1854	0-6-0T	1758, 1864
2021	0-6-0T	2040, 2060
517	0-4-2T	529, 539, 540, 545, 549, 551, 558, 576, 835, 837, 839, 842, 1154, 1427, 1436, 1440
Cornwall Min.	0-6-0T	1394, 1399

JANUARY 1938

Class	Type	No.
Star	4-6-0	4015, 4020, 4045
Saint	4-6-0	2902, 2927, 2935, 2939, 2945, 2947, 2951, 2971, 2975, 2978
Hall	4-6-0	4941, 4948, 5932, 5964
Bulldog	4-4-0	3306, 3421, 3433, 3452
Duke	4-4-0	3279
28XX	2-8-0	2849, 2873
30XX	2-8-0	3017, 3022, 3034
43XX	2-6-0	4365, 4368, 6347, 6354, 6374, 6384, 7300, 7314, 8359
2301	0-6-0	2347, 2415, 2473, 2529
51XX	2-6-2T	4113
45XX	2-6-2T	4532, 5529, 5534
Metro	2-4-0T	1498
57XX	0-6-0T	3724, 3737, 3739, 3748, 3764, 5716, 6716, 6737, 6738, 6739, 6740, 6741, 7749, 7762, 9790
74XX	0-6-0T	7418
655	0-6-0T	1786
850	0-6-0T	992, 1954, 2014, 2017
1854	0-6-0T	1731
2021	0-6-0T	2060, 2119
Whitland & Crdgn	0-6-0T	1331
1366	0-6-0T	1366, 1368, 1369, 1370
58XX	0-4-2T	5800, 5805
517	0-4-2T	1163, 1436, 1442
3571	0-4-2T	3571, 3580

JANUARY 1959

Class	Type	No.
Castle	4-6-0	5000, 5002, 5005, 5009, 5023, 5064, 5068, 7037
County	4-6-0	1004, 1012, 1019
Hall	4-6-0	4953, 4972, 5922, 5981, 5983, 5986, 5997, 6902, 6993
BR 5MT	4-6-0	73001, 73012, 73027
BR 4MT	4-6-0	75000, 75002
28XX	2-8-0	2818, 2835, 2852, 2865, 2879
43XX	2-6-0	5306, 5351, 6309, 6334, 6336, 6366, 9315
2251	0-6-0	2203
45XX	2-6-2T	5509, 5510, 5528, 5532, 5540, 5547, 5566
56XX	0-6-2T	6639
57XX	0-6-0T	3645, 3666, 3682, 3684, 3711, 3724, 3739, 3746, 3763, 3780, 4612, 4651, 4697, 6716, 6736, 6741, 7794, 8779, 8783, 8793, 9600, 9604, 9605, 9672, 9720, 9721, 9740, 9773, 9790, 9795
74XX	0-6-0T	7413, 7415, 7418, 7421, 7424
94XX	0-6-0T	8433, 8465, 8472, 9476
16XX	0-6-0T	1658
1361	0-6-0T	1365
1366	0-6-0T	1369, 1371
14XX	0-4-2T	1410, 1417, 1438, 1464
58XX	0-4-2T	5804, 5815
City (NRM, on loan)	4-4-0	3440

JANUARY 1949

Class	Type	No.
Castle	4-6-0	4081, 5009, 5068, 5083, 5084, 5091, 7015
Star	4-6-0	4015, 4017, 4022, 4036, 4055, 4057, 4062
Saint	4-6-0	2908, 2927, 2934, 2945, 2947, 2949, 2954
Hall	4-6-0	4905, 4925, 4945, 4956, 4972, 4973, 5934, 5943, 6908
90XX	4-4-0	9011, 9018, 9023
43XX	2-6-0	5367, 5371, 5396, 6322, 6358, 6374, 6384, 6387, 7321
2251	0-6-0	2224, 2250
2301	0-6-0	2568
45XX	2-6-2T	4507, 4521, 4538, 4544, 4550, 4551, 4590, 4592, 5510, 5534, 5566
Metro	2-4-0T	3561
57XX	0-6-0T	3645, 3666, 3682, 3684, 3724, 3739, 3748, 3780, 4651, 6716, 6737, 6739, 6741, 7794, 8733, 8779, 8793, 9600, 9720, 9721, 9773, 9790, 9795
74XX	0-6-0T	7415, 7418, 7424
94XX	0-6-0T	9400
850	0-6-0T	992, 2014, 2017
1501	0-6-0T	1542
1366	0-6-0T	1366, 1369, 1371
1854	0-6-0T	1731, 1758
2021	0-6-0T	2060
14XX	0-4-2T	1400, 1436
58XX	0-4-2T	5800, 5802, 5804
3571	0-4-2T	3575

Left: *Chippenham-based photographer Kenneth Leech with driver Tom Conduit, who started on the GWR as a lad porter at Monmouth in 1939. He was 13 years a fireman and spent much of that part of his career at Swindon, being able to miss part of the lower links when firing because of his experience. He attained driver status at Old Oak Common in 1955 and returned to Swindon in 1959. Kenneth Leech enjoyed many footplate trips and would always provide crews with large copies of his home-printed pictures. There must be thousands of his photographs in the homes of railway families in Swindon.* CTY. BARRY HAYWARD

ACKNOWLEDGEMENTS

In conclusion, Gordon and Mike would like to thank the following for their support, encouragement and assistance in the preparation of this work:

To families of Swindon railwaymen and folk who answered appeals — Sydney Sprules, Joan Thompson, Anthony Taylor, Celia Fraser, Beryl Wynn, Iris Hacker, June Lewis, Mary Thompson, Ron Hinder, with special thanks to Jim and Margaret Lowe.

To Gordon's former colleagues on the railway — Tom Conduit, Byron Williams, George Watts, Ken Watts, Colin Hawkins, Danny Williams, Colin Trembling, Pat Lawes, Mark Wilkins, Dave 'Brinkworth' Jones, Cyril Tarrant and Freddie Simpson.

To those who provided archival assistance and access to photograph collections — Barry Hayward, custodian of the Kenneth Leech Collection; Richard Casserley, for access to his father's wonderful photographs; Roger Trayhurn, Chief Librarian, Swindon Reference Library; Tom Morton of the *Swindon Evening Advertiser*, who was always helpful with publicity and appeals; David Postle, Curator, Kidderminster Railway Museum; and Rev. Canon Brian Arman.

To other researchers for sharing their material — Tom Smith, Peter Timms, Colin Dawson and especially Chris 'Beaver' Turner.

And, of course, the redoubtable Wild Swan team — Paul and Ann Karau, June Judge and John Copsey.

Freddie Simpson (right, on engine) was one of the back-up team for this book, helping fill gaps in the story enthusiastically on many occasions. He is seen here on pannier tank No. 7418 during World War Two on a factory pilot duty. The shunters with shunting poles are Bob Willis and Percy George. CTY. FREDDIE SIMPSON